Coursebook

Macroeconomics
Private & Public Choice
Tenth Edition

James D. Gwartney
Florida State University

Richard L. Stroup
Montana State University

Russell S. Sobel
West Virginia University

David A. Macpherson
Florida State University

THOMSON
SOUTH-WESTERN

Australia · Canada · Mexico · Singapore · Spain · United Kingdom · United States

THOMSON

SOUTH-WESTERN

Coursebook to accompany Macroeconomics: Private and Public Choice, 10th Edition

James D. Gwartney, Richard L. Stroup, Russell S. Sobel, David A. Macpherson

Editor-in-Chief:
Jack Calhoun

Team Leader:
Michael Roche

Acquisitions Editor:
Peter Adams

Developmental Editor:
Andrew McGuire

Senior Marketing Manager:
Janet Hennies

Production Editor:
Robert Dreas

Manufacturing Coordinator:
Sandee Milewski

Compositor:
Sheryl Nelson
OffCenter Concepts

Printer:
Globus Printing, Inc.
Minster, Ohio

Design Project Manager:
Michelle Kunkler

Cover Designer:
Bill Brammer, fusion 29 visual
communication

Preface

We are often asked why we call this book a *Coursebook* rather than a "study guide." We use this title because we feel the *Coursebook* goes well beyond the typical study guide in at least three ways:

1. *Critical Analysis.* We stress questions that require students to develop and use the economic way of thinking to come up with the answers, rather than having students passively choose between a group of prepared alternatives.

2. *Readings.* We include short, interesting readings by a broad spectrum of economists to provide a real-world context for applying the economic way of thinking to important issues.

3. *Explained Answers.* Except for the open-ended discussion questions, we include explanations of why a particular answer is correct and the alternatives incorrect.

In writing this *Coursebook,* we have attempted to strike a balance between economic reasoning and mechanics. Often a supplementary workbook is little more than a set of mechanical exercises. Such exercises lack substance and meaning for the student who has not yet acquired a firm foundation in the economic way of thinking. Our teaching experience has shown that stressing real-world situations, presenting actual data, providing selected short readings, and explaining why particular answers are correct—as we have done in the *Coursebook*—illuminate the power, and utility, of economic reasoning.

The *Coursebook* has been structured to maximize the student's comprehension of the concepts presented in each chapter of *Macroeconomics: Private and Public Choice,* Tenth Edition. The first section of each chapter is composed of approximately fifteen true/false questions. Although this section has a realistic flavor, mechanics primarily are emphasized. When possible, students are tested on their ability to reject common economic fallacies or "Myths of Economics," as they are often referred to in the highlighted discussion boxes in the text. The second section of problems and projects generally contains about five problems that emphasize both mechanics and economic reasoning. The problems and projects are specifically designed to foster the economic way of thinking by guiding students through a series of smaller, logical steps when approaching each larger economic problem. The third section contains approximately twenty-five multiple-choice questions of the type familiar to most students. We have tried to maximize the usefulness of these questions in preparing students for tests by making these questions similar in wording, context, and logic to the ones available to instructors in the test bank that accompanies the book. They represent a fair mix of questions designed to test mechanics and economic thinking. Finally, each chapter contains approximately five discussion questions that are intended to provoke further speculation on economic issues.

The *Coursebook* also serves as a reader, presenting a "Perspectives in Economics" section in about half of the chapters. These articles are readable and engaging, will reinforce the classroom presentation of economic lessons, and will expand on important concepts discussed in the text. Following each selection are questions asking the student to evaluate the position of the author. Is the reasoning sound? Is it opinionated? Does empirical evidence support the author's contention? This feature of the *Coursebook* again highlights the usefulness of economics in our everyday lives.

Answers to virtually every question are provided in the "Answer Key" at the back of the *Coursebook.* The answers are followed by an explanation of why that particular answer is correct. Students who take the time to master these questions—and who understand the rationale behind each answer—should do very well in introductory economics classes.

We would like to express our appreciation to Keri M. Cowan, A. H. Studenmund, and Mary Hirschfeld for their contributions to previous editions of the *Coursebook*, Sheryl Nelson of OffCenter Concept House for her help in production and composition, Andrew McGuire of South-Western, and especially Terri and Reagan Sobel for their patience, support, and understanding. This edition of the *Coursebook* is dedicated to the memory of Jon Vilasuso, a wonderful colleague, teacher, and friend.

Russell S. Sobel
James D. Gwartney
Richard L. Stroup
David A. Macpherson

Contents

Making the Grade in Economics

Here are some hints that will help you to greatly improve your grade in economics.

Do your coursebook for each chapter. Students who use the coursebook generally average exam grades at least one letter grade higher than those who do not use it. The coursebook questions will likely be very similar to what will be on your exams. If you have trouble with the wording, or don't understand why the right answers are indeed right, get help. Have a friend, your instructor, or a tutor help you with the specific questions.

Learning this "economic way of thinking" is more important than being able to memorize definitions. However, being familiar with the key terms and the jargon of economics will help. These terms, with their definitions, can be found in the margins of your textbook.

When grading your answers, ask yourself, "Did I miss several questions all regarding the same idea?" The quickest way to fail an exam is to miss a key concept that accounts for several exam questions. The coursebook should enable you to find these problem spots *before* your exam, so you can correct them. Get additional help on these problem spots.

Use the coursebook to improve the effectiveness of your study time. Suppose you get all the questions on opportunity cost correct, while you miss several questions on scarcity. Additional study time should focus on learning what you missed, not on restudying what you know. The coursebook can help you figure out which is which.

Do not focus too much on the specific example. Economics is a set of ideas that can, and should, be applied consistently. The law of demand (from Chapter 3) states that as the price of a good rises, consumers will buy less of it. So what will happen if the price of *funerals* in your town rises, will the quantity of funerals purchased rise, fall or stay the same? Students often deduce that death is unavoidable, so the quantity of funerals purchased will stay the same. WRONG! The world is full of substitutes: You can be buried in another town, or you could be cremated and have your ashes thrown over the ocean.

Because the specific example generally doesn't matter, a few key words generally determine the answer. Above, the key idea being tested is "a higher price causes . . ." find these key words in each question and ask what idea from the chapter is being tested. It isn't knowledge of the funeral home industry! That wasn't in the chapter.

Finally, remember what you already know from the real world. You have lived your entire life in an economy, and economic theory is meant to explain and give insights into the real world. Most students would know before ever taking economics that monopolies charge higher prices or that recessions are characterized by higher unemployment rates. Always double check the answer you get by applying economic theory against what you already know. Generally go with your first instinct on a question; students often read too much into questions when they overanalyze them.

CHAPTER 1

The Economic Approach

TRUE OR FALSE

T F

☐ ☐ 1. According to the economic guidepost that incentives matter, if there is an increase in the benefit derived from an activity, individuals will be more likely to choose that activity.

☐ ☐ 2. The opportunity cost of attending an economics class is the money spent on transportation (gasoline, parking, etc.) plus the cost of the books for the class.

☐ ☐ 3. Resources are inputs used to produce goods and services. They include human resources (such as labor), physical resources (such as capital), and natural resources (such as land).

☐ ☐ 4. The value of a good is objective; it is the same to everyone.

☐ ☐ 5. Economic activity often has secondary effects that are not initially observable.

☐ ☐ 6. Because public education is freely provided to students, it is by definition not a scarce good.

☐ ☐ 7. One's time is scarce and thus must be rationed among alternative activities.

☐ ☐ 8. If you like pizza and steak equally well, economizing behavior suggests you will purchase whichever is more expensive.

☐ ☐ 9. A good is scarce if human desire for it exceeds the amount freely available from nature.

☐ ☐ 10. In economics, the term *ceteris paribus* means that everything is changing.

☐ ☐ 11. The following is a positive economic statement: "An increase in the minimum wage will increase unemployment among unskilled workers."

☐ ☐ 12. The following is a positive economic statement: "The government should increase its funding of welfare programs to help the poor."

☐ ☐ 13. The following is an example of marginal thinking: "I was going to buy a taco and a drink, but the value meal with two tacos and a drink costs only $.30 *more* and has one *additional* taco."

T F

☐ ☐ 14. Whenever two events frequently happen together, this necessarily implies that one causes the other.

☐ ☐ 15. Economics assumes people will generally make decisions with limited information because information is costly to obtain.

PROBLEMS AND PROJECTS

1. The text lists eight guideposts to the economic way of thinking. They are summarized below.

    Guidepost 1: The use of scarce resources is costly; trade-offs must always be made. ("There is no such thing as a free lunch.")

    Guidepost 2: Individuals choose purposefully; they try to get the most from their limited resources.

    Guidepost 3: Incentives matter—choice is influenced in a predictable way by changes in incentives.

    Guidepost 4: Individuals make decisions at the margin.

    Guidepost 5: Although information can help us make better choices, its acquisition is costly.

    Guidepost 6: Economic actions often generate secondary effects in addition to their immediate effects.

    Guidepost 7: The value of a good or service is subjective.

    Guidepost 8: The test of a theory is its ability to predict.

    Read each of the statements below and indicate in the blank space to the left of the statement the number of the guidepost that best accounts for the statement.

    ___ a. The luxury tax placed on expensive boats in 1990 was meant to increase the tax burden on the rich, but it ended up hurting many blue-collar manufacturing workers in the boat industry as they lost their jobs when boat sales fell substantially.

    ___ b. I will usually not stop to pick up a penny laying on the ground but will stop to pick up a dollar bill.

    ___ c. While I would really like to buy that $100 name-brand shirt, I will instead buy a less expensive, $30 shirt and save the $70 for something else.

    ___ d. The Food and Drug Administration should stop requiring all new drugs for AIDS to be exhaustively tested for safety and effectiveness before approving their use. People who might have benefited from the drug are dying during the years required for the approval process.

    ___ e. I hate tomatoes, but my wife loves them. On the other hand, I love onions, and my wife hates them. When we go out to eat and order a salad, I give her my tomatoes and she gives me her onions.

    ___ f. Bill Gates spends hours each week caring for and growing grapes to make his own wine. That sure is some expensive wine!

    ___ g. Long ago people used to believe the earth was the center of the solar system, with the sun and the other planets orbiting around the earth. The sun-centered solar system was originally considered a radical theory that finally gained acceptance because it better predicted the positions of the planets observed in the night sky.

____ h. I love the beach, but because it is a six-hour drive, I don't go very often. However, each year when I visit my grandmother, I drive to the beach because she lives only one hour away from it.

2. Each of the following statements ignores or violates one of the eight guideposts to economic thinking (listed above in question 1). In each case, identify the guidepost and explain how it has been violated.

____ a. Before voting in an election, each voter should learn everything possible about the issues and candidates involved.

____ b. Reducing the prices of necessities would clearly benefit the poor. Therefore, it would help the poor if the government passed a law requiring landlords to reduce by half the rental rates for any tenant who makes less than $10,000 per year.

____ c. Full scholarships make education free.

____ d. Since I get the same satisfaction from reading a book, seeing a movie, or hearing a concert, there should be no reason for me to prefer one choice over the other.

____ e. Because criminals are irrational, increasing the punishment associated with a crime will not affect the amount of the crime committed.

____ f. Joe declares, "I'm not going to class today; I'd rather go to the beach." Sam responds, "But Joe, you are forgetting to consider the money you've already paid for tuition and books for the class."

____ g. I'm trying to find a ticket for Saturday's sold-out game, but everyone I call wants at least $75 for their ticket. Don't these people understand that their tickets are only worth the $15 price they originally paid for them?

____ h. Economics tries to explain the lower birth rate among educated women as being due to them having a higher opportunity cost of having children. This cannot be true because the decision to have a baby has nothing to do with economics.

3. The text discusses three common pitfalls to avoid in the economic way of thinking.

(1) Violation of the *ceteris paribus* condition.
(2) Association is not causation.
(3) The fallacy of composition.

Indicate which pitfall applies to each of the following statements. Briefly explain each case.

____ a. Since everyone buys a lottery ticket in hopes of winning a prize, the perfect lottery would pay back $1 to each player, making everyone a winner, instead of giving the money as only one big prize.

____ b. The price of typewriters has fallen over the last 10 years, but less typewriters are sold today than 10 years ago. This rejects the economic theory that people buy more as the price falls.

____ c. In the past, students who earn As in my class tend to be the ones who come up after class and ask questions. Perhaps I should require everyone to come up and ask questions to improve student grades.

4. [Note to students: The following problem relates to the addendum at the end of Chapter 1 on understanding graphs.] Exhibit 1 shows data on the relationship between gas consumption of a new Chevrolet and the number of miles traveled.

   a. Graph the relationship between miles traveled and gas consumption in the space provided. Measure miles traveled on the horizontal axis (*x* axis) and gasoline consumption on the vertical axis (*y* axis). Label the graph clearly.

   b. Is there a direct or inverse (that is, positive or negative) relationship between gasoline consumption and distance traveled?

   c. What is the slope of the line? How is it related to the miles per gallon obtained in the Chevrolet (that is, how many miles can be traveled on a gallon of gas)?

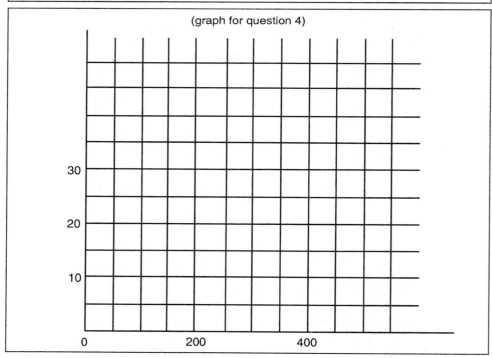

EXHIBIT 1

TOTAL DISTANCE TRAVELED (MILES)	AMOUNT OF GASOLINE CONSUMED (GALLONS)
0	0
75	5
150	10
225	15
300	20
375	25
450	30

(graph for question 4)

5. [Note to students: The following problem relates to the addendum at the end of Chapter 1 on understanding graphs.] Exhibit 2 shows how the quantity of

melons purchased by consumers depends on the price of melons and on average consumer income.

a.   In the space provided graph the relationship between price and quantity purchased if income is $10,000. Label this curve D_1.

b.   Are price and quantity purchased directly or inversely related to those with average incomes of $10,000 per year?

c.   Graph the relationship between price and quantity purchased if income is $15,000. Label this curve D_2.

d.   If price is fixed at 4 cents per pound, and consumer income rises from $10,000 to $15,000 per year, how much will quantity purchased change?

e.   For a person with an income of $15,000 per year, if the price rises from 4 cents to 5 cents per pound, how much will quantity purchased change?

EXHIBIT 2

PRICE (CENTS PER POUND)	QUANTITY PURCHASED (THOUSANDS OF TONS PER YEAR) FOR AVERAGE INCOME OF	
	$10,000/YEAR	$15,000/YEAR
1	900	1,100
2	800	1,000
3	700	900
4	600	800
5	500	700
6	400	600

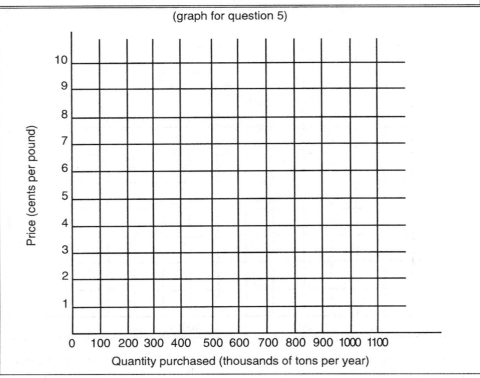

(graph for question 5)

Price (cents per pound)

Quantity purchased (thousands of tons per year)

MULTIPLE CHOICE

1. Which of the following is true?
   a. Scarcity and poverty are basically the same thing.
   b. Poverty implies that some basic level of need has not been attained.
   c. Scarcity is the result of prices being set too high.
   d. All of the above are true.

2. Economics is the study of how
   a. individuals make choices because of scarcity.
   b. to succeed in business.
   c. to make money in the stock market.
   d. the morals and values of people are formed.

3. When an economist states a good is scarce, she means that
   a. production cannot expand the availability of the good.
   b. it is rare.
   c. desire for the good exceeds the amount that is freely available from nature.
   d. people would want to purchase more of the good at any price.

4. When economists say an individual displays economizing behavior, they simply mean that the individual is
   a. making a lot of money.
   b. purchasing only those products that are cheap and of low quality.
   c. learning how to run a business more effectively.
   d. making choices to gain the maximum benefit at the least possible cost.

5. The national debt is too large. The government must stop spending so much money. This statement is
   a. a normative statement.
   b. a positive statement.
   c. a testable hypothesis.
   d. both b and c.

6. Which of the following is a guidepost to economic thinking?
   a. The value of a good can be objectively measured.
   b. Individuals should never make a decision without having complete information.
   c. Incentives matter.
   d. Goods are scarce for the poor but not for the rich.

7. Competitive behavior
   a. occurs as a reaction to scarcity.
   b. occurs only in a market system.
   c. occurs only when the government allocates goods and services.
   d. always generates waste.

8. In economics, the statement, "There is no such thing as a free lunch," refers to which of the following?
   a. Individuals must always pay personally for the lunch they consume.
   b. Production of a good requires the use of scarce resources regardless of whether it is supplied free to the consumers.
   c. Restaurant owners would never give away free lunches.
   d. All good theories are testable.

9. "If income were redistributed in favor of the poor, we would eliminate scarcity."
   The preceding statement is
   a. essentially correct.
   b. incorrect because shortages are always present.
   c. incorrect; it fails to recognize that poverty will be present as long as resources
      are scarce.
   d. incorrect; it confuses the elimination of poverty with elimination of the con-
      straint imposed by scarcity.

10. Which of the following is *not* scarce?
    a. an individual's time
    b. air
    c. pencils
    d. automobiles

11. People make decisions at the margin. Thus, when deciding whether to purchase
    a second car, they would compare
    a. the total benefits expected from two cars with the costs of the two cars.
    b. the additional benefits expected from a second car with the total cost of the
       two cars.
    c. the dollar cost of the two cars with the potential income that the two cars
       will generate.
    d. the additional benefits of the second car with the additional costs of the sec-
       ond car.

12. The basic difference between macroeconomics and microeconomics is that
    a. macroeconomics looks at how people make choices, and microeconomics
       looks at why they make those choices.
    b. macroeconomics is concerned with economic policy, and microeconomics is
       concerned with economic theory.
    c. macroeconomics focuses on the aggregate economy, and microeconomics
       focuses on small components of that economy.
    d. macroeconomics is associated with the fallacy of composition, and micro-
       economics has little to do with the fallacy of composition.

13. The highest valued alternative that must be given up in order to choose an action
    is called its
    a. opportunity cost.
    b. utility.
    c. scarcity.
    d. *ceteris paribus*.

14. Which of the following actions is consistent with the basic economic postulate
    (the guidepost) that incentives matter?
    a. Consumers buy fewer potatoes when the price of potatoes increases.
    b. A politician votes against a pay raise for himself because most of his con-
       stituents are strongly opposed to it and would vote against him in the next
       election.
    c. Farmers produce less corn because corn prices have declined.
    d. All of the above.

15. If Susan bought nine gallons of gasoline at $1.50 per gallon, the car wash cost $1, but if she bought 10 gallons of gasoline, the car wash was free. Given that Susan is going to get the car wash, the marginal cost of the tenth gallon of gasoline is
    a. zero.
    b. $.50.
    c. $1.00.
    d. $1.50.

16. Positive economics differs from normative economics in that
    a. positive economics deals with how people react to changes in benefits, and normative economics deals with how people react to changes in costs.
    b. positive economic statements are testable, and normative statements are not.
    c. positive economic statements tell us what we should be doing, and normative economics tells us what we should have done.
    d. positive economic statements focus on the application of the theory, and normative economic statements are theoretical.

17. Which of the following represents a normative statement?
    a. Incentives matter.
    b. The temperature in this room is 120 degrees.
    c. It is too hot in this room.
    d. People will buy less butter at $1.50 per pound than they will at $1.00 per pound.

18. The economic way of thinking stresses that
    a. changes in personal costs and benefits will exert a predictable influence on the choices of human decision makers.
    b. only direct monetary costs matter in making decisions.
    c. if a good is provided free to an individual, its production will not consume valuable scarce resources.
    d. secondary effects are not important to consider when making decisions.

19. Which of the following is a positive economic statement?
    a. The federal minimum wage should be raised $6.50 per hour.
    b. The United States spends too much on national defense.
    c. Higher rates of investment lead to higher rates of economic growth.
    d. Economics is more interesting to study than history.

20. When economists use the term *ceteris paribus*, they indicate
    a. the causal relationship between two economic variables cannot be determined.
    b. the analysis is true for the individual but not for the economy as a whole.
    c. all other factors are assumed to be constant.
    d. their conclusions are based on normative economics rather than positive economic analysis.

21. In economics, the benefit (or satisfaction) that an individual gets from an activity is called
    a. scarcity.
    b. utility.
    c. opportunity cost.
    d. *ceteris paribus.*

DISCUSSION QUESTIONS

1. When a good is scarce, there is not enough of it freely available from nature to satisfy human desires for the good. Thus, some means of rationing the limited quantity among those who desire it is necessary. A market system allows prices to perform this rationing function. Prices simply rise until the number of people willing to buy is equal to the quantity available. Can you think of other rationing systems other than price? Contrast the secondary effects of the alternative rationing systems with price rationing.

2. List three things that are not scarce. List three things that are commonplace but still scarce. How did you decide whether an item was scarce or not?

3. "Economics is of limited relevance. Most people will not be directly involved in management or the production of material goods. They will neither put much money in the stock market. Understanding the economic approach will be of limited value to the typical student." Do you agree or disagree with this view? Be honest. Explain your reasoning.

4. "The minimum wage makes it more expensive for businesses to hire unskilled labor. As a result of the higher cost, businesses will hire fewer unskilled workers. Because unskilled workers find it harder to get jobs under a minimum wage, we should eliminate the minimum wage." Indicate the positive and normative aspects of these three statements.

5. "Under our plan, health care in the United States will now be free. No citizen will be denied medical care because of an inability to pay. The program will be funded by increasing the employer's tax on the wages of his employees."
   a. Will health care be free? If so, why? If not, who do you think will end up paying for it?
   b. Will the total amount of health care consumption rise or fall? Do you consider this change in health care consumption desirable or not? Explain.

PERSPECTIVES IN ECONOMICS

ECONOMICS IN ONE LESSON

by Henry Hazlitt

[Reprinted with permission from Henry Hazlitt, *Economics in One Lesson,* (New York: Crown, 1979) pp. 15–17 (abridged).]

Economics is haunted by more fallacies than any other study. This is no accident. The inherent difficulties of the subject would be great enough in any case, but they are multiplied a thousandfold by a factor that is insignificant in, say, physics, mathematics or medicine—the special pleading of selfish interests. While every group has certain economic interests identical with those of all groups, every group has also interests antagonistic to those of all other groups. While certain public policies would in the long run benefit everybody, other policies would benefit one group only at the expense of all other groups. The group that would benefit by such policies, having such a direct interest in them, will argue for them plausibly and persistently. It will hire the best buyable minds to devote their whole time to presenting its case. And it will finally either convince the general public that its case is sound, or so befuddle it that clear thinking on the subject becomes next to impossible.

In addition to these endless pleadings of self-interest, there is a second main factor that spawns new economic fallacies every day. This is the persistent tendency to see only the immediate effects of a given policy, or its effects only on a special group, and to neglect to inquire what the long-run effects of that policy will be not only on that special group but on all groups. It is the fallacy of overlooking secondary consequences.

In this lies the whole difference between good economics and bad. The bad economist sees only what immediately strikes the eye; the good economist also looks beyond. The bad economist sees only the direct consequences of a proposed course; the good economist looks also at the longer and indirect consequences. The bad economist sees only what the effect of a given policy has been or will be on one particular group; the good economist inquires also what the effect of the policy will be on all groups.

From this aspect, therefore, the whole of economics can be reduced to a single lesson, and that lesson can be reduced to a single sentence. The art of economics consists in looking not merely at the immediate but at the longer effects of any act or policy; it consists in tracing the consequences of that policy not merely for one group but for all groups.

DISCUSSION

1. Rephrase Hazlitt's lesson in your own words. Is it really possible to reduce the whole of economics to one sentence?

2. Which "Guideposts to Economic Thinking" corresponds to Hazlitt's lesson? Explain your choice(s).

3. Can you think of applications of Hazlitt's lesson in your own life? What are they?

CHAPTER 2

Some Tools of the Economist

TRUE OR FALSE

T F

☐ ☐ 1. The opportunity cost of washing your car is the discomfort and drudgery associated with the task.

☐ ☐ 2. Time is a component of opportunity cost.

☐ ☐ 3. For most students, the largest component of the cost of college is the opportunity cost of forgone earnings.

☐ ☐ 4. In each trade there is a winner and a loser; trade cannot make both parties better off.

☐ ☐ 5. The law of comparative advantage helps explain why fathers often have their 12-year-old sons mow the lawn even though the fathers could do it in less time.

☐ ☐ 6. Private property rights give owners a strong incentive to disregard the wishes of others when using or employing their property.

☐ ☐ 7. Property that is privately owned tends to be much better cared for and better conserved for the future, than property that is not privately owned.

☐ ☐ 8. Middlemen add to the buyer's cost without producing anything of value.

☐ ☐ 9. A country gains by importing products that are relatively expensive for them to produce, while exporting products that are relatively inexpensive for them to produce.

☐ ☐ 10. The principle of comparative advantage causes both individuals and nations to specialize in the production of those things for which they are the lowest opportunity cost producer.

☐ ☐ 11. All economies must make decisions about what to produce, how to produce it, and to whom to distribute the goods produced.

☐ ☐ 12. Capitalism is the use of the political process and government planning to allocate goods and resources.

☐ ☐ 13. If an economy is operating efficiently, to produce more of one good it must produce less of another.

☐ ☐ 14. An increase in technology shifts the production possibilities curve inward.

PROBLEMS AND PROJECTS

1. Susan is a 30-year-old high-school graduate currently earning $20,000 at her job. She rents an apartment and pays for all of her own expenses (food, rent, transportation to and from work, etc.). She is considering quitting her job and enrolling in the local university to earn a college degree. The brochure for the local university gives the following table of the average cost of attending the university.

	EXHIBIT 1	
	PER YEAR	TOTAL FOR 4 YEARS
Tuition and fees	$2,191	$8,764
Books and supplies	$552	$2,208
Room and board	$4,434	$17,736
Transportation	$557	$2,228
Total	$7,734	$30,936

Using the economic tools of opportunity cost and the marginal way of thinking that you have learned in Chapters 1 and 2, evaluate Susan's cost of going to college relative to the table.

a. What important component of her cost of going to college is omitted from the table? (Hint: Think of opportunity cost.)

b. Are transportation and room and board (housing and food) really costs of going to college? Are they relevant costs in making her decision? (Hint: Use the marginal way of thinking.)

c. Adjust the table according to your answers to a and b. What is her relevant 1-year and 4-year costs of going to college?

d. What percent of this total cost is due to her forgone earnings?

e. Because a person's earnings usually increase with age, can you think of a reason why people generally chose to go to college when they are younger instead of waiting?

2. The text lists the following four important factors and incentives created by private property rights.

(1) Private owners can gain by employing their resources in ways that are beneficial to others, and they bear the opportunity cost of ignoring the wishes of others.

(2) The private owner has a strong incentive to care for and properly manage what he or she owns.

(3) The private owner has an incentive to conserve for the future if the property's value is expected to rise.

(4) With private property rights, the property owner is accountable for damage to others through the misuse of the property. Private ownership links responsibility with the right of control.

Now read each of the statements below and indicate in the blank space to the left of the statement the number of the above feature or incentive of private property rights that best accounts for the statement.

____ a. Before selling their home, most people fix it up and do needed repairs.

____ b. You cause an automobile accident and must pay to repair the damage to the other automobile.

____ c. When sharing an apartment with others, the common areas such as the living room and kitchen are usually not kept as clean as each person keeps their own room.

____ d. John and Mary love to eat popcorn and watch movies on their VCR. However, they note that when they put the popcorn in one big bowl it gets eaten more quickly than if it is divided and each gets their own bowl of popcorn.

____ e. Cows, pigs, and chicken are slaughtered in massive quantities each year for human benefit. Whales and African elephants are also killed for human benefit, but at much lower rates. However, whales and elephants are facing extinction while cows, pigs, and chicken are everywhere.

____ f. People generally take better care of housing that they own than housing that they rent.

____ g. Sam uses spray paint to paint his car pink and purple and puts bumper stickers all over the outside of the car. When he goes to sell it, he has trouble finding a buyer and ends up getting a much lower price than the average used value for his make and model car.

3. Bob needs to go from Atlanta to Miami. A bus ticket costs $200, and the bus takes 56 hours, while an airplane ticket costs $450 and takes 6 hours.

   a. What is the marginal cost of taking the plane? That is, how much *more* additional money does the plane ticket cost over the bus?

   b. What is the marginal benefit of taking the plane? That is, how many hours does he save over taking the bus?

   c. For 50 hours of Bob's time to be worth $250, how much must he value his time?

   d. If Bob's value of his time is $8 per hour, should he fly or take the bus?

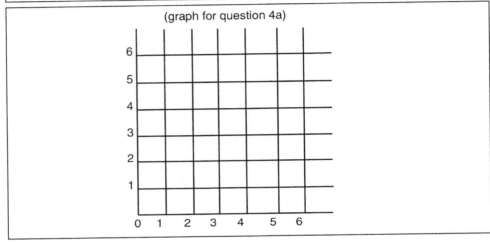

SAM'S WEEKLY PRODUCTION POSSIBILITIES		LARRY'S WEEKLY PRODUCTION POSSIBILITIES	
TABLES	CHAIRS	TABLES	CHAIRS
5	0	4	0
4	2	3	1
3	4	2	2
2	6	1	3
1	8	0	4
0	10		

4. Sam and Larry operate a furniture shop. They specialize in the production of tables and chairs. The data representing their respective production possibilities schedules are presented in Exhibit 2.
   a. Plot the data given in the exhibit for Larry in the graph to graphically show his production possibilities curve.
   b. If Larry produces no tables, and instead devotes all of his time to producing chairs, how many chairs can he produce? If Larry produces one table, how many chairs can he produce with his remaining time? How many chairs did Larry have to give up to produce this one table?
   c. If Sam produces no tables, and instead devotes all of his time to producing chairs, how many chairs can he produce? If Sam produces one table, how many chairs can he produce with his remaining time? How many chairs did Sam have to give up to produce this one table?
   d. Who gives up the fewest chairs to produce one table (that is, who has the comparative advantage in producing tables, or equivalently, who is the lowest opportunity cost producer of tables)?
   e. Using the same process as above in parts b through d, can you find both Larry's and Sam's opportunity cost of producing one *chair*? Who has the comparative advantage in producing chairs?
   f. Sam currently produces 2 tables and 6 chairs, and Larry produces 1 table and 3 chairs. Total production is 3 tables and 9 chairs. Using your answers to parts d and e, allow Larry and Sam to specialize in the area of their comparative advantage and see how much they can produce in total if they specialize. Is it more or less total output than now?

EXHIBIT 3

	HOURS OF WORK REQUIRED PER TON OF	
	COFFEE	TOBACCO
United States	15	45
Brazil	25	50

5. The following questions relate to the data given in Exhibit 3 on the hours of work required to produce tons of coffee and tobacco in the United States and Brazil.
    a. If it takes the United States 15 hours to produce a ton of coffee and 45 hours to produce a ton of tobacco, how many tons of coffee must the United States give up to produce one ton of tobacco? (Hint: How many tons of coffee could be produced in the same 45 hours?)
    b. How many tons of coffee must Brazil give up to produce one ton of tobacco?
    c. Which country has the lowest opportunity cost (in terms of forgone coffee) of producing tobacco?
    d. Which country has the lowest opportunity cost (in terms of forgone tobacco) of producing coffee?
    e. What implications does this have for trade between the United States and Brazil?

EXHIBIT 4

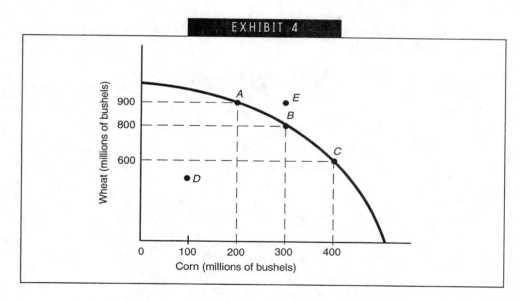

6. Exhibit 4 shows the production possibilities curve for growing wheat and corn.
    a. Are resources efficiently employed at point *A?* At point *B?* At point *D?*
    b. At point *A*, how much wheat is being produced? How much corn?
    c. To increase corn production from *A* to *B*, how much wheat must be sacrificed? What is the opportunity cost of one bushel of corn when production moves from point *A* to *B?*
    d. Can the country produce 900 million bushels of wheat and 300 million bushels of corn (the output shown at point *E*)?

7. The division of labor enhances the value that citizens contribute to an economy. Each of the five statements below is a potential answer to a question about the division of labor; read them before going on.

(1) According to the laws of physics, matter is neither created or destroyed, it is only rearranged. Manufacturing reshapes matter; distribution relocates it. Both activities, done wisely, rearrange matter in a way that increases its value.

(2) Deciding which activities to undertake and how to undertake them are risky and costly decisions.

(3) "You measure the worth of a ballplayer by how many fannies he puts in the seats." (George Steinbrenner, baseball team owner).

(4) For jobs that are not inherently pleasant, groups of workers left on their own may not accomplish much.

(5) Lots of activities generate value without being exchanged in the marketplace.

Now read each of the questions below and indicate in the blank space to the left of the question the number of the statement above that best answers the question.

____ a. How can a baseball player ever be worth over $6 million a year?

____ b. Why not buy direct more often and cut out the wasteful middleman?

____ c. Why do so many house spouses just "sit at home" instead of going out and getting a "real" job?

____ d. Why don't we encourage more labor-managed firms so we can eliminate unproductive jobs like shift leaders and supervisors?

____ e. Why does the compensation of presidents and owners of corporations often rise and fall with the profitability of their firms instead of being fixed like most salaries?

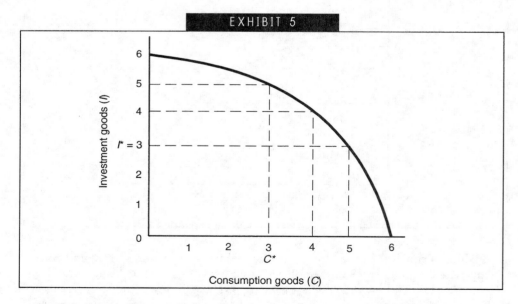

EXHIBIT 5

8. Exhibit 5 contains a production possibility curve, but instead of for two consumption goods as usual, it is specified in terms of a country's production of goods for current consumption (C) such as pizza and beer, and investment (I) goods such as new buildings and machines. Output is measured in millions of units.

$C^* = 3$ indicates the minimum level of the consumption good C that must be produced in order to avoid starving its citizens.

$I^* = 3$ indicates the amount of the investment good I necessary to replace capital equipment and resources that wear out each year. If investment falls short of I^*, the economy's production possibilities curve will shrink from its present position. If investment exceeds I^*, the economy's production possibilities curve will expand.

a. What will be the consumption/investment good production point(s) if the country wants to (1) grow as rapidly as possible without starving its citizens, or (2) wants to enjoy as much consumption as possible without reducing its future production capabilities?

b. Circle the portion of the production possibilities curve that corresponds to all points that have both more I than is needed for replacement and more C than is required to avoid starvation.

MULTIPLE CHOICE

1. The opportunity cost to the United States of placing a man on the moon was
   a. the loss of government revenues that were allocated to the mission.
   b. the cost of all production involved in the space program.
   c. the loss of utility from the highest valued bundle of products that had to be forgone because of the moon mission.
   d. less than zero, since the long-run benefit of the project will be greater than the cost.

2. When Benjamin Franklin wrote, "Remember that time is money!" he understood
   a. the incentives created by property rights.
   b. the law of comparative advantage.
   c. the concept of opportunity cost.
   d. that watches cost money.

3. An airline ticket from Seattle to Miami costs $525. A bus ticket is $325. Traveling by plane will take 5 hours, compared with 25 hours by bus. Thus, the plane costs $200 more but saves 20 hours of time (Hint: Note how we are "thinking at the margin" here by looking at the changes). Other things constant, an individual will gain by choosing air travel if, and only if, each hour of her time is valued at more than
   a. $10 per hour.
   b. $13 per hour.
   c. $20 per hour.
   d. $105 per hour.

4. Which of the following best describes the implications of the law of comparative advantage? If each person sells goods for which he or she has the greatest comparative advantage in production and buys those for which his or her comparative advantage is least, the
   a. total output available to each person can be expanded by specialization and exchange.
   b. total output will fall.
   c. buyers of goods will gain at the expense of sellers.
   d. sellers of goods will gain at the expense of buyers.

5. Keri decided to sleep in today rather than attend her 9 A.M. economics class. According to economic analysis, her choice was
   a. irrational, because economic analysis suggests you should always attend classes that you have already paid for.
   b. irrational, because oversleeping is not in Keri's self-interest.
   c. rational if Keri has not missed any other classes.
   d. rational if Keri values sleep more highly than the benefit she expects to receive from attending the class.

6. Which of the following is *not* one of the basic economic questions that all economies must answer?
   a. What will be produced?
   b. To whom will the goods produced be allocated?
   c. How will goods be produced?
   d. Which government agency will set the prices of the goods produced?

7. The owners of private property will
   a. use their property for selfish ends, taking no account of the impact their behavior has on others.
   b. use their property in ways that others value because the market will generally reward them with profits (or a higher selling price) if they do so.
   c. find very little incentive to take care of the property or conserve it for the future.
   d. lose profits when they take the wishes of others into consideration.

8. Ken values his boat at $5,000, and Monica values it at $8,000. If Monica buys it from Ken for $7,000, which of the following is true?
   a. Ken gains $2,000 of value, and Monica gains $1,000 of value.
   b. Ken gains $7,000 of value, and Monica loses $7,000 of value.
   c. Ken gains $7,000 of value, and Monica gains $3,000 of value.
   d. Ken and Monica both gain $7,000 of value.

9. When collective decision making (the political process) is used to resolve economic questions regarding the allocation of resources,
   a. decentralized decision making is present.
   b. central planning and political bargaining will replace market forces.
   c. individual preferences are of no importance.
   d. economic equality will result.

10. The law of comparative advantage suggests that
    a. individuals, states, and nations can all benefit if they trade with others.
    b. free trade among nations is harmful to an economy.
    c. each economy should strive to be self-sufficient.
    d. each country should attempt to produce roughly equal amounts of all goods.

11. When resources are being used wastefully or inefficiently, the
    a. production possibilities curve shifts inward.
    b. production possibilities curve shifts outward.
    c. economy is operating at a point inside its production possibilities constraint.
    d. economy is operating at a point outside its production possibilities constraint.

12. Which of the following is a transaction cost?
    a. price of a ticket to a concert
    b. price of food eaten before a concert
    c. time spent standing in line to buy the ticket
    d. price of a T-shirt at the concert

13. Middlemen, such as grocers, stockbrokers, and Realtors
    a. specialize in reducing transactions costs.
    b. provide nothing of value to either the buyer or the seller.
    c. have no effect on economic output in society.
    d. do not exist in capitalist economies.

14. Private property rights exist when property rights are
    a. exclusively controlled by the owner or owners.
    b. transferable to others.
    c. protected by legal enforcement.
    d. all of the above.

15. When an economy is operating efficiently, the production of more of one good
    will result in the production of less of some other good because
    a. consumers do not want more of both goods.
    b. resources are limited (scarce) and efficiency implies that all are already in use.
    c. the production possibilities curve shifts inward as more of one good is produced.
    d. technological improvement can only improve the production of a single good.

16. Which of the following would allow the production possibilities curve for an
    economy to shift outward?
    a. a better social organization of economic activity, such as conversion from
        socialism to capitalism
    b. an increase in the labor force or resource base
    c. more investment leading to better technology and more innovation
    d. all of the above

17. "If I didn't have a date tonight, I would save $10 and spend the evening playing
    tennis." The opportunity cost of the date is
    a. the other things that could be purchased with the $10.
    b. the other things that could be purchased with the $10 plus the forgone value
        of a night of tennis.
    c. dependent upon how pleasant a time one has on the date.
    d. the forgone value of a night of tennis.

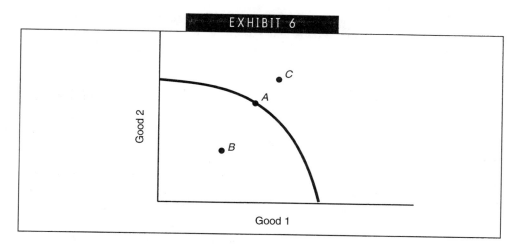

EXHIBIT 6

18. Use Exhibit 6 to answer the following question: In the above figure showing the
    production possibilities curve,
    a. *A* is efficient.
    b. *B* is inefficient.
    c. *C* is unattainable.
    d. all of the above are true.

19. Dr. Jones, a dentist, is choosing between driving and flying from Pittsburgh to New York City. If Jones drove, she would have to close her office four hours earlier than if she flew by airplane. Her expected income (after taxes) from her practice is $50 per hour. Assuming all other factors are equal, if Jones was a rational decision maker, she would drive if the price differential (air cost minus driving) was greater than
    a. $50.
    b. $100.
    c. $150.
    d. $200.

20. According to the law of comparative advantage,
    a. each producer should strive toward self-sufficiency in order to maximize the total production of the economy.
    b. each product should be produced by the lowest opportunity cost producer in order to maximize output.
    c. one should never compare one's abilities with those of another.
    d. each product should be produced by the individual who can produce more of that product than any other individual.

21. "The economic wealth of this country was built primarily by some individuals profiting from a transaction, whereas others were harmed by that transaction." This statement indicates the speaker
    a. fails to comprehend the idea that all voluntary trades benefit both parties involved.
    b. fails to comprehend the fallacy of composition.
    c. fails to understand the significance of the production possibilities curve.
    d. uses the economic way of thinking. The statement is essentially correct.

22. (I) When individuals engage in a voluntary exchange, both parties are made better off. (II) By channeling goods and resources to those who value them most, trade creates value and increases the wealth created by a society's resources.
    a. I is true; II is false.
    b. I is false; II is true.
    c. Both I and II are true.
    d. Both I and II are false.

The next two questions relate to the material in the addendum to Chapter 2. Use the following production possibilities data for Lebos and Slavia to answer these questions.

LEBOS		SLAVIA	
FOOD	CLOTHING	FOOD	CLOTHING
0	8	0	8
2	6	1	6
4	4	2	4
6	2	3	2
8	0	4	0

23. Which of the following is correct?
    a. In Lebos, the opportunity cost of producing one unit of food is equal to one unit of clothing.
    b. In Slavia, the opportunity cost of producing one unit of food is equal to two units of clothing.
    c. The opportunity cost of producing food in Lebos is less than the opportunity cost of producing food in Slavia.
    d. All of the above are correct.

24. Which of the following is correct?
    a. Lebos has the comparative advantage in both goods.
    b. Slavia has the comparative advantage in food.
    c. Lebos has the comparative advantage in food.
    d. Lebos has the comparative advantage in clothing.

DISCUSSION QUESTIONS

1. As an individual, you will ultimately take part in determining how your economy answers its three basic economic decisions. What will help you choose what *you* should produce, how *you* should produce it, and *for whom* you should produce it? Are these answers at all interrelated?

2. Consider the cost of this economics course to you.
    a. About how much money did you spend on tuition and books for this course? When did you incur these costs?
    b. What is the cost of actually attending the class once you've paid your tuition and purchased your books?
    c. Use your answer to part b to comment on the following quote: "I could earn $15 if I worked during today's economics class, but tuition averages out to $20 per lecture, so I can't afford to go. If only I went to a university where tuition is lower, I could skip class and earn the money." Do you agree or disagree? Explain your answer.

3. Explain why it is often efficient for faculty members with training in computer programming to hire student programmers to do their computer work.

4. Consider the following quote by a medical doctor who knows something about economics: "It doesn't make sense for me to care for my own lawn when my opportunity cost is $80 per hour."
    a. Do you agree with the doctor's view? Explain.
    b. Would you be surprised to find this doctor's lawn exquisitely maintained? Explain.

5. When the Khmer Rouge came to power in Cambodia in 1975, they sought to eliminate the evils of money. One part of their strategy was to eliminate those jobs that dealt primarily in money rather than the production of goods and services. In other words, they got rid of the "middlemen." What would happen to an economy that had no middlemen? What would happen to the standard of living of the average consumer? Explain.

PERSPECTIVES IN ECONOMICS

UNFAIR COMPETITION WITH THE SUN

By Frederic Bastiat

[From Frederic Bastiat, "Petition of the Manufacturers of Candles, Wax-Lights, Lamps, Candlesticks, Street Lamps, Snuffers, Extinguishers, and of the Producers of Oil, Tallow, Resin, Alcohol, and Generally, of Everything Connected with Lighting." To messieurs the members of the Chamber of Deputies.]

Gentlemen,—You are on the right road. You reject abstract theories, and have little consideration for cheapness and plenty. Your chief care is the interest of the producer. You desire to protect him from foreign competition, and reserve the *national market for national industry.*

We are suffering from the intolerable competition of a foreign rival, placed, it would seem, in a condition so far superior to ours for the production of light that he absolutely *inundates* our *national market* with it at a price fabulously reduced. The moment he shows himself our trade leaves us—all consumers apply to him; and a branch of native industry, having countless ramifications, is all at once rendered completely stagnant. This rival, who is no other than the sun, wages war to the knife against us, and we suspect that he has been raised up by *perfidious Albion* (a good policy as times go); inasmuch as he displays towards that haughty island a circumspection with which he dispenses in our case.

What we pray for is, that it may please you to pass a law ordering the shutting up of all windows, skylights, dormer-windows, outside and inside shutters, curtains, blinds, bull's-eyes, in a word, of all openings, holes, chinks, clefts, and fissures, by or through which the light of the sun has been in use to enter houses, to the prejudice of the meritorious manufactures with which we flatter ourselves we have accommodated our country—a country, which, in gratitude, ought not abandon us now to a strife so unequal.

We trust, Gentlemen, that you will not regard this our request as a satire, or refuse it without at least previously hearing the reasons which we have to urge in its support.

And, first, if you shut up as much as possible all access to natural light, and create a demand for artificial light, which of our French manufacturers will not be encouraged by it?

We foresee your objections, Gentlemen, but we know that you can oppose to us none but such as you have picked up from the effete works of the partisans of Free Trade. We defy you to utter a single word against us which will not instantly rebound against yourselves and your entire policy.

You will tell us that, if we gain by the protection which we seek, the country will lose by it, because the consumer must bear the loss.

We answer:

You have ceased to have any right to invoke the interest of the consumer for, whenever his interest is found opposed to that of the producer, you sacrifice the latter. You have done so for the purpose of encouraging workers and those who seek employment. For the same reason you should do so again.

You have yourselves obviated this objection. When you are told that the consumer is interested in the free importation of iron, coal, corn, textile fabrics—yes, you reply, but the producer is interested in their exclusion. Well, be it so; if consumers are interested in the free admission of natural light, the producers of artificial light are equally interested in its prohibition.

If you urge that the light of the sun is a gratuitous gift of nature, and that to reject such gifts is to reject wealth itself under pretense of encouraging the means of acquiring it, we would caution you against giving a death-blow to your own policy. Remember that hitherto you have always repelled foreign products, *because* they approximate more nearly than home products to the character of gratuitous gifts.

Nature and human labour cooperate in various proportions (depending on countries and climates) in the production of commodities. The part which nature executes is very gratuitous; it is the part executed by human labour which constitutes value, and is paid for.

If a Lisbon orange sells for half the price of a Paris orange, it is because natural, and consequently gratuitous, heat does for the one what artificial, and therefore expensive, heat must do for the other.

When an orange comes to us from Portugal we may conclude that it is furnished in part gratuitously, in part for an onerous consideration; in other words, it comes to us at *half-price* as compared with those of Paris.

Now, it is precisely the gratuitous *half* (pardon the word) which we contend should be excluded. You say, How can national labour sustain competition with foreign labour, when the former has all the work to do, and the latter only does one-half, the sun supplying the remainder. But if this *half*, being gratuitous, determines you to exclude competition, how should the *whole*, being gratuitous, induce you to admit competition? If you were consistent, you would, while excluding as hurtful to native industry what is half gratuitous, exclude a *fortiori* and with double zeal, that which is altogether gratuitous.

One more, when products such as coal, iron, corn, or textile fabrics are sent us from abroad, and we can acquire them with less labour than if we made them ourselves, the difference is a free gift conferred upon us. The gift is more or less considerable in proportion as the difference is more or less great. It amounts to a quarter, a half, or three-quarters of the value of the product, when the foreigner only asks us for three-fourths, a half or a quarter of the price we should otherwise pay. It is as perfect and complete as it can be, when the donor (like the sun is furnishing us with light) asks us for nothing. The question, and we ask it formally, is this: Do you desire for our country the benefit of gratuitous consumption, or the pretended advantages of onerous production?

Make your choice, but be logical; for as long as you exclude as you do, coal, iron, corn, foreign fabrics, in proportion as their price approximates to zero what inconsistency it would be to admit the light of the sun, the price of which is already at zero during the entire day!

DISCUSSION

1. What does the Bastiat reading have to do with this chapter? [*Hint:* The text states that the law of comparative advantage applies to nations as well as to individuals.] Does comparative advantage mean that *all* trade is good? Explain your answer.

2. Do you think that individuals or industries ever need protection from competition? If so, how would we decide whether an industry (like the lighting industry or the automobile industry) deserves to be protected from competition?

3. What economic arguments can you use to argue against the proposal?

CHAPTER 3

Supply, Demand, and the Market Process

TRUE OR FALSE

T F

☐ ☐ 1. Consumers will purchase fewer tacos at higher prices than at lower prices if other factors remain the same.

☐ ☐ 2. If the price of bananas increased, the demand for substitutes such as oranges and apples would increase.

☐ ☐ 3. The law of supply reflects the willingness of producers to expand output in response to an increase in the price of a product.

☐ ☐ 4. When consumer purchases of a good are highly responsive to a change in the price of a good, the demand for that good is said to be relatively inelastic.

☐ ☐ 5. An increase in demand for coffee would cause its price to rise and producers to expand output.

☐ ☐ 6. A reduction in the supply of beef would cause the price of beef to fall.

☐ ☐ 7. Hamburgers and hot dogs would be considered substitutes, while peanut butter and jelly would be considered compliments.

☐ ☐ 8. If Terri would be willing to pay up to $50 for a pair of jeans and finds them for $30, her purchase would give her $20 in consumer surplus.

☐ ☐ 9. If an increase in the price of pizza resulted in fewer pizzas being sold, this would be considered a reduction in quantity demanded, not a reduction in demand.

☐ ☐ 10. Three factors that will each cause the supply curve for Napa county wine to shift to the left include a drought in Napa county, higher wages for Napa county grape pickers, and lower prices for Napa county wine.

☐ ☐ 11. If an increase in the cost of lumber resulted in fewer new homes being produced, this would be considered a reduction in quantity supplied, not a reduction in supply.

☐ ☐ 12. An increase in the price of lumber used in the construction industry would cause housing prices to rise and the demand for housing to decline.

☐ ☐ 13. An increase in consumer income would cause the demand for new cars to increase.

☐ ☐ 14. Government regulation is the only way to coordinate economic activity in complex societies like the United States with millions of individuals buying and selling goods and services.

PROBLEMS AND PROJECTS

1. Exhibit 1 presents hypothetical supply and demand schedules for shoes in a local market area.
   a. Graph the initial demand curve (column 2) on the chart below.
   b. Graph the initial supply curve (column 3) on the chart below.
   c. What is the initial equilibrium price?
   d. The region experiences a boom and consumer income increases, causing an increase in demand. The new demand schedule is indicated in column 4. Graph the new demand curve in the chart.
   e. What is the new equilibrium price?
   f. What has happened on the demand side of the market? Is it a change in demand or a change in quantity demanded?

EXHIBIT 1

PRICE (1)	INITIAL QUANTITY DEMANDED (2)	QUANTITY SUPPLIED (3)	NEW QUANTITY DEMANDED (4)
$ 6	60	20	80
9	50	30	70
12	40	40	60
15	30	50	50
18	20	60	40
21	10	70	30

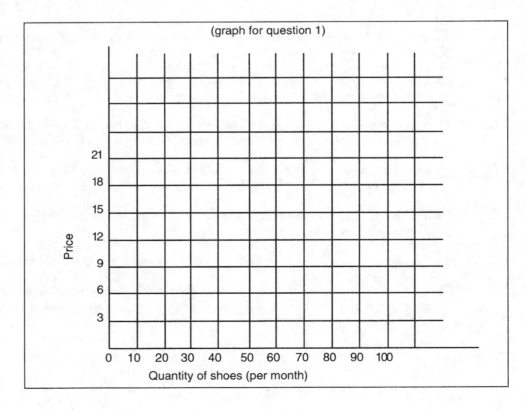

(graph for question 1)

g. What has happened on the supply side of the market? Is it a change in supply or a change in quantity supplied?

2. As indicated by Exhibit 2, the initial demand for hot dogs is D_1. The supply is S.
   a. What is the initial equilibrium price? Quantity sold?
   b. Hamburgers are a substitute for hot dogs. Higher hamburger prices cause the demand for hot dogs to increase to D_2. What is the new equilibrium price? Quantity sold?
   c. Suppose instead of hamburger prices rising, hot dog *bun* prices have fallen. Would the impact of the lower hot dog bun prices on the market for hot dogs be the same?

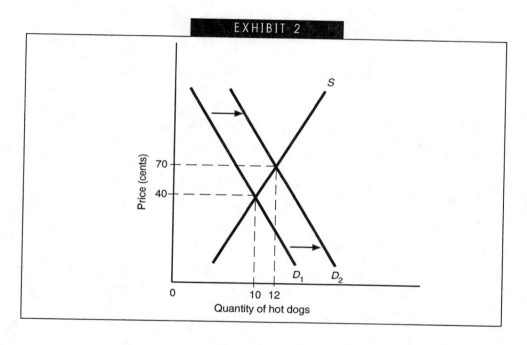

EXHIBIT 2

3. The pricing system sends out signals that influence the decisions of producers and consumers. Understanding the secondary effects of a change in market conditions is essential if one is to understand how a market system works. Suppose that the price of gasoline rose sharply. What do you think would happen to
   a. the demand for smaller, more fuel efficient cars relative to large cars?
   b. the demand for other leisure goods (such as home swimming pools), relative to cross-country driving vacations?
   c. employment in the tourism industry?
   d. the prices of consumer goods that require transportation?
   e. the demand for alternative energy sources (such as solar power) and the incentive to produce them?
   f. the incentive to find and develop new oil reserves to produce gasoline?
   g. the price of electricity, firewood, and other substitute fuels?

4. Use the diagrams below to indicate the changes in demand (*D*), supply (*S*), equilibrium price (*P*), and equilibrium quantity (*Q*) in response to the events described to the left of the diagrams. First show in the diagrams how supply and/or demand shift in response to the event, and then fill in the table to the right of the diagrams using a plus sign (+) to indicate an increase, a negative sign (–) to indicate a decrease, and 0 to indicate no change. As an example, the first question has been answered.

Market	Event	Diagrams	D	S	P	Q
a. Automobiles	The wages of autoworkers increases.		0	=	±	=
b. Oranges	Frost destroys half the Florida orange crop.		—	—	—	—
c. Butter	There is a decrease in the price of margarine (a substitute for butter)		—	—	—	—
d. Lumber	Lower interest rates cause a housing construction boom.		—	—	—	—
e. Wine	A technological advance lowers the cost of growing grapes		—	—	—	—

5. Exhibit 3 illustrates two different demand curves with different slopes, D_1 and D_2.
    a. If the price rises from $5 to $15, by how much will consumer purchases fall if the demand curve is given by D_1?
    b. If the price rises from $5 to $15, by how much will consumer purchases fall if the demand curve is instead given by D_2?
    c. Which of the demand curves represents consumers being more responsive in their purchases to a change in the price of the good?
    d. Which of the demand curves would be considered relatively elastic? Which would be considered relatively inelastic?

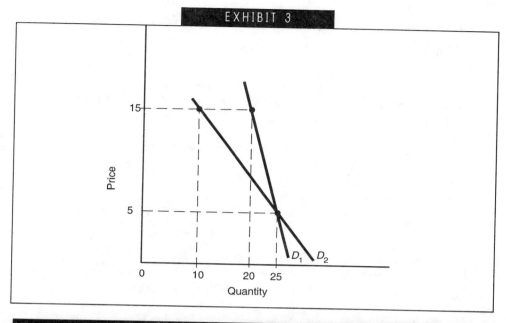

EXHIBIT 3

MULTIPLE CHOICE

1. If the price of tickets to the World Series were set below the equilibrium price,
    a. the quantity demanded would be smaller than the quantity supplied.
    b. the demand for World Series tickets would be highly responsive to the price.
    c. there would be no transactions between buyers and sellers of the tickets.
    d. the number of persons seeking to obtain tickets to World Series games would be greater than the number of tickets available.

2. Which of the following would cause the price of automobiles to rise?
    a. a decrease in the wages of autoworkers
    b. a reduction in the price of bus travel
    c. an increase in the price of gasoline
    d. an increase in consumer income

3. Which of the following would be the best example of consumer surplus?
    a. Jane pays $30 a month for phone service even though it is worth $70 to her.
    b. Sam refuses to pay $10 for a haircut because it is only worth $8 to him.
    c. Fred buys a car for $4,000, the maximum amount that he would be willing to pay for it.
    d. When Sue purchases a candy bar for $.50, she uses a $20 bill to pay for it.

4. If cigars and cigarettes are substitute goods, an increase in the price of cigars would result in
    a. an increase in the demand for cigarettes.
    b. a decrease in the price of cigarettes.
    c. a decrease in the demand for cigarettes.
    d. a decrease in the demand for cigars.

5. Which of the following would most likely cause the current demand for video cassette recorders (VCRs) to fall?
   a. an increase in consumer income
   b. an increase in the price of VCRs
   c. an increase in the price of laser disc players, a substitute good
   d. the expectation that the price of VCRs will decrease sharply during the next six months

6. Which of the following would be most likely to cause the demand for Miller beer to increase?
   a. an increase in the price of Budweiser beer
   b. a decrease in consumer income
   c. a decrease in the price of barley used to make Miller beer
   d. a decrease in the price of Miller beer

7. (I) The height of the demand curve for a commodity indicates the maximum amount the consumer would be willing to pay for each unit of the good. (II) The height of the supply curve for a commodity indicates the minimum price the seller would accept for each unit of the good.
   a. I is true; II is false.
   b. I is false; II is true.
   c. Both I and II are false.
   d. Both I and II are true.

8. All things constant, a decrease in bus, train, and airplane fares will
   a. shift the demand curve for automobiles to the left.
   b. cause a movement along the demand curve for automobiles.
   c. shift the demand curve for automobiles to the right.
   d. have no impact on the demand curve for automobiles.

9. If coffee and cream are complements, a decrease in the price of coffee will cause
   a. the demand for cream to decrease.
   b. the demand for cream to increase.
   c. the demand for coffee to increase.
   d. no change in the demand for cream; only quantity demanded would be affected.

10. If the market price is above the equilibrium price, there will be a tendency for price to decrease, causing
    a. the quantity demanded to decrease and the quantity supplied to increase until they are equal.
    b. the quantity demanded to increase and the quantity supplied to decrease until they are equal.
    c. both quantity demanded and quantity supplied to decrease until they are equal.
    d. both quantity demanded and quantity supplied to increase until they are equal.

11. According to the law of supply, as the price of a good decreases
    a. buyers will buy more of the good.
    b. sellers will produce more of the good.
    c. buyers will buy less of the good.
    d. sellers will produce less of the good.

12. John advertises his used car for $3,000 in the newspaper. He would be willing to sell his used car for as low as $2,000. He is offered $2,600 for it from a buyer and accepts it. In this trade, John receives
    a. producer surplus of $3,000.
    b. producer surplus of $2,600.
    c. producer surplus of $600.
    d. consumer surplus of $400.

13. Economic efficiency requires that
    a. individuals take all actions within their power.
    b. only long-lasting, high-quality products be produced.
    c. income be distributed equally among individuals.
    d. all economic activity generating more benefits than costs to individuals in the economy be undertaken.

14. If the demand for beer increased, what would be the effect on the equilibrium price and quantity of beer?
    a. price increases, quantity decreases
    b. price decreases, quantity decreases
    c. price increases, quantity increases
    d. price decreases, quantity increases

15. In Exhibit 4, there are two triangular areas indicated by the letters *A* and *B*. Which of the following is true?
    a. *A* represents consumer surplus; *B* represents producer surplus.
    b. *A* represents producer surplus; *B* represents consumer surplus.
    c. Both areas *A* and *B* represent consumer surplus.
    d. Both areas *A* and *B* represent producer surplus.

EXHIBIT 4

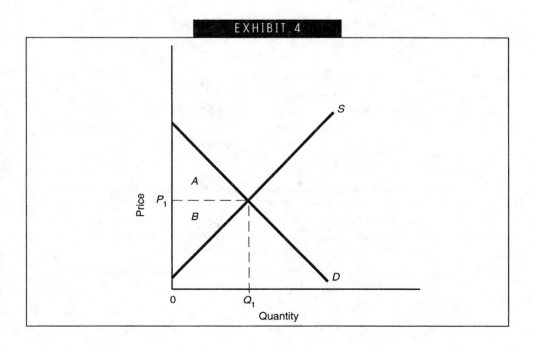

16. "Falling consumer income from the recent recession has hurt automakers in more ways than one. Not only have sales of new cars fallen, but car prices have fallen as well. As a result, the major automakers have announced cutbacks in production and layoffs of workers." Which of the following places these statements in the proper economic terminology within the context of the supply and demand model? [Note: It may help to graph this first.]
    a. a decrease in demand and a decrease in supply
    b. a decrease in demand and a decrease in quantity supplied
    c. a decrease in quantity demanded and a decrease in quantity supplied
    d. a decrease in quantity demanded and a decrease in supply.

17. "If gasoline were taxed, the price of gasoline would rise. Consequently, the demand for gasoline would fall, causing the price to fall to the original level." This statement is
    a. essentially correct.
    b. incorrect—after the demand falls, the price would fall but to some level higher than the original level.
    c. incorrect—demand and quantity demanded are confused. The price increase would reduce quantity demanded, not demand.
    d. incorrect—after the demand falls, the price would fall but to some level lower than the original level.

18. Over the past 20 years both the quantity of health care provided and health care prices have been rising rapidly. Economic theory would suggest that the observed data could best be explained as
    a. an increase in supply, while demand remained relatively constant.
    b. a decrease in both supply and demand.
    c. an increase in demand, while supply remained relatively constant.
    d. a sharp increase in both supply and demand.

19. A decrease in the supply of a good will
    a. decrease the demand for the good.
    b. cause the price of the good to fall.
    c. lead to an increase in the price of the good.
    d. increase the quantity of the good bought and sold.

20. Which of the following would most likely decrease the price of beef?
    a. lower prices of grains used to produce cattle feed
    b. higher prices for chicken, a substitute for beef
    c. a cow disease that destroys millions of cattle (and makes their meat unfit for consumption) before they are ready for market
    d. an increase in consumer income

21. The price of gasoline increases. Purchasers of gasoline will probably
    a. reduce their purchases more in the long run than in the short run.
    b. reduce their purchases more in the short run than in the long run.
    c. reduce their purchases equally in both the short and long run.
    d. increase their purchases, since the higher gasoline price will increase supply.

22. When Adam Smith said economic activity was directed by an "invisible hand," he was referring to the fact that
    a. competitive markets motivate altruistic individuals to pursue productive activities that only serve their private interests.
    b. when economic activity is directed by competitive markets, the actions of self-interested individuals will generally serve the public interest.
    c. invisible forces will lead to economic chaos unless wise central planning directs economic activity.
    d. scarcity is largely the result of invisible forces that would be eliminated if individuals were free to pursue their own self-interests.

23. A hurricane damaged much of the housing in Miami. Shortly thereafter, the price of plywood rose significantly. The events suggest that
    a. a decrease in the supply of plywood caused the price of plywood to rise.
    b. an increase in the supply of plywood caused the price of plywood to rise.
    c. a decrease in the demand for plywood caused the price of plywood to rise.
    d. an increase in the demand for plywood caused the price of plywood to rise.

24. If the demand for a good increases, which of the following will generally occur in a market setting?
    a. The price of the good will decrease.
    b. The supply of the good will increase.
    c. The quantity supplied will increase.
    d. Producer profits will fall.

DISCUSSION QUESTIONS

1. In an effort to increase the number of students going to college, the federal government is considering legislation that would give a large tax credit to low-income families with college tuition payments. What impact would the legislation have on the
    a. number of students attempting to enroll in college?
    b. price of tuition for other students?
    c. salaries earned by college graduates?
    d. wage rates in low-skilled occupations that only require a high school degree?
    e. salaries earned by college professors?

2. Consider the following statement: "Campus parking permits and meters are inefficient and unfair. Campus parking should be free, with parking spaces allocated on a first-come, first-served basis."
    a. Is "free" parking that requires time to hunt for a space (or requires students to get into school earlier) really free?
    b. Is "free" parking more efficient than permit or meter parking? In other words, is rationing the spaces by price more or less efficient than rationing them by the cost of student time?
    c. With "free" parking, who, if anyone, gains? Who loses?
    d. Would you favor "free" parking on your campus? Why or why not?

3. Explain what is wrong with the following reasoning: "When meat prices rise due to a decrease in the supply of meat, the demand for meat decreases, so meat prices end up falling."
    a. Suppose a price is temporarily above its equilibrium level. How do you think producers figure out the price is in fact "too high"? Explain how a lower price

causes both production and consumption adjustments to help correct the situation.

   b.   Suppose a price is temporarily below its equilibrium level. How do you think producers figure out the price is in fact "too low"? Explain how a higher price causes both production and consumption adjustments to help correct the situation.

4.   People often use the term "demand" when they actually mean "quantity demanded"; the same is true of "supply" and "quantity supplied."

   a.   What causes a change in quantity demanded but not a change in demand?

   b.   With market determined prices, can the following statement be true: "The demand for oil is expected to exceed supply by 2050"?

   c.   How can you rephrase the statement of part b so that it makes economic sense?

5.   Define both consumer and producer surplus, and give an example of each. Define economic efficiency, and show graphically how it relates to the consumer and producer surplus areas within a supply and demand graph.

6.   There are some occasions when shortages or surpluses appear. For example, there is routinely a shortage of tickets to "hot" concerts or sporting events—people who want the tickets at the listed price are unable to get them. Can you think of any other situations you have seen where the market had either a shortage or a surplus (in other words, out of equilibrium)? Was the situation temporary? What caused the problem, was the price set too high or too low?

PERSPECTIVES IN ECONOMICS

THE USE OF KNOWLEDGE IN SOCIETY

by Friedrich A. Hayek

[Abridged from "The Use of Knowledge in Society," *American Economic Review*, volume 35, number 4, September 1945, pp. 519–530. Reprinted with permission.]

What is the problem we wish to solve when we try to construct a rational economic order?

On certain familiar assumptions the answer is simple enough. *If* we possess all the relevant information, *if* we can start out from a given system of preferences and *if* we command complete knowledge of available means, the problem which remains is purely one of logic.

This, however, is emphatically *not* the economic problem which society faces. The reason for this is that the "data" from which the economic calculus starts are never for the whole society "given" to a single mind which could work out the implications, and can never be so given.

The peculiar character of the problem of a rational economic order is determined precisely by the fact that the knowledge of the circumstances of which we must make use never exists in concentrated or integrated form, but solely as the dispersed bits of incomplete and frequently contradictory knowledge which all the separate individuals possess. The economic problem of society is thus not merely a problem of how to allocate "given" resources—if "given" is taken to mean given to a single mind which deliberately soles the problem set by these "data." It is rather a problem of how to secure the best use of resources known to any of the members of society, for ends whose relative importance only these individuals know. Or, to put it briefly, it is a problem of the utilization of knowledge not given to anyone in its totality.

If we can agree that the economic problem of society is mainly one of rapid adaptation to changes in the particular circumstances of time and place, it would seem to follow that the ultimate decisions must be left to the people who are familiar with these circumstances, who know directly of the relevant changes and of the resources immediately available to meet them. We cannot expect that this problem will be solved by first communicating all this knowledge to a central board which, after integrating *all* knowledge, issues its orders. We must solve it by some form of decentralization. But this answers only part of our problem. We need decentralization because only thus can we ensure that the knowledge of the particular circumstances of time and place will be promptly used. But the "man on the spot" cannot decide solely on the basis of his limited but intimate knowledge of the facts of his immediate surroundings. There still remains the problem of communicating to him such further information as he needs to fit his decisions into the whole pattern of changes of the larger economic system.

There is hardly anything that happens anywhere in the world that *might* not have an effect on the decision he ought to make. Be he need not know of these events as such, not of *all* their effects. It does not matter for him *why* at the particular moment more screws of one size than of another are wanted, *why* paper bags are more readily available than canvas bags, or *why* skilled labor, or particular machine tools, have for the moment become more difficult to acquire. All that is significant for him is *how much more or less* difficult to procure they have become compared with other things with which he is also concerned, or how much more or less urgently wanted are the alternative things he produces or uses. It is always a question of the relative importance of the particular things with which he is concerned, and the causes which alter their relative importance are of no interest to him beyond the effect on those concrete things of his own environment.

Fundamentally, in a system where the knowledge of the relevant facts is dispersed among many people, prices can act to coordinate the separate actions of different people in the same way as subjective values help the individual to coordinate the parts of his plan. It is worth contemplating for a moment a very simple and commonplace instance of the action of the price system to see what precisely it accomplishes. Assume that somewhere in the world a new opportunity for the use of some raw material, say tin, has arisen, or that one of the sources of supply of tin has been eliminated. It does not matter for our purpose—and it is very significant that it does not matter—which of these two causes has made tin more scarce. All that the users of tin need to know is that some of the tin they used to consume is now more profitably employed elsewhere, and that in consequence they must economize tin. There is no need for the great majority of them even to know where the more urgent need has arisen, or in favor of what other needs they ought to husband the supply. If only some of them know directly of the new demand, and switch resources over to it, and if the people who are aware of the new gap thus created in turn fill it from still other sources, the effect will rapidly spread throughout the whole economic system and influence not only all the uses of tin, but also those of its substitutes and the substitutes of these substitutes, the supply of all the things made of tin, and their substitutes, and so on; and all this without the great majority of those instrumental in bringing about these substitutions knowing anything at all about the original cause of these changes. The whole acts as one market, not because any of its members survey the whole field, but because their limited individual fields of vision sufficiently overlap so that through many intermediaries the relevant information is communicated to all.

We must look at the price system as such a mechanism for communicating information if we want to understand its real function. The most significant fact about this system is the economy of knowledge with which it operates, or how little the individual participants need to know in order to be able to take the right action. In abbreviated form, by a kind of symbol, only the most essential information is passed on, and passed on only to those concerned. It is more than a metaphor to describe the price system as a kind of machinery for registering change, or a system of telecommunications which enables individual producers to watch merely the movement of a few pointers, as an engineer might watch the hands of a few dials, in order to adjust their activities to changes of which they may never know more than is reflected in the price movement.

Of course, these adjustments are probably never "perfect" in the sense in which the economist conceives of them in his equilibrium analysis. But I fear that our theoretical habits of approaching the problem with the assumption of more or less perfect knowledge on the part of almost everyone has made us somewhat blind to the true function of the price mechanism and led us to apply rather misleading standards in judging its efficiency. The marvel is that in a case like that of a scarcity of one raw material, without an order being issued, without more than perhaps a handful of people knowing the cause, tens of thousands of people whose identity could not be ascertained by months of investigation, are made to use the material or its products more sparingly; *i.e.*, they move in the right direction. This is enough of a marvel even if, in a constantly changing world, not all will hit it off so perfectly that their profit rates will always be maintained at the same constant or "normal" level.

I have deliberately used the word "marvel" to shock the reader out of the complacency with which we often take the working of this mechanism for granted. I am convinced that if it were the result of deliberate human design, and if the people guided by the price changes understood that their decisions have significance far beyond their immediate aim, this mechanism would have been acclaimed as one of the greatest triumphs of the human mind. Its misfortune is the double one that it is not the product of human design and that the people guided by it usually do not know why they are made to do what they do. But those who clamor for "conscious direction"—and who cannot believe that anything which has evolved without design (and even without our understanding it) should solve problems which we should not be able to solve consciously—should remember this: The problem is precisely how to extend the span of our utilization of resources beyond the span of the control of any one mind; and, therefore, how to dispense with the need of conscious control and how to provide inducements which will make the individuals do the desirable things without anyone having to tell them what to do.

The price system is just one of those formations which man has learned to use (though he is still very far from having learned to make the best use of it) after he had stumbled upon it without understanding it. Through it not only a division of labor but also a coordinated utilization of resources based on an equally divided knowledge has become possible. The people who like to deride any suggestion that this may be so usually distort the argument by insinuating that it asserts that by some miracle just that sort of system has spontaneously grown up which is best suited to modern civilization. It is the other way round: man has been able to develop that division of labor on which our civilization is based because he happened to stumble upon a method which made it possible. Had he not done so he might still have developed some other, altogether different, type of civilization, something like the "state" of the termite ants, or some other altogether unimaginable type. All that we can say is that nobody has yet succeeded in designing an alternative system in which certain features of the existing one can be preserved which are dear even to those who most violently assail it-such as particularly the extent to which the individual can choose his pursuits and consequently freely use his own knowledge and skill.

DISCUSSION

1. What does the Hayek reading have to do with this chapter? How does it relate to Adam Smith's invisible hand principle?

2. Are prices an effective mechanism to communicate information? Do they save people time in having to acquire information about events to adjust their behavior?

3. Do the signals sent by price changes cause people to adjust their behavior in ways that are consistent with what is best for society in the face of the new events?

CHAPTER 4

Supply and Demand: Applications and Extensions

T F

☐ ☐ 1. Wage rates, interest rates, and exchange rates are all market prices determined by the relative supply and demand in those markets.

☐ ☐ 2. If the demand for housing increased, the demand for resources used to produce housing (such as lumber) would fall.

☐ ☐ 3. A sudden increase in the willingness of individuals to save would cause the market interest rate to rise.

☐ ☐ 4. If the current exchange rate is one dollar equals three Mexican pesos, the cost of purchasing a 60 peso product in dollars is $20.

☐ ☐ 5. An increase in foreign demand for products made in the United States would cause the dollar to appreciate.

☐ ☐ 6. A depreciation of the U.S. dollar would make U.S. products more expensive to foreigners, thus causing U.S. exports to decline.

☐ ☐ 7. If the government imposed a price ceiling of $1 on compact discs, there would be a surplus of compact discs.

☐ ☐ 8. Shortages arise when prices are legally set above the equilibrium level.

☐ ☐ 9. The minimum wage increases unemployment among unskilled workers.

☐ ☐ 10. As illegal drug markets illustrate, the lack of contract and private property right enforcement causes harmful secondary effects that keep these black markets from operating as smoothly as legal markets.

☐ ☐ 11. The individuals on whom a tax is imposed are always the ones who end up bearing the burden of the tax.

☐ ☐ 12. The actual burden of a tax does not depend on the original legal (or statutory) assignment of the tax, but it does depend upon the elasticities of demand and supply.

☐ ☐ 13. Because taxes reduce the number of mutually beneficial trades in a market, they create an excess burden (or deadweight loss) in addition to the direct revenue burden of the tax.

☐ ☐ 14. A proportional tax is one in which everyone pays the same dollar amount of taxes regardless of income.

☐ ☐ 15. When marginal tax rates are very high, the Laffer curve suggests that lowering tax rates will result in an *increase* in tax revenue.

PROBLEMS AND PROJECTS

1. Using the supplied diagrams, show how the indicated events would affect these markets.

    a. Exhibit 1A shows the job market for accountants. Using Exhibit 1A (i) show how an increase in the number of students majoring in accounting would affect the wage rate and employment of accountants. Using Exhibit 1A (ii) show how a tax reform that vastly increased the simplicity of the tax code would affect the wage rate and employment of accountants.

EXHIBIT 1A

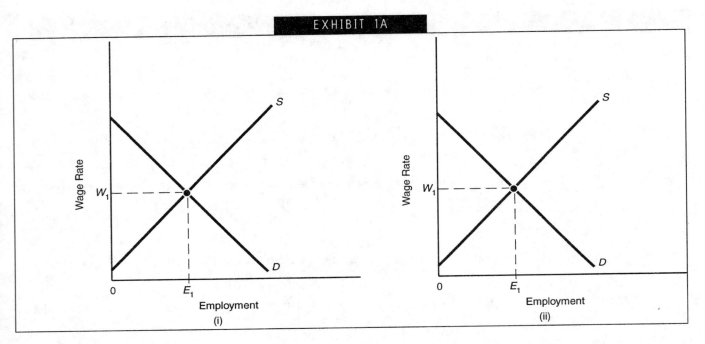

(i)

(ii)

    b. Exhibit 1B shows the market for loanable funds. Using Exhibit 1B (i) show how a decrease in the number of persons seeking new automobile loans would affect the interest rate and quantity of loans. Using Exhibit 1B (ii) show how an increase in the desire of households to save their income would affect the interest rate and quantity of loans.

    c. Exhibit 1C shows the foreign exchange market for the Mexican peso. Using Exhibit 1C (i) show how an increase in the desire of Americans to go on vacation to Mexico would affect the value of the peso and the quantity exchanged. In Exhibit 1C (i), has the peso appreciated or depreciated relative to the U.S. dollar? Using Exhibit 1C (ii) show how an increase in the desire of Mexicans to purchase foreign-made goods (for instance, U.S. automobiles) would affect the value of the peso and the quantity exchanged. In Exhibit 1C (ii), has the peso appreciated or depreciated relative to the U.S. dollar?

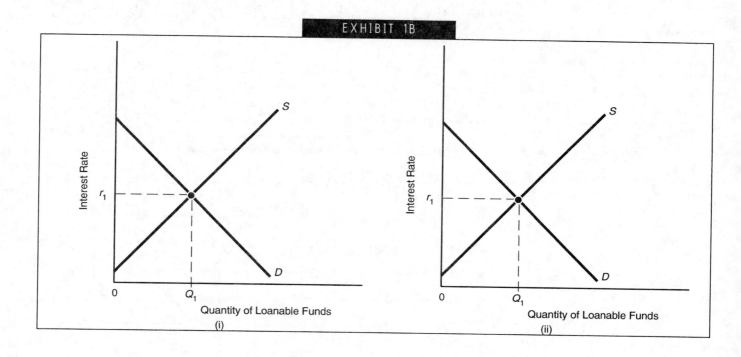

EXHIBIT 1B

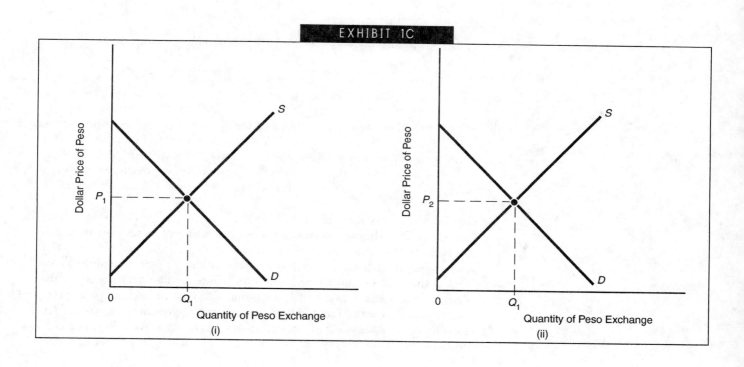

EXHIBIT 1C

2. Exhibit 2 shows the market for rental housing in a college town.
   a. Indicate in the diagram the equilibrium price and quantity for rental housing.
   b. If a law is passed setting a maximum monthly rental rate at $100, what would happen to the quantity of rental housing supplied? The quantity demanded? Is there a surplus or a shortage?
   c. What would you expect to happen to the rate of new rental housing construction in the future?

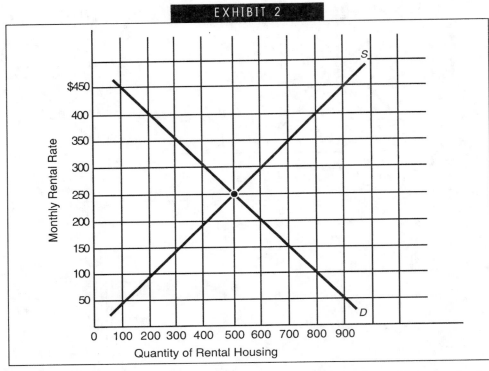

EXHIBIT 2

d. What would you expect to happen to the quality of rental housing in the area?
   e. With so many renters hunting after only a very limited number of apartments, what criterion do you think landlords will use to ration the apartments now that they are forbidden by law from rationing them by price?

3. Exhibit 3 shows the market for unskilled labor.
   a. Indicate in the diagram the equilibrium wage and level of employment for unskilled labor.
   b. Suppose a minimum wage of $6 per hour is enacted for unskilled labor. What would happen to the number of workers searching for jobs in this market (that is, the quantity of labor supplied)? What would happen to the number of job openings available at this higher wage rate (that is, the quantity of labor demanded)?
   c. Does the imposition of the minimum wage create a shortage or a surplus of labor?
   d. Are the workers who are able to retain their jobs at this higher wage better off or worse off?
   e. Are the workers who are now no longer able to find jobs at this higher wage better off or worse off?

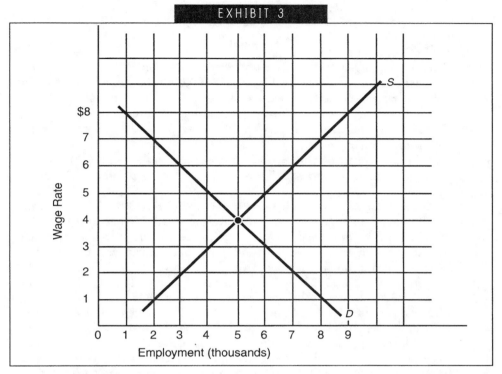

EXHIBIT 3

4. Exhibit 4 shows how a $1 per beer tax, statutorily imposed on beer sellers, affects the market for beer. Use the exhibit to answer the following questions.
   a. What was the original price of beer prior to the imposition of the tax?
   b. What is the new price that a consumer must pay for a beer after the imposition of the tax on sellers? How much has the price to consumers risen?
   c. After selling a beer at the new market price, the seller must send the government $1 in tax for the beer. What is the new net (after-tax) price the seller receives from selling a beer? How much has the price a seller receives fallen?
   d. Who has borne the larger share of the actual burden of the tax, beer buyers or sellers?
   e. How much revenue has the government raised from this tax? Shade in the area that represents tax revenue in the exhibit.
   f. How much has this tax reduced beer consumption? Shade in the area in the exhibit representing the losses to buyers and sellers from the reductions in these trades (that is, the area representing the deadweight loss of the tax).
   g. Show in the exhibit how the market would have appeared had an equal tax have been imposed on buyers instead of sellers (so that there would be a tax amount added on your purchase, just as is the regular consumer sales tax). What would have been the new market price of beer? How much would sellers have received per beer sold? How much would consumers pay for a beer considering both the price of a beer and the additional $1 tax?
   h. How would the actual burden of the tax differed had the tax been imposed on buyers rather than sellers?

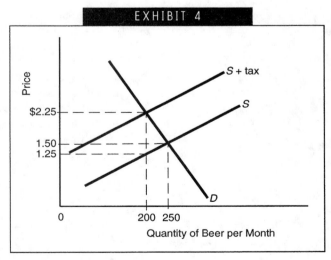

EXHIBIT 4

5. Reagan currently makes $50,000 in taxable income and pays $10,000 in taxes on her income. Her boss offers her a promotion that would double her taxable income to $100,000 per year.
    a. What is Reagan's current average tax rate on her income?
    b. Suppose that at her new level of income ($100,000) she will owe $15,000 in taxes. What will be her new average tax rate? What is the marginal tax rate on this additional income? What percent of her additional income does she get to keep in the form of additional take-home pay? Is this tax code regressive, proportional, or progressive?
    c. Explain how in part b above the tax is regressive even though she is now paying more taxes than before ($15,000 in taxes as opposed to her old taxes of $10,000).
    d. Instead, now suppose that at her new level of income ($100,000) she will owe $20,000 in taxes. What will be her new average tax rate? What is the marginal tax rate on this additional income? What percent of her additional income does she get to keep in the form of additional take-home pay? Is this tax code regressive, proportional, or progressive?
    e. Instead, now suppose that at her new level of income ($100,000) she will owe $35,000 in taxes. What will be her new average tax rate? What is the marginal tax rate on this additional income? What percent of her additional income does she get to keep in the form of additional take-home pay? Is this tax code regressive, proportional, or progressive?
    f. Instead, now suppose that at her new level of income ($100,000) she will owe $60,000 in taxes. What will be her new average tax rate? What is the marginal tax rate on this additional income? What percent of her additional income does she get to keep in the form of additional take-home pay? Is this tax code regressive, proportional, or progressive? Under this final case, would you suggest she take the promotion if it required additional responsibilities and longer work hours?

6. When a tax is imposed on a product, the price rises and consumers cut back on their purchases of the product. Exhibit 5 shows this relationship for a tax on candy bars.
    a. For each tax rate, calculate the total tax revenue raised by the tax and put your numbers in the spaces provided in the table.
    b. Now, using your answers from part a, plot the relationship between the tax rate and tax revenue in the space provided. Connect the data points with a curved line, this is the Laffer curve for the candy bar tax.
    c. If the government's objective was to maximize the revenue from this tax, what tax rate should be chosen?
    d. If the current tax rate on candy bars was $5, what would you suggest the government do if it wanted to increase its revenue, lower or raise the candy bar tax?

EXHIBIT 5

TAX PER CANDY BAR	QUANTITY OF CANDY BARS SOLD	TAX REVENUE
$0	600	$_____
1	500	_____
2	400	_____
3	300	_____
4	200	_____
5	100	_____
6	0	_____

MULTIPLE CHOICE

1. An increase in the demand for a product will cause output to
   a. increase and both the demand for and prices of the resources used to produce the product to increase.
   b. increase and both the demand for and prices of the resources used to produce the product to decrease.
   c. decrease; the demand for the resources used to produce the product will remain constant.
   d. decrease; the price of resources used to produce the product will decrease.

2. Suppose business decision makers become more optimistic about future economic conditions and desire additional funds to expand their plant capacity. What is the likely effect on the loanable funds market?
   a. The demand for loanable funds will rise and the interest rate will rise.
   b. The demand for loanable funds will fall and the interest rate will fall.
   c. The supply for loanable funds will rise and the interest rate will fall.
   d. The supply for loanable funds will fall and the interest rate will rise.

3. An increase in the dollar price of the Mexican peso (an appreciation of the peso) would cause
   a. Mexico's imports to increase and exports to decline.
   b. Mexico's exports to increase and imports to decline.
   c. both Mexico's imports and exports to decline.
   d. both Mexico's imports and exports to rise.

4. During the imposition of price controls in the 1970s, long gasoline lines were common. In the absence of price controls, markets would have eliminated such excess demand by
   a. allowing the price to rise, so gas was rationed to those willing to pay the most for it.
   b. increasing the gap between supply and demand.
   c. allowing price to decline, so the poor could afford to buy more gas.
   d. mandating a 50-mile-per-hour speed limit to reduce consumption.

5. If an increase in the government-imposed minimum wage pushes the price (wage) of unskilled labor above market equilibrium, which of the following will most likely occur in the unskilled labor market?
   a. an increase in demand for unskilled labor
   b. a decrease in the supply of unskilled labor
   c. a shortage of unskilled labor
   d. a surplus of unskilled labor

6. With a price ceiling above the equilibrium price,
   a. quantity demanded would exceed quantity supplied.
   b. quantity supplied would exceed quantity demanded.
   c. the market would be in equilibrium.
   d. the equilibrium price would be expected to fall over time.

7. Rent controls generally fix the price of rental housing below market equilibrium. Economic analysis suggests these controls
   a. are effective in helping the poor find housing.
   b. improve the quality of housing available to consumers.
   c. create a surplus of rental housing.
   d. reduce the future supply of rental housing.

8. Because illegal drug markets operate outside the legal system,
   a. the quality of these drugs has increased.
   b. the sellers of illegal drugs earn less money.
   c. there is less violence in these markets than if they were legal.
   d. none of the above.

9. Currently, federal and state gasoline taxes (imposed statutorily on the sellers of gasoline) amount to about $.45 per gallon. Suppose the current price of gasoline is $1.20 per gallon, and that if the tax was not in place, the price would be only $.80.
   a. The full incidence of the tax is falling on consumers.
   b. The full incidence of the tax is falling on suppliers.
   c. A $.05 burden is being borne by sellers and $.40 by consumers.
   d. A $.05 burden is being borne by consumers and $.40 by sellers.

10. The deadweight loss resulting from levying a tax on an economic activity is
    a. the tax revenue directed to the government as the result of the tax.
    b. the loss of potential gains from trade from activities forgone because of the tax.
    c. the increase in the price of an activity as the result of the tax levied on it.
    d. the marginal benefits derived from the expansion in government activities made possible by the increase in tax revenues.

11. Suppose there is an increase in the excise tax imposed on cigarettes, a good for which the demand is relatively inelastic. The short-run burden of the tax increase will be borne primarily by
    a. consumers, because the increase in market price will be large relative to the increase in the excise tax.
    b. firms, because the increase in market price will be large relative to the increase in the excise tax.
    c. consumers, because the increase in market price will be small relative to the increase in the excise tax.
    d. firms, because the increase in market price will be small relative to the increase in the excise tax.

12. An income tax is regressive if
    a. the tax liability of high-income recipients exceeds the tax liability of those with low incomes.
    b. the tax liability of high-income recipients is less than the tax liability of those with low incomes.
    c. high-income recipients pay a higher percentage of their incomes in taxes than those with low incomes.
    d. high-income recipients pay a lower percentage of their incomes in taxes than those whose incomes are low.

13. Use the table below to choose the correct answer.

INCOME	TAX LIABILITY
$10,000	$1,000
20,000	2,000
30,000	3,000
40,000	4,000

    For the income range illustrated, the tax shown here is
    a. regressive.
    b. proportional.
    c. progressive.
    d. progressive up to $30,000 but regressive beyond that.

14. In the mid-1940s, the marginal income tax rate in the top income tax bracket was 94 percent. In the 1960s, the top rate was lowered to 70 percent, and in the 1980s, the top rate was again lowered to 28 percent. The data show that as a result of these tax rate reductions, tax revenue (particularly from the rich) increased. This is consistent with the idea illustrated with the
    a. Laffer curve.
    b. production possibilities curve.
    c. supply of loanable funds curve.
    d. demand for unskilled labor curve.

15. The Laffer curve illustrates the principle that
    a. when tax rates are quite high, reducing tax rates will increase tax revenue.
    b. when tax rates are quite low, reducing tax rates will increase tax revenue.
    c. when tax rates are quite high, reducing tax rates will decrease tax revenue.
    d. increasing tax rates always increases tax revenue.

16. If Joan pays $5,000 in taxes when she earns $20,000 and must pay $12,000 in taxes when she earns $30,000, she faces a marginal tax rate in this income range of
    a. 25 percent.
    b. 30 percent.
    c. 40 percent.
    d. 70 percent.

17. A legal minimum wage is an example of
    a. the invisible hand principle.
    b. a price floor.
    c. a price ceiling.
    d. a fringe benefit.

18. Both price floors and price ceilings, when effective, lead to
    a. shortages.
    b. surpluses.
    c. an increase in the quantity traded.
    d. a reduction in the quantity traded.

19. If there was an increase in the excise tax on beer, what would be the effect on the equilibrium price and quantity of beer?
    a. price increases, quantity decreases
    b. price decreases, quantity decreases
    c. price increases, quantity increases
    d. price decreases, quantity increases

20. The more elastic the supply of a product, the more likely it is that the burden of a tax will
    a. fall on sellers.
    b. fall on buyers.
    c. fall equally on both buyers and sellers.
    d. be borne by the public sector, and not by market participants.

DISCUSSION QUESTIONS

1. Many uninformed people believe that the reductions in the income tax rates during the 1980s were the cause of the large budget deficits during that period. However, data show that the effect of the tax rate reductions was to increase tax revenue, not lower it.
   a. Use the Laffer curve to illustrate how a reduction in tax rates can increase tax revenue.
   b. Explain in words how it is possible to obtain more revenue when tax rates are lowered. (Hint: What must happen to the tax base?)
   c. Had the tax rate reductions not have been enacted, would the budget problems have been worse or better?

2. Evaluate the following statements. "Currently there are 100,000 six-packs of soda sold per year in our state. We are going to impose a $10 tax on each six-pack and require that the seller of the soda pays the tax. In this way we will raise $1,000,000 for the state budget, and none of the burden will be borne by our state consumers."
   a. Will the tax raise $1,000,000 in revenue? Explain.
   b. How much revenue would you expect the state to get from this tax?
   c. Is it true that consumers will bear none of the burden of this tax because it is legally imposed on the sellers? Show using a graph.

3. Consider the health care industry. We could allow the market to allocate health care through the price mechanism (*rationing by price*), or we could have the government set the price of health care at a low level so that it would be "affordable" for all citizens. Assume that when the government sets a low price for health care, health care services are allocated on a first-come, first-served basis (*rationing by waiting*).
   a. What type of waste occurs with rationing by waiting?
   b. Suppose there is a surge in demand for health care services. Which rationing system provides health care providers with better information and incentives? Explain.
   c. Health care involves a variety of services including preventive care (checkups and diagnostic procedures), treatment of illness and injuries, expensive and/or experimental procedures to care for the critically ill and injured, and plastic surgery or other elective procedures. What mix of these services would you expect to see in a system rationed by price? What mix of health care services would you expect to see in a system rationed by waiting? [Hint: Who would get more health care in a system rationed by price? By waiting?]
   d. What other rationing schemes are possible? What effects would they have on the efficiency of health care delivery? What effects would they have on the mix of health care services provided?
   e. Why should health care be rationed at all? Why not provide unlimited health care to everyone?

4. In an effort to control rising prices during the 1970s, many governments adopted price controls, fixing prices (and wages) for extended periods of time and thereby causing shortages of some goods and surpluses of others. Respond to the following statement: "Shortages are a disadvantage of price controls, but surpluses are an offsetting advantage."

5. Market prices coordinate economic activity by providing the proper incentives and bringing into harmony the desires of buyers and sellers. Explain how market prices coordinate the following:
    a. the actions of those wanting to save with those wanting to borrow.
    b. the relationship between a country's imports and exports.
    c. the markets for labor in terms of job seekers and employment offerings.
    d. the desires of the buyers and sellers of a product of your choosing.

PERSPECTIVES IN ECONOMICS

THE DRUG PROBLEM

by Randall G. Holcombe

[Abridged from "The Drug Problem," Chapter 10 in Randall G. Holcombe, *Public Policy and the Quality of Life.* (Westport, CT: Greenwood Press, 1995). Reprinted with permission.]

The public policy response to the drug problem has been to make recreational drug use illegal and then to enforce drug laws by arresting both users and sellers, even going overseas to nations supplying the underground drug markets to try to stop the supply at the source. The war on drugs is now decades old, and there is no evidence that the war is being won, or can be won.

As the very limited success of the war on drugs shows, drug use will continue to be extensive although drugs are illegal. Along with the law enforcement campaign against underground drug markets has come a public relations campaign to dissuade people from drug use. The public relations campaign appears more successful than the law enforcement campaign, and public relations campaigns can help to curtail the use of both illegal drugs and legal drugs such as alcohol and tobacco. This shows that there are alternative strategies to legal prohibition for those who want to use the government to reduce drug use. The costs of continuing to make recreational drug use illegal are many. The war on drugs is taking its toll on the individual rights our Constitution was designed to protect. Many of the negative consequences if illegal drug use stem from the fact that illegal drugs are illegal rather than that they are drugs. Because of the history of the legal prohibition on recreational drug use, it is reasonable to consider alternatives to help solve many of the problems that are a part of the drug problem.

The creation of illegal markets for recreational drugs has the obvious effect of making prices higher than they would be with legal markets. Higher prices contribute to property crime because high prices can push users into criminal activity to finance their drug purchases. The news often portrays drug users as criminals who steal to support their habit but rarely shows stories of alcoholics who steal to support their addictions. One reason is that alcohol prices are not forced upward artificially by legal prohibition.

Before considering some of the pros and cons of legalization, consider the question of whether it would ever be possible to win the war on drugs. One of the problems often cited in fighting the war on drugs is that users tend to be relatively insensitive to the price of drugs. If drugs become more costly, users will engage in various types of theft to acquire them. In the terminology of economists, the demand for recreational drugs is relatively inelastic, so that even a relatively large increase in the price will result in only a small decrease in the quantity of drugs demanded by users.

If users in the recreational drug market do not want to alter their consumption habits very much in response to price changes, consider the results of winning some battles in the war on drugs. Surely, sellers in the black market for drugs will charge whatever the market will bear, and if government efforts succeed in removing a small percentage of the supply of drugs from the market, competition among buyers for drugs will push prices up by a greater percentage than the decline in quantity, with the result that the drug market will take in more total money by selling fewer drugs.

Trade in illegal markets creates huge profits that entice people into the market. Legalization would take the glamour out of drug dealing, it would eliminate the problems produced by the profitability of dealing, and it would be more likely to keep children out of the drug market.

Another disadvantage to users of trading in illegal markets is that there is no legal protection for the transaction. This means, at a minimum, that there is no recourse in case of a faulty product but also means that a buyer risks being the victim of other crimes in an attempt to purchase drugs. Users might be reluctant to tell the police that they were robbed by someone from whom they were trying to buy drugs.

One major disadvantage to drug users of trading in illegal markets is that their activities make them criminals. There are several negative side effects. First, there is a stigma attached to drug use simply because it is illegal. One need only remember the 1980s to recall that Judge Douglas Ginsberg's nomination to the Supreme Court was torpedoed because he had used marijuana. There was no evidence that it had affected his legal activities or his judgment in any other way. Simply the stigma attached to marijuana use was enough to keep him off the Supreme Court. If, instead, he had admitted to trying bourbon there would have been no issue raised.

This stigma will also make users more reluctant to seek treatment. People must admit not only that they cannot seem to get off drugs but also that they have been violating the law. Legalization would make it easier for people to seek treatment for drug problems if they desired it.

Another negative aspect of the profits generated by drug prohibition is they create an opportunity for corrupting law enforcement officers. Law enforcement is not a notably high-paid profession, and drug profits can be spent to pay law enforcement officers for protection or to look the other way while drug dealers transact their business.

Corruption of law enforcement officers is most serious with victimless crimes, such as drug sales, prostitution, gambling, and the like. Crimes with victims, like assault and burglary, have individuals who want to cooperate with law enforcement officers and who have an incentive to monitor the law enforcement system to see that justice is done. With victimless crimes nobody directly involved in the activity wants law enforcement. If an individual who commits an assault is able to buy his way out of an arrest, the assault victim will want to call that corruption to the attention of someone higher up in the political chain of command. The potential problems would be severe enough that there would be a high likelihood that the corrupt law enforcement officer would not benefit from the corrupt activity. With victimless crimes, nobody directly involved in the crime has an incentive to complain about corrupt activity. Therefore, corruption is more likely.

Corruption may not be the major problem related to the legal enforcement of drug crimes. Incentives in the legal system may lead law enforcement officers to pursue drug crimes at the expense of other types of crime, with the result that other crimes increase. The most obvious incentive is that often property confiscated by law enforcement officers through drug arrests remains with the law enforcement agency. Law enforcement officers will have more incentive to pursue these types of crimes if the budgets of their agencies can be directly enhanced as a result.

The incentives are structured so law enforcement officers can benefit from putting more law enforcement effort into drug crimes and less effort into property crimes. As a result of reduced effort fighting property crimes robbery and burglary will become less risky, and crime rates in those areas will increase.

Dealing in illegal drugs is a very profitable business for the dealers, but it is a business that has no access to legal protection. Whereas the legal system is, for the most part, designed to protect property and to defend the rights of individuals to engage in voluntary exchange and retain ownership over what they receive through market transactions, in the drug market, the legal system is worse than neutral toward protecting participants. Rather than just not offering those transactions any protection, the legal system actively seeks to confiscate any money and goods exchanged in the market. Because the government's legal system is openly hostile to drug markets those who participate in those markets must take steps to actively protect themselves.

Non-users suffer considerably because drugs are bought and sold on black markets, which offers no legal protection to those who deal in them. There is big money to be made dealing in drugs, and, without legal protection, those dealing in the markets must find ways to protect themselves. This is what leads to the gang warfare, the drive-by shootings, and the unsafe neighborhoods filled with criminal activity.

The consequences of the illegal profits in drug markets are overwhelmingly negative. The location of drug markets tends to be in poorer neighborhoods and in inner cities. The resulting crime harms those who do not participate in the markets but have a limited ability to move from the area. However, in poor neighborhoods, there is also the negative side effect of the incentives established by drug markets. In areas where unemployment may be high and employed people work for relatively low wages, much more money can be made by dealing in drugs than working in legal markets. The people with the new cars and the people with the gold chains will likely be those involved in the drug market. This entices others to enter the market and makes those who deal in drugs neighborhood role models. Why work for low wages, if one can find a job at all, when by working for dug dealers one can make more money?

If recreational drugs were legal, there would be no high profits to lure individuals into the market. There would still be drug users, to be sure, but those individuals would tend to be the losers—the equivalent of the skid row alcoholic—rather than the people to envy. Without the illegal profits, those involved in drugs would no longer look like role models to individuals in drug-infested neighborhoods. This is one argument for legalization. If all drugs were legalized, the drug culture would not look nearly as attractive because it would be stripped of its excess profits caused by government efforts to reduce supply.

If drugs were legalized, their quality would be controlled better because they would be sold in commercial markets. Firms would have an incentive to develop reputations for quality, and drugs would be packaged in standardized doses, which would reduce the incidence of accidental overdoses. Because drugs would be sold under brand names, sellers would have an incentive to distinguish their products and to be concerned about the health of their customers.

If drugs were legalized, there would not be the same incentives to produce drugs in concentrated doses. Transportation is more costly for illegal drugs because they must be concealed from law enforcement officers. Drugs that can contain more doses in a given volume will be more valuable, and one of the motivations of designer drugs is to allow easier transportation through more concentrated doses. Using alcohol as an example, high-proof liquor was more often produced than beer with low alcohol content during prohibition. Legalization would result in drugs that are not as strong.

If drugs were legalized, there would be an incentive for research and development in the recreational drug industry to produce designer drugs that cause better feelings but with fewer harmful side effects. The designer drug industry today shows the possibilities for research and development in recreational drugs, but, as just noted, the incentives today are to produce more concentrated drugs rather than less harmful drugs. This push toward less harmful designer drugs would be amplified if drug manufacturers were allowed to advertise their products.

Finally, if drugs were legalized, manufacturers would have an incentive to innovate because they could take advantage of patent protection and other legal protections that would go to producers in any legal industry. As it is, the incentives do not exist because drugs are illegal.

Legalization would bring the same benefits to users and non-users. Violence and unpredictable behavior from drug use should be reduced because of better information about drugs, quality control, increased variety, and the tendency for drugs to be packaged in less potent forms. Accidental deaths should fall, which would reduce costs to those with drug users in the family. Thus, the effects of drug use should be less burdensome to non-users if drugs were legalized.

Earlier, it was argued that the demand for recreational drugs is relatively inelastic meaning that a reduction in the price would not cause large increases in consumption. This suggests that legalization would have relatively little effect on drug use taking only the money price into account. For some people, however, the violation of drug laws might appear as a powerful and prohibitive deterrent because legalization would entice people who never had a desire to do so to try recreational drugs.

An important argument in favor of legalization, regardless of how many new users would be created, is that in a free society people should have the right to behave as they choose as long as their behavior does not harm others. People engage in many activities that are hazardous to their health, but society does not ban skydiving or motorcycle riding. One of the casualties of the war on drugs has been individual rights.

This discussion of drug policy considers a controversial issue but one that is worthwhile considering within the context of an examination of public policy and the quality of life. For one thing, a general framework should be able to deal with controversial issues, but a larger reason is that the issue of drug policy directly confronts the issue of the degree to which individual freedom contributes to the quality of life. Freedom is important enough to the quality of life to want to defend it as a goal of its own, but the protection of individual freedoms also indirectly enhances the quality of life. Freedom allows people to pursue their own interests as they understand them, and it allows them to profit from activities that benefit others. The protection of individual rights is necessary for a market system to operate, and the market system has proven itself to be an indispensable component in enhancing the welfare of a nation's citizens.

DISCUSSION

1. Using a demand and supply diagram, show how drug enforcement policies aimed at reducing the supply of drugs affect the price of drugs and the quantity traded. How do the effects on price and quantity compare with policies aimed at reducing demand (such as education and "Just say no" campaigns)?

2. Do you think the demand for illegal drugs is fairly inelastic? What does this imply about the ability to reduce consumption by supply-side policies that increase the price of drugs?

3. Police departments have a fixed amount of resources that must be allocated across different crimes and laws that must be enforced. Use a production possibilities curve to show how increased enforcement of drug laws reduces the enforcement of other laws. What effect does this have on the amount of these other crimes committed?

4. If drugs were made legal, what do you think would happen to the following?
    a. the quantity of drugs consumed
    b. the profits of drug sellers
    c. the amount of gang violence
    d. the presence of street corner drug dealers (Hint: Could they compete with Wal-Mart?)
    e. the quality of drugs in terms of side-effects and tainted products
    f. the number of users willing to admit their problem and get help

5. During prohibition in the 1920s, alcohol was made illegal. As a result, gangsters controlled the alcohol trade, the murder rate rose substantially, high-potency moonshine was created, and deaths from tainted alcohol rose. Compare and contrast each of these with (1) the current market and usage of alcohol now that it is legal again (Are these problems gone or at least reduced?), and (2) with the current market and usage of illegal drugs.

CHAPTER 5

The Economic Role of Government

TRUE OR FALSE

T F

☐ ☐   1. The total social cost of an action includes the costs to the voluntary participants and any costs imposed on third parties.

☐ ☐   2. When production of a good results in externalities that impose a cost on others, the output level of the good often exceeds the socially ideal amount.

☐ ☐   3. It is often difficult to exclude nonpaying customers from receiving the benefits of a public good.

☐ ☐   4. Anything provided by the government (the public sector) is called a public good.

☐ ☐   5. When an activity generates external costs, government intervention in the form of establishing private property rights or imposing a tax that would reduce the level of the activity could improve economic efficiency.

☐ ☐   6. National defense is an example of a public good.

☐ ☐   7. Poor information on the part of buyers is very seldom a factor in real-world markets.

☐ ☐   8. Spillover, or third-party effects, are the same thing as externalities.

☐ ☐   9. Getting accurate information is often difficult for consumers, but sellers offering good products have an incentive to provide this information to consumers.

☐ ☐ 10. *Consumer Reports* is an example of a government solution to the problems for the market created by information costs.

☐ ☐ 11. Externalities are the result of poorly defined or poorly enforced private property rights.

☐ ☐ 12. Externalities can be either negative (costs) or positive (benefits).

☐ ☐ 13. The free-rider problem occurs when it is easy to exclude nonpaying customers.

☐ ☐ 14. The market and public sector are similar in that individuals must pay exactly for the benefits they receive.

☐ ☐ 15. Scarcity is not present in the public sector because the government pays for all goods and services it provides free to citizens.

PROBLEMS AND PROJECTS

1. Public goods are goods that are both (1) joint-in-consumption and (2) nonexcludable. For each of the goods listed below, indicate whether it meets each of these criterion with a "yes" or a "no" in the space provided. In the final column indicate whether the good is a public good or a private good based upon your answers.

GOOD	JOINT-IN-CONSUMPTION	NONEXCLUDABLE	PUBLIC GOOD OR PRIVATE GOOD
a. National defense	_____	_____	_____
b. A rock concert	_____	_____	_____
c. Mail and package delivery	_____	_____	_____
d. A cup of coffee	_____	_____	_____
e. A radio broadcast	_____	_____	_____
f. A movie at a theatre	_____	_____	_____
g. A taco	_____	_____	_____
h. A toll road	_____	_____	_____

2. Exhibit 1 shows the supply and demand schedules for pulp paper in Academia, a hypothetical country.

EXHIBIT 1

PRICE (PER TON)	QUANTITY (TON/YEAR) DEMANDED	SUPPLIED
$150	1,000	7,000
140	2,000	6,000
130	3,000	5,000
120	4,000	4,000
110	5,000	3,000
100	6,000	2,000

a. Diagram the supply and demand curves and show the equilibrium price and quantity for pulp paper in Academia.

b. Suppose the production of pulp paper results in external pollution costs of $20 per ton produced. In your diagram show a supply curve that includes these external costs. What are the socially ideal (efficient) price and quantity for pulp paper? Show these in your diagram.

c. Explain in your own words why the private market equilibrium you found in part a is inefficient.

   d. Suppose the government levies a tax of $20 per ton on producers of pulp paper. How will this affect the market? How will the outcome compare with efficiency?

3. Exhibit 2 below depicts the market for baseball teams, with the total number of teams on the horizontal axis and the price of each team (in millions of dollars) on the vertical axis.

EXHIBIT 2

PRICE (MILLIONS)	QUANTITY DEMANDED	QUANTITY SUPPLIED
$68	17	35
62	20	32
56	23	29
50	26	26
44	29	23
38	32	20
32	35	17

   a. Diagram the supply and demand curves and determine the values of the free market equilibrium price and quantity.

   b. Some have argued that a baseball team generates external benefits for a city by increasing the city's morale and pride and by bringing in extra tourist revenue. Suppose the value of these external benefits turns out to be $24 million per team. Use your diagram from part a to depict these externalities. What is the efficient total number of baseball teams?

   c. What type of policy could a city government use to attract a baseball team?

   d. Suppose there really are no external benefits associated with baseball teams but that city governments subsidize them anyway. Will the resulting outcome be consistent with economic efficiency? Explain.

4. The book presents the following two conditions as necessary for economic efficiency:

Rule 1: Undertaking an economic action will be efficient if it produces more benefits than costs for the individuals in the economy.

Rule 2: Undertaking an economic action will be inefficient if it produces more costs than benefits to the individuals.

Using these criterion, for each of the following cases, decide whether the action is efficient or inefficient and which rule applies.

   a. Buying a pair of jeans for $25 that you value at $30

   b. Building a new public park that generates $100 million in benefits to the public, but costs $150 million in tax revenue to build

   c. Making a $1,500 repair to your home that will allow you to sell it for $2,000 more

d. Operating a recycling program that costs $50 million per year and creates benefits (such as energy savings) of $20 million per year

e. The production of a good that yields $20 in benefits to a consumer, costs the firm $15 to produce, and generates $10 in external pollution costs when it is produced

f. The production of a good that yields $20 in benefits to a consumer, costs the firm $5 to produce, and generates $10 in external pollution costs when it is produced

g. Imposing a tax that costs the government $10 million to enforce and administer to correct an externality that was generating $5 million in external costs

h. Purchasing an issue of *Consumer Reports* magazine for $3 that contains a review of writing pens to help you decide whether to purchase a Bic pen or a Papermate pen, both of which cost 50 cents

i. Purchasing an issue of *Consumer Reports* magazine for $3 that contains a review of new automobiles to help you decide whether to purchase a Ford Explorer or a Jeep Cherokee

MULTIPLE CHOICE

1. Which one of the following would *reduce* the efficiency of the market process?
   a. promoting competitive markets
   b. protecting persons from fraud and theft
   c. providing a stable monetary environment
   d. protecting consumers by imposing legally mandated price ceilings

2. It is difficult for the market process to provide public goods because
   a. private firms generally cannot undertake large-scale projects.
   b. it will be difficult to get potential consumers to pay for such goods since there is not a direct link between payment for and receipt of the good.
   c. consumers do not really want public goods, even though such goods are best for them.
   d. individuals are generally made worse off by the production of public goods.

3. Which of the following is true about the market and public sectors?
   a. Competitive behavior is present in both sectors.
   b. The public sector utilizes the price mechanism more than the private sector.
   c. In both sectors, individuals always pay for the goods and services they consume.
   d. There is more free choice for individual consumers in the public sector than in the private sector.

4. Despite many differences, the market and public sectors are *similar* in which one of the following respects?
   a. In both sectors, income (or power) is distributed on the basis of the same criterion.
   b. Consumers in the market sector and voters in the public sector are equally well informed.
   c. Voluntary exchange, rather than compulsion, is characteristic of both sectors.
   d. It will be costly to use scarce goods, whether through the private or the public sector.

5. Which of the following activities is *least* likely to give rise to external costs or benefits?
   a. spraying to control mosquitos in your backyard
   b. driving one's car during rush hour
   c. inoculating your children during a flu epidemic
   d. buying a hamburger and eating it for lunch

6. Driving your automobile in Los Angeles during the rush hour causes externalities because
   a. it adds congestion and pollution from auto exhaust, reducing the welfare of others.
   b. gasoline is scarce and you must pay for it.
   c. gasoline is a public good.
   d. your actions will benefit others even though you will be unable to charge them for the service.

7. Criteria of ideal economic efficiency requires that (I) all actions generating more social benefit than cost be undertaken and (II) no actions generating more social cost than social benefit be undertaken.
   a. Both I and II are true.
   b. Both I and II are false.
   c. I is true; II is false.
   d. II is true; I is false.

8. Which of the following "goods" is the best example of a pure public good?
   a. highways
   b. national defense
   c. mail delivery
   d. welfare programs

9. In the absence of government intervention, goods with external costs tend to be
   a. overproduced.
   b. underproduced.
   c. efficiently produced.
   d. offset by goods generating external benefits.

10. The *absence* of well-defined and enforceable private property rights often
    a. causes people to work together for the common good.
    b. improves society because it avoids the selfish actions of private property owners.
    c. causes difficulties for society due to externalities.
    d. brings about efficiency by providing incentives to conserve resources.

11. The major distinction between private and public goods is that
    a. private goods are goods produced by private firms while public goods are goods produced by government—the public sector.
    b. unlike private goods, public goods are nonexcludable—it is difficult or impossible to prevent nonpaying customers from receiving the good.
    c. unlike private goods, public goods are joint-in-consumption—the consumption of a unit by one person does not detract from the amount available to others.
    d. both b and c are correct.

12. New products provide a classic case of the consumer information problem. However, in some cases consumers partially solve the problem by trusting the "brand name" of the producer of the new product. Since firms spend millions of dollars advertising and maintaining their brand names, the likelihood of a "brand name" firm's intentionally selling a dangerous or shoddy new product is
    a. high because big firms are always after a quick dollar.
    b. high because their brand name is a communal property right.
    c. low because big firms do not make mistakes.
    d. low because the firm with a brand name has a lot to lose if word spreads about bad consumer experiences.

13. Which of the following is legally permitted to use coercive force to modify the actions of adults against their will?
    a. banks
    b. corporations
    c. governments
    d. all of the above

14. Which of the following correctly describes an *external benefit* resulting from an individual's purchase of a winter flu shot?
    a. The flu shot is cheaper than the cost of treatment when you get the flu.
    b. The income of doctors increases when you get the flu shot.
    c. The flu shot reduces the likelihood of others catching the flu.
    d. The flu shot reduces the likelihood you will miss work as the result of sickness; therefore, you will earn more income.

15. Which of the following would be a protective function of government?
    a. providing national defense
    b. welfare programs and income redistribution
    c. mail delivery
    d. all of the above

16. Consider two goods—one that generates external benefits and another that generates external costs. A competitive market economy would tend to produce too
    a. much of both goods.
    b. little of both goods.
    c. much of the good that generates external benefits and too little of the good that generates external cost.
    d. little of the good that generates external benefits and too much of the good that generates the external cost.

17. Externalities are due to which of the following?
    a. poorly defined or enforced private property rights
    b. individuals not caring sufficiently about the welfare of others
    c. the choice of a capitalist, rather than socialist, economy
    d. poor information on the part of buyers and sellers

18. The problem created when it is difficult to exclude nonpaying customers is called the
    a. consumption-payment link problem.
    b. free-rider problem.
    c. public sector dilemma.
    d. asymmetric information problem.

19. General agreement exists that the legitimate economic functions of government include
    a. protection against invasions from a foreign power.
    b. provision of goods that cannot easily be provided through markets.
    c. the maintenance of a framework of rules within which people can interact peacefully with one another.
    d. all of the above.

DISCUSSION QUESTIONS

1. Provide a specific example for each of the reasons why unregulated markets might fail to be efficient. For each case explain how government intervention might promote efficiency.

2. List as many goods as you can think of that have substantial public good characteristics that are provided by the private sector. Try weather forecasts and radio broadcasts for starters. Pick two of these goods and answer the following questions: How does the market cope with the public goods aspect of the good? Does the market produce enough of the good? Would government provision of the good be more efficient?

3. For decades, smokers were free to smoke almost everywhere—at work, at parties, on airplanes, and in restaurants. Today, smokers face increasing restrictions about where they can smoke. Some of these restrictions are the result of government policy, but many have arisen without legislation and are simply imposed by private companies (such as airlines, restaurants, and private employers). The latter set of restrictions represent a nongovernmental solution to the externalities created by smokers. Can you think of other activities that generate negative externalities that are regulated in a similar manner?

4. Your decision about which college to attend is an example of a non-repeat, major purchase about which few individuals have full information. Do you feel like you made a good choice? Is there any way for you to know that you made the best choice? What sources did you use to obtain information about the various colleges and universities? How many of these sources were provided by the market? by the government? Does poor information pose a problem for the market for higher education?

5. In general, it has been argued that private sector markets will allocate too few resources to public goods like national defense. Do you think the public sector allocates too few, too many, or just the right amount of resources to such goods? What is your evidence? How should you go about determining the socially optimal amount of public goods to produce? Does government intervention necessarily imply that the good will be produced efficiently?

6. Consider each of the following quotes:

    "Following the example set by the ending of Prohibition, we should legalize marijuana, cocaine, and certain other drugs we have failed to control. Excise taxes and punishments could hold drug use to tolerable levels and discourage their use prior to engaging in activities that might harm others." (Gary Becker, economist)

"Drug use is out of control in our society. Making it legal would only reinforce the erroneous perception that drugs such as marijuana and cocaine can be used without consequences." (Lee I. Dogoloff, Executive Director, American Council for Drug Education)

Assume you are the vice president of the United States and have to cast a vote to break a tie in the Senate on the issue of legalization of marijuana and cocaine. In a single paragraph, state your decision, and carefully and clearly support your position. Be sure to address both points of view expressed above.

CHAPTER 6

The Economics of Collective Decision Making

TRUE OR FALSE

T F

☐ ☐ 1. Well-organized special interest groups may be able to use the political process for their own gain even though the action is inefficient and results in a net social loss.

☐ ☐ 2. The shortsightedness effect implies that a policy providing immediate, readily identified benefits at the expense of costs in the future that are difficult to identify tends to be very attractive to a legislator seeking reelection.

☐ ☐ 3. Logrolling and pork-barrel legislation are rules designed to prevent individual legislators from getting special interest policies for their districts passed.

☐ ☐ 4. Rent seeking is when an individual spends time and money in an effort to influence government policy in their favor.

☐ ☐ 5. When an individual votes, they will attempt to gain all available information about the candidate and the issues involved.

☐ ☐ 6. The efficiency of the political process would be enhanced if the costs of government action (taxes) were more closely linked to the benefits people receive from government action.

☐ ☐ 7. Government failure strengthens the case for use of the market system.

☐ ☐ 8. An individual voter has a strong economic incentive to fight special interest legislation with his or her own time and money because such legislation is costly to all members of society.

☐ ☐ 9. The majority of government income transfer programs are directed toward the poor.

☐ ☐ 10. The assumption that politicians behave in a self-interested fashion is premised largely on the fact that politicians who fail to do so will often also fail to be reelected.

☐ ☐ 11. A voter usually must choose among candidates whose positions represent complex bundles of goods, services, and costs to the voter.

☐ ☐ 12. When voters pay in proportion to benefits received, all voters gain from productive (i.e., efficient) government action.

☐ ☐ 13. The exchange between politicians of political support for issues (vote trading) is called pork-barrel legislation.

☐ ☐ 14. Even if a policy is inefficient, government is likely to enact it if the benefits are concentrated in a small interest group and if the costs are widespread.

T F

☐ ☐ 15. Even if a policy is efficient, government is *not* likely to enact it if the costs are concentrated in a small interest group and if the benefits are widespread.

PROBLEMS AND PROJECTS

1. Exhibit 1 presents data on the benefits received by three voters for two different proposals up for vote, A and B. Also shown in the table are two possible tax-sharing arrangements for each project. The equal tax is if they split the total cost of the project equally, while the benefit tax is the case where each person pays the same percent of the total tax bill as the percent of the benefits they receive from the project.

   a. Proposal A creates a total benefit of $200, and the total cost of the project (as shown by the total tax needed) is $150. Is project A efficient? Is project B efficient?

   b. Suppose only the equal tax plans are considered and majority rule is used to make the decisions. Would proposal A pass (win majority approval) under the equal tax-sharing arrangement? Would proposal B pass under the equal tax-sharing arrangement?

   c. Are the outcomes in part b consistent with the criterion of efficiency in part a?

   d. Under the benefit tax shown, each taxpayer is assessed the same proportion of the total tax as the proportion of the benefits they receive from the project. For example, Bob receives one-half the benefits from project B ($50 of $100), so is charged one-half the total tax ($60 of $120). Under the ben-

EXHIBIT 1

| | PROPOSAL A | | | PROPOSAL B | | |
VOTER	BENEFIT	EQUAL TAX	BENEFIT TAX	BENEFIT	EQUAL TAX	BENEFIT TAX
Adam	$140	$50	$105	$5	$40	$6
Bob	40	50	30	50	40	60
Cathy	20	50	15	45	40	54
Totals	$200	$150	$150	$100	$120	$120

efits tax plan, would proposal A pass? Would proposal B pass under the benefits tax?

   e. Are the outcomes in part d consistent with the criterion of efficiency in part a? If you want government to pass only efficient projects, would it be better to use equal taxes or taxes in proportion to benefits received?

2. Exhibit 2 shows the net benefits (benefits minus tax cost) from three different government projects for three districts.
   a. By looking at the Totals row at the bottom of the table, which of these projects are efficient? Which are inefficient?
   b. If each project was put up for vote individually (by majority rule), which would pass? Which would fail?
   c. Suppose you were the representative of district A and wanted to get your new road passed. You only need one more vote for a majority. Would both you and the representative of district B be willing to "trade" votes to get your projects passed? That is, would you be willing to vote for B's park if he voted for your road? Would he agree to the trade as well?

EXHIBIT 2

	NET BENEFITS (+) OR COSTS (−) TO DISTRICT		
REPRESENTATIVE OF DISTRICT	NEW ROAD IN DISTRICT A	NEW PARK IN DISTRICT B	NEW DAM IN DISTRICT C
A	$+10	$−5	$−2
B	−6	+9	−2
C	−6	−5	+13
Totals	−2	−1	+9

   d. Now, consider a "pork-barrel" bill that contained all three projects. How would each representative vote on the total bill containing all three projects?

3. Consider the supply and demand for public sector action, and decide whether each of the following illustrates
   (1) rent-seeking behavior by private parties,
   (2) vote-seeking behavior by elected officials, or
   (3) the rational ignorance effect.
   ____ a. Members of Congress rejected bills that would have restricted the lobbying activities of political action coalitions (PACs).
   ____ b. Election results are often distorted by poorly informed voters and low voter turnouts.
   ____ c. Liquor wholesalers in most states have lobbied for state laws that compel retailers to buy their liquor supplies only from the nearest available wholesaler, instead of shopping around.
   ____ d. Many voters support import tariffs and quotas on foreign goods even though such protectionism costs consumers billions of dollars.
   ____ e. A steel company sends a $50 million campaign contribution to a legislator in a year in which a bill is being debated that would affect the steel industry.

4. Exhibit 3 shows the classification of government actions into four types depending upon how concentrated or widespread the benefits and costs of the action are.
    a. For which types of action is government likely to work the best (that is most consistent) with economic efficiency?

EXHIBIT 3

Distribution of Benefits

		Widespread	Concentrated
Distribution of Costs	Widespread	Type 1	Type 2
	Concentrated	Type 4	Type 3

---

b. For which type of action is government likely to have a bias toward adopting the actions even if they are inefficient?
c. For which type of action is government likely to have a bias against adopting the actions even if they are efficient?

Classify each of the following as type 1, 2, 3, or 4 according to the above exhibit.
d. A $1 tax on every citizen to provide large subsidies to tobacco farmers
e. A 10 percent tax on the profits of major gasoline retailers (BP, Shell, Exxon, etc.) to finance government-funded research on solar energy
f. An increase in the income tax to finance an increase in national defense spending
g. A $5 increase in student tuition to finance increases in professor salaries
h. A law allowing consumers to buy prescription drugs on the advice of their pharmacist without a visit to a medical doctor (who are strongly represented by the American Medical Association)
i. A 1 percent increase in Social Security taxes on current workers to finance large benefit increases for those currently receiving Social Security payments
j. Reductions in subsidies to sugar farmers to finance the increases in Social Security benefits

---

MULTIPLE CHOICE

The following quotation relates to questions 1 and 2.

"The ideal policy, from the viewpoint of the state, is one with identifiable beneficiaries, each of whom is helped appreciably, at the cost of many unidentifiable persons, none of whom is hurt very much." (George Stigler, *A Dialogue on the Proper Economic Role of the State*)

1. This statement is probably
    a. incorrect because voters are well informed on a wide range of political issues.
    b. incorrect because the political process dilutes the influence of special interest groups, since like other citizens, their members have only one vote.
    c. correct because the well-informed voter will favor policies that cater to the views of small groups of people.
    d. correct because voters who have a strong personal interest in an issue will tend to support candidates who cater to their views, whereas most other voters ignore the issue.

2. Which of the following groups does the above quotation suggest would have the most influence on public sector action?
    a. taxpayers
    b. nonunion workers
    c. special interest groups
    d. consumers

3. Economists use the term *shortsightedness effect* to describe which one of the following phenomena?
    a. Politicians tend to support actions that have immediate and easily recognized current benefits.
    b. Individuals are apt to spend their income on goods that bring immediate personal benefits.
    c. Voters elect politicians on the basis of campaign promises, regardless of what they may do once they are in office.
    d. Politicians support the programs of special interest groups in order to get elected; however, special interest support may be detrimental later, costing politicians popularity after the programs are implemented.

4. Economic theory leads us to expect that the typical voter will be uninformed on many issues because
    a. most issues are so complex that voters will be unable to understand them.
    b. even though information is free, most voters do not care.
    c. information is costly, and the individual voter casting a well-informed vote can expect negligible personal benefit.
    d. citizen apathy about political matters is inevitable, except when decisions are made by referendum.

5. Public choice theory suggests that politicians will be most likely to favor redistribution of income from
    a. the rich to the poor.
    b. disorganized individuals to well-organized special interest groups.
    c. middle-income taxpayers to both rich and the poor.
    d. well-organized business and labor groups to consumers.

6. Giving local governments more power is less dangerous than giving the same power to the national government because
    a. local governments generally have more strict constitutional rules they must operate under.
    b. it is easier to vote in local elections than national elections.
    c. only national-level governments are allowed to use coercive force.
    d. higher exit options exist at the local level—it is easier for people to move away from a bad local government.

7. Assume that you are a member of the U.S. House of Representatives from your home state and district. Which of the following best explains why you have a strong incentive to get the federal government to finance pork-barrel projects in your district?
   a. Most of the benefits of pork-barrel projects within your district will accrue to your constituents, while most of the costs will be imposed on voters from other districts.
   b. Most of the costs of pork-barrel projects within your district will be imposed on your constituents, while most of the benefits will accrue to voters from other districts.
   c. Pork producers are a powerful political lobby that will influence the actions of legislators in all districts.
   d. This is a trick question; in a representative democracy, there is little incentive for legislators to support pork-barrel projects.

8. The theory of public choice
   a. analyzes the likelihood that various public sector alternatives will be instituted.
   b. assumes that economic incentives influence the choices of voters.
   c. applies the tools of economics to the collective decision-making process.
   d. all of the above

9. When analyzing public sector decision making, economic theory assumes that voters, politicians, and government officials will
   a. respond to changes in personal benefits and costs when making public sector choices.
   b. pursue the public interest even when it conflicts with their private interests.
   c. pursue primarily public interests since competition is less intense in the public sector.
   d. do none of the above.

10. Public choice theory indicates that competitive forces between candidates in elections provide a politician with a strong incentive to offer voters a bundle of political goods that she believes
    a. is best for the economic and political situations the country faces.
    b. will most likely clear the legislative process.
    c. will increase the welfare of society.
    d. will increase her chances of winning elections.

11. When voters pay in proportion to the benefits received from an economic action of the government, if the government activity is productive,
    a. all voters will gain.
    b. only a smaller proportion of voters will gain.
    c. less than a simple majority of voters will gain.
    d. approximately 50 percent of the voters will gain.

12. In which case is the political process most likely to result in the acceptance of productive programs and rejection of unproductive political activities?
    a. when the benefits are highly concentrated and costs widespread among voters
    b. when the costs are highly concentrated and the benefits widespread among voters
    c. when both the benefits and costs are widespread among voters
    d. when the benefits accrue primarily in the future, while the costs are more visible during the current period

13. When is representative democracy most likely to lead to the adoption of an inefficient government program?
    a. when the program provides substantial benefits to a small proportion of voters and the costs are widespread among voters
    b. when both the benefits and costs of the program are widespread among voters
    c. when the program is financed by a user charge
    d. when a close relationship exists between the personal benefits received from the program and the tax cost imposed on each voter

14. Legislators often gain by bundling a number of projects benefiting local districts at the expense of general taxpayers. Such legislation is called
    a. market failure legislation.
    b. the rational ignorance effect.
    c. public goods legislation.
    d. pork-barrel legislation.

15. Which of the following refers to when legislators trade votes on legislation?
    a. logrolling
    b. the special interest effect
    c. rational ignorance
    d. the shortsightedness effect

16. Which of the following is a predictable side effect of increased government activity (e.g., taxes and subsidies) designed to redistribute income among citizens?
    a. improvement in the operational efficiency of government agencies
    b. budget surpluses
    c. reduction in the poverty rate
    d. an increase in rent-seeking activity

17. Legislation that offers immediate and easily recognized benefits, at the expense of uncertain costs that are in the distant future (such as financing by government debt), is often enacted even when economic inefficiency results. This can be expected because of
    a. a lack of incentive for operational efficiency in the public sector.
    b. market failure.
    c. the special-interest effect.
    d. the shortsightedness effect.

18. Public choice analysis indicates that
    a. because government action provides public goods, it always increases the wealth of the citizenry.
    b. unconstrained democratic governments often enact special-interest programs that waste resources and impair the standard of living.
    c. constitutional rules limiting public-sector activity generally lower the economic efficiency of the overall economy.
    d. Politicians and voters are better able to judge the public interest than their own private interest.

DISCUSSION QUESTIONS

1. Do you find the public choice theory of political behavior convincing? What do you see as its strengths? its weaknesses? Do you think most politicians are motivated by personal self-interest? Cite evidence in support of your answer.

2. Why are well-organized special interest groups likely to be politically powerful? Why will vote-seeking politicians have an incentive to cater to their views?

3. "Government bureaucrats are only as important as the size of their departments, so they will always spend their entire budget allocation to avoid having their budgets cut in the next year."
    a. Do you agree with this quote? Why or why not?
    b. If bureaucrats act this way, what are the implications for the efficiency of government-run bureaus? Will they minimize their costs?

4. What are the major factors that contribute to market failure? What are the major factors that contribute to government failure? Which type of failure do you think is more common? more costly?

5. In recent years there has been a widespread discontent with the large size of income transfer programs in the United States. Welfare programs for the poor are subject to much heated criticism, whereas other transfer programs, like farm subsidies, are less often and less heatedly criticized. At the same time, large transfer programs like Social Security and Medicare are labeled as politically "untouchable." What explains why there is a greater clamor to cut welfare programs rather than farm subsidy programs? To what extent can public choice theory explain the difference? In an era when many are calling for substantial reductions in income transfer programs, why is it considered politically impossible to cut Social Security or Medicare?

CHAPTER 7

Taking the Nation's Economic Pulse

TRUE OR FALSE

T F

□ □ 1. Gross domestic product (GDP) is a measure of the market value of all final goods and services that were produced domestically during a year.

□ □ 2. The consumer price index (CPI) and the GDP deflator are price indexes used to convert nominal values to real values when attempting to correct data for the effects of inflation.

□ □ 3. If you paid $800 for a used motorcycle last year, the sale contributed $800 toward last year's GDP.

□ □ 4. One way to raise GDP would be for everyone to give up their leisure time and spend more time working.

□ □ 5. Gross investment measures all expenditures on investment, while net investment subtracts depreciation to arrive at only expenditures on new investment. Thus, net investment excludes expenditures for replacement of worn-out capital equipment.

□ □ 6. When Social Security payments are given to retired persons, this transfer payment is added to GDP.

□ □ 7. If domestic citizens live and work in foreign countries, their income is counted as part of GDP.

□ □ 8. If Joe buys 100 shares of stock at $5 each, GDP rises by $500.

□ □ 9. Increases in real output give rise to increases in real income and thus increase a nation's standard of living.

□ □ 10. If one wanted to measure the change in the annual output of goods and services between 1995 and 2000, nominal GDP would be a more reliable indicator than real GDP.

□ □ 11. During a period of rising prices (inflation), the increase in nominal GDP will be larger than the increase in real GDP.

□ □ 12. If a person gets a 2 percent raise in their nominal salary in a year in which consumer prices rise by 5 percent, their real income (or real purchasing power) falls by 3 percent.

PROBLEMS AND PROJECTS

EXHIBIT 1

EXPENDITURE APPROACH		RESOURCE COST-INCOME APPROACH	
Personal consumption expenditures	$6,728	Employee compensation	$5,715
Gross private investment	1,768	Proprietors' income	715
Government consumption and		Rents	142
gross investment	1,741	Corporate profit	876
Net exports	−364	Interest income	533
		Indirect business taxes	763
		Depreciation	1,117
		Net income of foreigners	12

1. Exhibit 1 presents economic data for the United States (in billions of dollars) for 2000.
   a. Calculate GDP using the expenditure approach by adding up the data in the left set of columns.
   b. Calculate GDP using the resource cost-income approach by adding up the data in the right set of columns.
   c. Explain why the same result for GDP can be obtained by either adding up spending in the economy or by adding up income in the economy.
   d. Gross investment includes all investment expenditures. However, these expenditures can be divided into (1) expenditures to replace current capital equipment that has worn out and (2) net investment expenditures on new additions to capital equipment. Find net investment expenditures by subtracting depreciation from gross investment.
   e. In the table, net exports are negative. Explain why this is negative given that exports were $1,103 and imports were $1,467.
   f. Economists use several other measures of economic activity that you can derive from the data above:
      (1) gross national product, equal to gross domestic product minus the net income of foreigners.
      (2) net national product, equal to gross national product minus depreciation.
      (3) national income, equal to net national product minus indirect business taxes.

2. Exhibit 2 shows the hourly wage earned by Bob when he was twenty years old in 2001 and his father and grandfather when they were the same age. The consumer price index (CPI) for each year is also given in the table.
   a. Convert all of the wages shown to their real value in the base year of the CPI (the year when the price index was equal to 100, which is now defined as an average of 1982 through 1984). Place your answers in the spaces provided in the table.
   b. Who had the highest real wage? Who was able to buy the most goods and services with the money they earned from an hour's work?
   c. Now, consider the grandfather who made $0.75 per hour in 1961. Using the CPI for 1961 and the CPI for 2001, figure out the grandfather's real salary in 2001 dollars. Note that this shows how much a person would need to earn in 2001 to have an identical real salary to a person earning $0.75 in 1961.

EXHIBIT 2

PERSON	YEAR	HOURLY WAGE (NOMINAL)	CONSUMER PRICE INDEX (CPI)	REAL HOURLY WAGE (IN BASE YEAR DOLLARS)
Bob's grandfather	1961	$0.75	29.9	_____
Bob's father	1981	3.00	90.9	_____
Bob	2001	6.50	177.1	_____

3. Exhibit 3 shows actual data for the U.S. economy between 1990 and 1993.
   a. Fill in the missing information in the left half of the table regarding the values of nominal GDP, the GDP deflator, and real GDP.
   b. Fill in the missing information in the right half of the table regarding the percentage changes in these variables (Hint: Recall the percent change formula is [(new value − old value) ÷ old value].)
   c. Given that the percentage change in the GDP deflator is the inflation rate for that year, what can you say about inflation during this period? Did it rise or fall?
   d. Explain why the percentage growth in real GDP was smaller than the percentage change in nominal GDP for these years.
   e. Interpreting your results for the percentage changes in real GDP, what can you say about the state of the economy during 1991? During 1992?

EXHIBIT 3

	NOMINAL GDP (BILLIONS)	GDP DEFLATOR (1996 = 100)	REAL GDP (BILLIONS OF 1996) DOLLARS	PERCENTAGE CHANGE FROM PREVIOUS YEAR		
				NOMINAL GDP	GDP DEFLATOR	REAL GDP
1990	$5,803	86.5	$6,709	5.7%	3.8%	1.8%
1991	_____	89.7	6,673	3.2	3.7	_____
1992	6,319	_____	6,883	_____	2.3	3.1
1993	6,642	94.0	_____	5.1	_____	2.7

4. In the blank preceding each event described below, indicate whether the event would increase (+) or cause no change (0) in measured GDP for the United States.
   ____ a. Mary cleans her house.
   ____ b. Mary hires someone to clean her house.
   ____ c. Jim sells cocaine on the black market and earns $30,000 per year.
   ____ d. Rachel buys $5,000 worth of IBM stock from Steve.
   ____ e. A burglar steals your stereo.
   ____ f. You buy a new stereo to replace the one that was stolen.
   ____ g. You purchase a German clock by mail-order from a German company.
   ____ h. Instead of paying for your dinner at a local restaurant, you wash dishes for them in exchange for your meal.
   ____ i. Gary receives a $1,000 social security check from the government.
   ____ j. The federal government buys a new stealth bomber for $2 billion.
   ____ k. You lose $500 playing blackjack in your dorm.
   ____ l. You wreck your car and pay $5,000 to have it repaired.

____ m. You buy an antique desk from a friend for $300.

____ n. You buy some flour to make a loaf of bread.

____ o. IBM purchases some new equipment for $10 million.

____ p. You pay your landlord $300 for this month's rent.

____ q. A hurricane destroys a family's home, and they pay $100,000 to rebuild it.

MULTIPLE CHOICE

1. Real GDP refers to nominal GDP
   a. minus gifts to other countries.
   b. minus total unemployment compensation.
   c. adjusted for price changes.
   d. adjusted for unemployment changes.

2. Assume that between 1995 and 2000 nominal GDP increased from $1,000 to $2,500, and the index of prices increased from 100 to 200. Which of the following expresses GDP for 2000 in terms of 1995 prices?
   a. $1,000
   b. $1,250
   c. $2,500
   d. $5,000

3. Which of the following transactions would be counted toward this year's GDP?
   a. General Motors purchases 10,000,000 tires from Firestone.
   b. A three-hundred-year-old painting is sold for $12 million.
   c. A street gang earns $2 million from selling illegal drugs.
   d. Your real estate agent earns $5,000 commission when you sell your hundred-year-old house for $100,000.

4. The consumer price index (CPI) and the GDP deflator are designed to measure the degree to which
   a. there have been changes in the proportions of national income generated by (and thus earned by) the rich relative to the poor.
   b. the cost of purchasing a bundle of goods has changed over time.
   c. consumption patterns have changed with time.
   d. consumer prices have risen over and above increases in worker wages.

5. If you wanted to take 2000 nominal GDP and convert it to 1995 prices, you would take 2000 nominal GDP and
   a. multiply it by (GDP deflator$_{1995}$ ÷ GDP deflator$_{2000}$).
   b. multiply it by (GDP deflator$_{2000}$ ÷ GDP deflator$_{1995}$).
   c. divide it by GDP deflator$_{2000}$.
   d. divide it by (GDP deflator$_{2000}$ + GDP deflator$_{1995}$).

6. Which of the following would *not* be counted as part of this year's GDP?
   a. the increase in the value of an antique automobile that was restored this year
   b. the value of a new automobile at its sale price
   c. the value of a used car at its sale price
   d. a family's replacement of a worn-out washing machine with a new one

7. Jim, a U.S. citizen, gets a summer job working in Germany. His summer earnings
   a. would count as part of U.S. GDP and German GNP.
   b. would count as part of U.S. GNP and German GDP.
   c. would count as part of U.S. GDP but would have no effect on Germany's GNP or GDP.
   d. would be double-counted, raising both U.S. GDP and German GDP.

Use the following information to answer questions 8 and 9.

Personal consumption expenditures	$900
Personal taxes	180
Government consumption and gross investment	300
Interest income	60
Exports	40
Imports	75
Depreciation	60
Gross investment	200

8. What is this country's *net* exports?
   a. 35
   b. −35
   c. 115
   d. −115

9. What is this country's gross domestic product?
   a. 1,225
   b. 1,305
   c. 1,365
   d. 1,440

10. Which of the following is *not* a problem or shortcoming of GDP?
    a. Goods produced in one period that are sold in the following period fail to get counted in any period.
    b. It tends to understate the growth of economic welfare because it does not fully and accurately account for improvements in the quality of products.
    c. GDP is not an accurate measure of welfare because it makes no adjustment for harmful side effects (such as pollution) or destructive acts of nature.
    d. GDP understates output because it does not include nonmarket production such as takes place in the household or in illegal markets.

11. If you were required to write a paper for your history class (or a report for your job) in which you were using dollar valued data across different years, you would
    a. use a price index to remove the effects of inflation to have reliable data measuring changes in the real value of things.
    b. never attempt to correct for inflation because inflation is a key indicator of economic activity.
    c. tell your teacher or boss that you never learned how to correct data for inflation.
    d. assume that prices did not change during the period you are studying.

12. Suppose that nominal GDP increased by 3 percent, but the real GDP increased by only 1 percent during that same period. Which of the following best explains the phenomenon?
    a. Prices increased by approximately 1 percent.
    b. Prices increased by approximately 2 percent.
    c. Prices increased by approximately 3 percent.
    d. Prices increased by approximately 4 percent.

13. If tax rates were raised substantially, we would expect which of the following scenarios to result?
    a. Measured GDP would fall relative to the actual amount of true economic activity.
    b. Measured GDP would come closer to reflecting the actual amount of true economic activity.
    c. GDP would increase by the amount of the new tax revenue because of the higher level of government spending it allows.
    d. Personal consumption expenditures would rise, while government spending would fall.

14. Which of the following would increase U.S. GDP?
    a. The city government of New York buys file cabinets directly from a Mexican company.
    b. A Mexican citizen buys stock in a U.S. company.
    c. A Japanese automobile company produces cars within the U.S.
    d. A U.S. automobile company produces cars in a foreign country.

15. You buy one hundred shares of IBM stock at $100 per share and pay $250 commission. How much will this transaction add to GDP?
    a. zero
    b. $250
    c. $10,000
    d. $10,250

16. If a used-car dealer purchases a used car for $1,000, restores it, and resells it for $1,500, the dealer contributes
    a. value added equal to $500, but nothing is added to GDP.
    b. value added equal to $500, and consequently $500 is added to GDP.
    c. nothing to production because only existing goods are involved.
    d. value added equal to $1,500, but only $500 is added to GDP.

17. Gross domestic product is the sum of
    a. the purchase price of all goods and services exchanged during the period.
    b. the purchase price of all final goods and services produced domestically during the period.
    c. the purchase price of all goods and services produced during the period minus depreciation of productive assets during the period.
    d. the purchase price of all final goods and services produced by a country's citizens during the period.

18. If the base year for the GDP deflator is 1996, the value of the GDP deflator for 1996
    a. is 10.
    b. is 100.
    c. is 150.
    d. cannot be determined from the data given.

19. If the base year for the GDP deflator is 1996 and the value of the GDP deflator in 2000 was 107, this indicates that the general level of prices
    a. declined between 1996 and 2000.
    b. was approximately 7 percent lower in 2000 than in 1996.
    c. was approximately 7 percent higher in 2000 than in 1996.
    d. was approximately 107 percent higher in 2000 than in 1996.

20. Your grandfather tells you he earned $0.65 per hour at his job when he was a boy in 1929. Given that the CPI was 17.1 in 1929 and 177.1 in 2001, how much would you have had to make in 2001 to have the same real hourly wage as your grandfather?
    a. $0.65
    b. $3.80
    c. $6.73
    d. $11.12

21. Assume that between 1990 and 2000 the money GDP of an economy increased from $3 trillion to $8 trillion and that the appropriate index of prices increased from 100 to 200. Which of the following expresses GDP for 1990 in terms of 2000 prices?
    a. $1 trillion
    b. $3 trillion
    c. $4 trillion
    d. $6 trillion

22. Suppose that Mike earned $15,000 in 2000 and $15,600 in 2001. If the consumer price index was 100 in 2000 and 103 in 2001, by approximately what percent did Mike's *real* salary increase?
    a.   1 percent
    b.   3 percent
    c.   4 percent
    d.   5 percent

23. In a country where many families make their own clothes, GDP will be understated because the clothes making represents
    a.   economic bads.
    b.   leisure.
    c.   the underground economy.
    d.   nonmarket production.

24. The *primary* value of GDP lies in its ability to
    a.   reflect the welfare of a society relative to a previous period.
    b.   compare the quality of a nation's products between two periods widely separated in time.
    c.   indicate short-term changes in the output rate of a nation.
    d.   indicate how much leisure time the people of a nation have.

25. Which of the following is true regarding GDP per capita?
    a.   Economists generally use GDP per capita to make comparisons of the average standard of living across different countries.
    b.   GDP per capita will generally tend to understate the standard of living in countries with large underground economies.
    c.   GDP per capita will generally tend to understate the standard of living in countries where there is a significant household production.
    d.   All of the above are true regarding GDP per capita.

DISCUSSION QUESTIONS

1. What is the difference between the income approach to calculating GDP and the expenditure approach? Why do both methods yield the same answer?

2. Would you expect real GDP to grow faster or slower over time than nominal GDP? Why? Which do you think better measures changes in the level of economic activity? Why?

3. What are some of the deficiencies of GDP as a measure of aggregate output? Consider the following statement: "In terms of measuring *changes* in the level of economic activity, these deficiencies are not important as long as the present method of measuring GDP is applied consistently over time."
   a. Is this statement correct if the structure of our economic activity (the way we operate and the types of things we produce) is fairly stable over time? Why or why not?
   b. Two major changes in recent years include sizeable increases in (1) efforts to control pollution and (2) the proportion of households with two working parents who pay for services such as child care, housecleaning, and gardening. Is the above quotation correct under these circumstances? Why or why not?

4. Suppose that a farmer grows $0.30 worth of wheat and sells it to a miller who makes it into flour. The miller then sells it for $0.50 to a baker who makes bread with it and sells the bread to a customer for $0.75. How much GDP results from this chain of events? If intermediate transactions were counted at their market sales prices, how much GDP would be reported? What is wrong with counting the intermediate transactions?

5. Until recently, Gross National Product was the most frequently cited measure of the aggregate output of an economy. What is the main difference between GDP and GNP? Do you agree with the choice to switch (that is, do you think GDP is the preferred measure)? Why or why not?

6. Think of three events that would raise GDP but that would make people in the economy worse off. Given that increases in GDP do not always reflect an improvement in living standards, why does anyone care about GDP? What is GDP really designed to measure, welfare or production?

7. When making comparisons of the average standard of living across countries, economists generally compare GDP per capita of the countries. How do rankings using GDP per capita compare to rankings based on other social and economic indicators such as life expectancy, adult illiteracy, and infant mortality? What factors for a country might make GDP per capita a poor measure of the accurate standard of living?

PERSPECTIVES IN ECONOMICS

GDP: PLUSES AND MINUSES

Morgan Guaranty Trust Company

[From *Morgan Guaranty Survey,* June, 1970, pp. 9–13. Reprinted
with permission of the Morgan Guaranty Trust Company.]

The gross domestic product in recent years has basked in the warm
glow of nearly universal praise. Economists, quite naturally, have been
freest with the encomiums. Where else but the GDP could they get in
one tidy number a measure of the growth in the mammoth U.S. economy? Businessmen, though not entirely persuaded of the value of statistics, especially esoteric statistics, nevertheless have been known to
quote the GDP—possibly because of its powers to impress audiences
with the speaker's grasp of the "big picture." Politicians, too, have been
extravagant in their admiration of GDP, most especially when it was
rising at a brisk pace. Even the ubiquitous cocktail party has paid
homage to the GDP as assorted junior executives, research assistants,
housewives, and dancing instructors have pronounced on the latest
GDP numbers with a solemn and knowing air.

Now all that seems to be changing. GDP increasingly is coming
under attack. Dr. Arthur F. Burns, Chairman of the Federal Reserve
Board, told Congress recently: "The gross domestic product—which
has been deceiving us all along—is a good deal lower than we think it
is." Richard A. Falk, a professor of international law at Princeton, told
a Congressional committee not long ago: "If the U.S. were to double
its GDP, I would think it would be a much less livable society than it
is today." And Representative Henry S. Reuss of Wisconsin warned earlier this year that "as our GDP grows, national pollution also grows
every year."

Such comments suggest a need to take a new hard look at GDP,
at what it is and—equally significant—what it is not.

Amoral GDP. At the outset, it is important to realize that GDP is
an estimate of the *market value* of goods and services produced. The
unit of account is always dollars. What is equally important to remember is the GDP measures only those goods and services which are
exchanged for money in the market place. In other words, what people, or business, or government are willing to *pay for* gets into the
national income and product accounts. Few distinctions are made
among the types of expenditures. Thus, the dollars spent in dedicated
pursuit of a cancer cure carry the same weight in the GDP as the wages
of lackadaisical ecdysiast. Official compilers of the GDP routinely
calculate money spent for medical care, new homes, whiskey, tobacco,
and plastic objects d'art. To those who object on aesthetic or even
moral grounds, the standard reply is that GDP measures what people
actually buy, not what they *ought* to buy. The latter is thought by economists to be more the province of a higher occupational order, such as
saints. It should be noted, however, that the accounting rules are not
entirely indifferent to moral considerations. Hence, GDP does not
include economic activity from illegal operations—such as a bookie
parlor, an illicit still, or a doxy's den.

Janus-Faced GDP. Thus it is clear that estimating the value of the
nation's total spending depends on application of some fairly rigid—
some would say arbitrary—rules of inclusion and exclusion. Economic
scholars over the years have discussed ways to improve the GDP. Their
suggestions can be conveniently split into two groups, the "pluses" and
the "minuses." The former school argues that more items should be
added to the accounts when striking a total. This school thinks that the
GDP, by excluding nonpaid items such as work done by housewives,
significantly *understates* the nation's output. Those in the "minuses"
group, while not necessarily unreceptive to the other group's proposals,
nevertheless see a different set of deficiencies. They charge that GDP is

overstating national income and progress because it does not, for example, take account of the deterioration of the environment.

At present, the "minuses" school seems to be dominating the
headlines. Dr. Burns, for example, while strongly backing maximum
production, is suggesting that the nation develop and stress a more
meaningful *net* domestic product, or NDP. This is GDP after deduct-
ing the value of capital goods used up in the production process. Such
depreciation or capital consumption currently is running about $80
billion a year. From this NDP (published quarterly along with GDP
data), Dr. Burns would additionally deduct some unspecified amount
that would represent depreciation in the environment.

To illustrate the point, assume that a manufacturer flushes waste
products into a river. If $1,000 were spent to remove the sludge from
the waterway, such spending would increase GDP by a like amount. If
no effort is made to deal with the pollution, there is no effect on GDP.
Economists argue that this is improper since, in fact, the situation is
analogous to the depreciation of capital assets. In the waterway case,
however, the fixed asset is the environment and its depreciation is called
pollution. What is wrong with present accounting procedures, according to these analyses, is that pollution has not been removed from GDP
in the calculations of NDP.

Admittedly, adjusting GDP accounting rules to embrace
allowances for social values presents some abstruse conceptual
problems. Until fairly recently, such social costs were not overwhelmingly important. The elements of the environment were so vast that
they appeared to be inexhaustible. Air, for example, was considered to
be a "free good." Although air is necessary to life, it was so abundantly
available that no one could sell it at a positive price. As a consequence,
the destruction of the usefulness of such a prevalent commodity
imposed no costs on society.

Now, of course, things are different. There is much concern about
the air these days as more and more people in urban areas have come
to realize that they cannot breathe deeply without some risk to lung tis-
sue. Air no longer is "free": There is some "cost" to the user.

But how much do you deduct from GDP for dirty air? Or for
streams that no longer support fish or waterfowl? Or for a scenic view
bulldozed out of existence? For such as these (the list could easily be
expanded), any reasonable person would agree that some deduction
should be made. But how much? Calculated in what way?

Goodies and Baddies. The only practical method so far discovered is to follow the simple test of marketability—can it be sold for a
price? Presumably, if people want breathable air, drinkable water, and
the noise levels of a sternly supervised library, then they will spend the
money needed to pay for it all. Such spending is included in the GDP.
But the offsetting "depreciation" that makes these expenditures necessary is not now deducted from GDP in arriving at NDP. This is not to
say, of course, that the market value approach to calculating environmental depreciation would be easy to apply or entirely satisfactory. But
inspired intellectual effort surely could produce a method to account
for what one observer has called "man-made-bads" to offset the "man-
made-goods" that go into the GDP.

It is undoubtedly true, as Dr. Burns states, that a GDP which does
not take account of environmental pollution overstates growth and
progress of the nation. The affluent society, measured by an expanding
GDP, is not so affluent as the official numbers indicate.

Or is it? There are, after all, a number of sizable "pluses" not in the
GDP which could be added. If this were done, the "minus" of environmental pollution might very well be more than offset.

The single largest item not counted in GDP is the value of work
done in the home by housewives. However, much of this may appear as
an antifeminist manifestation, suitable for protestations by women's lib-
eration groups, the plain fact is that placing a value on home tending
presents some very tricky problems in estimation. Besides, unpaid

productive work done by husbands in the home, too, does not get into the GDP. An example of such work would be the turning of a basement into a finished playroom. Only the purchased material would swell GDP; the husband's work would add nothing to GDP even though his house would increase in value as a consequence of the added playroom. However, if the housewife or husband hired someone to clean the house or finish off the basement, such spending would find its way into GDP.

Other examples of "pluses" that are left out: no allowance is made in GDP for volunteer work, and it is only the out-of-pocket cost, rather than the time spent or the wisdom acquired, that measures the contribution of education. Similarly, no estimates are made of the "income" received by people from services in the public sector—such as use of a park, highway, or library. People receive benefits from such facilities year after year, and yet GDP records only the initial cost when the facility is built and its subsequent maintenance. Here again there are immense problems of estimation. Not all people have access to public facilities, the quality of which, in any case, varies widely all across the nation.

Finally, GDP treats the value of spending on consumer durable goods in different ways depending on their ownership. For instance, money spent by an auto rental agency for its fleet of automobiles is included in the GDP. So is money spent by people and businesses to rent the autos year after year. On the other hand, money spent by an individual purchasing a car for himself gets into the GDP only once—as a personal consumption expenditure at the time of purchase, even though the buyer will get a stream of services, no different from those he would get from a rental auto, for several years. In other words, the "service income" to the owner of any consumer durable good—auto, refrigerator, washing machine, TV—is left out of GDP.

An exception is made in the case of an owner-occupied house. Since the rent on rented dwellings goes into GDP, the comparable service enjoyed by homeowners from their own dwellings is also included so that the total is not subject to variation resulting merely from changes in the proportion of home ownership. Homeowners simply are regarded as landlords who rent to themselves at going local rates. If all consumer durable goods were to be treated the same way as housing, the result, of course, would be a larger GDP.

Policies that would produce no growth in GDP undoubtedly would hold down pollution. But "costs" to society would be heavy. For one thing, antipollution efforts themselves cost money. Only increased production can provide the resources to tackle pollution—and to reduce poverty, keep up the nation's defenses, meet housing needs, and a thousand other things. Suggestions that consumption of goods be restricted to lessen pollution have a surface kind of logic. But, in practice, what goods would be restricted? From the hands of what groups of people? Would this require the setting up of a new agency: The Department of Consumer Privation? The nation's poor do not have the feeling that they are consuming to an excessive degree. Nor do the millions in the middle class who, after paying taxes and making the mortgage payment, are barely able to keep their heads above water. They would find little comfort if the quagmire that engulfed them when GDP stopped growing were a little purer.

Those who are asking whether the nation can survive with pollution are asking the wrong question. It is unfortunate but true that the nation cannot survive without pollution. The answer is not to jettison growth and push for an anemic GDP, but rather to channel economic growth in new directions. More resources and more talent can be applied to reducing pollution to tolerable levels. In the case of automobiles, for example, increased inputs of capital and labor to produce autos that do not emit noxious fumes would be more sensible than closing down assembly lines to produce fewer automobiles. In short, there need not be a basic contradiction between growth and a livable environment. It is not necessary or even possible to choose one and abandon the other.

DISCUSSION

1. What does the author mean when he says that "air no longer is 'free': There is some 'cost' to the user"?

2. The author appears to belittle the concern of many economists that omitting the value of work done in the home causes a sexist bias in GDP calculations. With whom do you agree? Why?

3. Which group do you agree with considering the improvement of GDP, the "pluses" or "minuses"?

4. Which concerns about GDP revolve around its ability to accurately measure current production versus around its ability to measure economic well-being? Is there a difference? Is there value in having a separate measure of both, or can one measure perform both functions?

CHAPTER 8

Economic Fluctuations, Unemployment, and Inflation

TRUE OR FALSE

T F

☐ ☐ 1. The term business cycle refers to the fluctuations in economic output known as expansion, boom, contraction, and recession.

☐ ☐ 2. Inflation decreases the purchasing power of the dollar.

☐ ☐ 3. During a recession, both frictional and structural unemployment will be zero.

☐ ☐ 4. If the actual current rate of unemployment is equal to the natural rate of unemployment, actual *employment* will be equal to the full-employment level and actual GDP will be equal to potential GDP.

☐ ☐ 5. A nonworking student or a retired person is not counted as unemployed in the official figures.

☐ ☐ 6. If a country has a population of 100 of which 75 are employed, the unemployment rate must be 25 percent.

☐ ☐ 7. Potential GDP is the level of output associated with the full employment of resources.

☐ ☐ 8. When the economy is in a recession, unemployment will be higher than the natural rate and actual GDP will be below potential GDP.

☐ ☐ 9. Inflation can be harmful to an economy when it lowers the willingness of individuals to enter into long-term contracts and requires individuals to devote resources toward protecting themselves against the effects of the inflation.

☐ ☐ 10. The natural rate of unemployment is composed of frictional unemployment and cyclical unemployment, but structural unemployment is excluded.

☐ ☐ 11. Inflation is an increase in the general level of prices in an economy.

☐ ☐ 12. If the price index rose from 120 to 132, the inflation rate was 12 percent.

☐ ☐ 13. Through time, inflation hurts the average worker because it raises the prices of consumer goods without increasing their income.

☐ ☐ 14. The labor force is equal to the number employed plus the number unemployed.

☐ ☐ 15. The GDP of an economy can never exceed the potential GDP level.

PROBLEMS AND PROJECTS

1. Classify the following workers as either *F*, frictionally unemployed; *S*, structurally unemployed; *C*, cyclically unemployed; or *O*, out of the labor force.

    ____ a. A worker moves to a new town and has spent two weeks searching for a new job.

    ____ b. Environmental regulations have resulted in a coal miner losing his job. He has not been able to find a job that he can perform with his current skills.

    ____ c. A mother is reentering the labor force after having a baby but has not yet found work.

    ____ d. An auto worker is laid off because of a sharp decline in GDP during the last six months.

    ____ e. A 40-year-old man quits his current job to return to college and get his degree. He does not currently hold a job.

    ____ f. An airline pilot is laid off after an economic slowdown caused by a sharp reduction in the demand for air transportation.

    ____ g. After unsuccessfully searching for a job for eight weeks, a woman decides to stop looking for work.

    ____ h. A person retires after working for his employer for twenty years.

2. Exhibit 1 presents data on the population, employment, and unemployment in three hypothetical countries.

    a. Using the data supplied, calculate and fill in the labor forces of the countries.

    b. Using your results, find the unemployment rates for the countries.

    c. Based upon the unemployment rates, which country has the best performing economy and which has the worst?

    d. Now find the labor force participation rates for the countries.

    e. Calculate the employment to population ratios for each country.

    f. Explain why these "employment rates" from part e are not simply 100 percent minus the unemployment rates.

EXHIBIT 1

Country	Population	Employed	Unemployed	Labor Force	Unemployment Rate	Labor Force Participation Rate	Employment to Population Ratio
Abos	200	100	50	____	____	____	____
Bela	100	76	4	____	____	____	____
Copa	100	54	6	____	____	____	____

3. For each of the situations listed, look at the data given and classify the economy as either *R*, in a recession; *F*, at full employment; or *B*, in an economic boom.

    ____ a. An economy with a natural rate of unemployment of 5 percent currently has an actual unemployment rate of 7 percent.

    ____ b. An economy with a full employment (or potential) level of GDP equal to $5 billion has an actual GDP of $4 billion.

    ____ c. An economy with a natural rate of unemployment of 5 percent currently has an actual unemployment rate of 5 percent.

    ____ d. An economy with a potential GDP of $2 billion has actual GDP of $3 billion.

MULTIPLE CHOICE

1. Frictional unemployment results from
   a. not enough jobs in the economy.
   b. not enough employers.
   c. not enough employees.
   d. scarce information about job opportunities and the time it takes to acquire that information.

2. The definition of the unemployment rate is
   a. the number of persons in the country who are not employed.
   b. the number of persons in the civilian labor force who are not employed.
   c. the percentage of persons in the country who are not employed.
   d. the percentage of persons in the civilian labor force who are not employed.

3. Inflation is *best* described as
   a. high prices.
   b. an increase in the general level of prices as indicated by a price index.
   c. an increase in the purchasing power of money.
   d. an increase in the price of a particular good or service that is necessary for all consumers.

4. The natural rate of unemployment equals
   a. the sum of frictional and structural unemployment.
   b. frictional unemployment.
   c. full employment minus all those unemployed.
   d. the sum of frictional and cyclical unemployment.

5. If the Consumer Price Index in 2001 was 150 and the CPI in 2002 was 165, the rate of inflation between 2001 and 2002 would be
   a. 9.09 percent.
   b. 10 percent.
   c. 15 percent.
   d. 110 percent.

6. The labor force participation rate is
   a. the number of persons employed divided by the number of persons unemployed.
   b. the number of persons 16 years of age and older who are either employed or actively seeking work divided by the total noninstitutional population 16 years of age and older.
   c. the number of persons employed divided by the number of persons 16 years of age and older.
   d. the number of persons who are actively seeking work divided by the number of persons who are employed.

7. Structural unemployment means that
   a. employment in the construction industry is insufficient.
   b. there are simply not enough jobs to go around.
   c. worker qualifications do not match available jobs.
   d. jobs are plentiful, but workers are scarce.

8. Actual GDP
   a. is greater than potential GDP during recessions.
   b. is less than potential GDP during recessions.
   c. and potential GDP have identical meanings.
   d. is equal to potential GDP during economic booms.

9. During periods of high and variable inflation, which of the following is *unlikely* to occur?
   a. Resources will be diverted from economically productive activities towards activities designed to protect individuals from inflation.
   b. Individuals will find it difficult to know whether a price change is due to the general inflation or due to shifts in supply or demand in a given market.
   c. Individuals will want to make long-term contracts in order to enjoy the benefits of higher prices.
   d. Some resources will be wasted as suppliers have to reprint menus and price catalogues to reflect the new, higher prices.

10. In a properly operating, dynamic economy
    a. the unemployment rate should remain near zero.
    b. we would expect to have some unemployment due to normal structural and frictional factors.
    c. the rate of unemployment will be very high during economic booms.
    d. the employment/population ratio should average 100 percent.

11. The period of declining growth in real GDP between the peak of the business cycle and the trough is called the
    a. contractionary phase.
    b. boom.
    c. expansionary phase.
    d. lost phase.

12. Which of the following will most likely occur during the expansionary phase of a business cycle?
    a. Real GDP rises and unemployment falls.
    b. Real GDP declines and inflation rises.
    c. Interest rates rise and the number of business failures rise.
    d. Inflation rises and employment falls.

13. In the early 1990s, the U.S. government substantially reduced defense expenditures. The resulting unemployment of defense-related workers, who possessed skills no longer needed by the economy, is an example of
    a. cyclical unemployment.
    b. frictional unemployment.
    c. seasonal unemployment.
    d. structural unemployment.

14. Which of the following would be officially classified as unemployed?
    a. a school administrator who has been working as a substitute teacher one day per week while looking for a full-time job in administration
    b. a mathematician who returned to graduate school after failing to find a job the last four months
    c. a 60-year-old former steel worker who would like to work but has given up actively seeking employment
    d. None of the above would be officially classified as unemployed.

Use the following data to answer the next four questions.

Population	200 million
Number employed	120 million
Number unemployed	30 million

15. What is the labor force of the economy?
    a.   30 million
    b.   120 million
    c.   150 million
    d.   200 million

16. What is the unemployment rate of the economy?
    a.   15 percent
    b.   20 percent
    c.   60 percent
    d.   75 percent

17. What is the labor force participation rate of the economy?
    a.   25 percent
    b.   60 percent
    c.   75 percent
    d.   80 percent

18. What is the employment/population ratio of the economy?
    a.   25 percent
    b.   60 percent
    c.   75 percent
    d.   80 percent

19. (I) Changes in the age composition of the labor force will affect the natural rate of unemployment (for example, an increase in the relative number of youthful workers). (II) Institutional changes such as an increase in the minimum wage may increase cyclical unemployment but will not affect the natural rate of unemployment.
    a.   Both I and II are true.
    b.   I is true; II is false.
    c.   I is false; II is true.
    d.   Both I and II are false.

20. Which of the following is true?
    a.   During a boom, the natural rate of unemployment falls below the actual rate of unemployment.
    b.   During a boom, the output of the economy will exceed its long-run potential output.
    c.   During a boom, there will be widespread unemployment.
    d.   During a boom, the actual rate of unemployment will exceed the natural rate of unemployment.

21. The natural rate of unemployment
    a.   is fixed; it cannot be changed with public policy.
    b.   fluctuates substantially over the business cycle.
    c.   is associated with the economy's maximum sustainable output rate.
    d.   declines when youthful workers (under age 25) become a larger proportion of the labor force.

DISCUSSION QUESTIONS

1. a. What is inflation? How is it measured? What would a negative inflation rate mean?
    b. Could you predict what would happen to the price of swimsuits and the price of coats during a hot, dry summer, all else equal? How would these changes affect the overall inflation rate? Explain both answers.

2. List the major factors that determine the natural rate of unemployment. Based on those factors, do you expect the natural rate of unemployment to rise or fall over the next decades?

3. If you were to ask most people what the optimal rate of unemployment was, they would be likely to respond "zero, of course!" Do you agree? What drawbacks might zero unemployment have for workers? For firms? For the economy as a whole?

4. In 1998, the U.S. unemployment rate was 4.5 percent. Was the economy in a recession or boom? Explain your reasoning.

5. When Ronald Reagan took office, the nation's unemployment rate was 7.4 percent. When it reached 9.8 percent two years later, Reagan joked that he would take responsibility for the 2.4 percent increase in the unemployment rate during his term if the Democrats would accept blame for the other 7.4 percent. Should Reagan's joke be taken literally? Explain.

6. Respond to each of the following statements:
    a. "We could eliminate the economic cost of recessions by setting up unemployment compensation so that all unemployed workers receive the same income that they earn when working."
    b. "We could eliminate the economic cost of inflation by indexing all payments, such as wages, interest, retirement benefits, and taxes."

PERSPECTIVES IN ECONOMICS

THE EFFICIENCY COSTS OF INFLATION: MYTH AND REALITY

by Alan S. Blinder

[Reprinted with permission from Alan S. Blinder, *Soft Hearts: Tough Minded Economics for a Just Society* (Reading, MA: Addison-Wesley, 1987), pp. 45–51 (abridged).]

It is pretty clear that inflation is unloved. The question is why. More precisely, is the popular aversion to inflation based on fact and logic or on illusion and prejudice? After all, public opinion also lines up solidly behind the existence of flying saucers, angels, and extrasensory perception.

Economists, naturally, have been thinking about, studying, and trying to measure the social costs of inflation for decades. A central conclusion of the research is that the costs of inflation depend very much on whether it proceeds at a steady, predictable rate or is volatile and takes people by surprise.

Unexpected changes in inflation are widely decried because they capriciously create and destroy large chunks of wealth. When borrowers

pay back loans in cheaper dollars then they borrowed, they reap a bonanza at the expense of lenders. During hyperinflation, the wealth redistributions from inflation swamp all other sources of wealth creating. The profit to be made by designing and marketing useful products becomes trivial next to the rewards for clever cash management. Accordingly, entrepreneurial talent is channeled into outsmarting inflation rather than outsmarting the competition. When that happens, the invisible hand is amputated.

Similar things happen in the more moderate inflations we are used to in the United States, though on a muted scale. Americans who provided for their retirement by purchasing long-term bonds in the 1950s and 1960s saw the purchasing power of their savings decimated by the unexpectedly high inflation in the 1970s. In stark contrast, Americans who acquired fixed-interest mortgages at 3 percent and 4 percent interest rates in the 1950s and 1960s discovered to their delight that inflation reduced their mortgage payments to insignificance.

Winners and losers arise whenever there are large swings in the inflation rate. And the resulting redistributions of wealth are rank violations of the principle of (horizontal) equity. Because they are the product of neither the smooth functioning of an efficient market economy nor deliberate government interventions to assist the poor, the arbitrary redistributions caused by unanticipated changes in inflation deserve their bad reputation.

One example is especially important. When people are uncertain about the future course of inflation, long-term contracts calling for payment in dollars become hard to write and even harder to live by. Again, the case of hyperinflation makes the point graphically: When contracts lasting more than a few days become infeasible because no one can predict what money will buy, the economy is in deep trouble. But even modest inflation creates substantial uncertainties and engenders insecurity. In terms of today's money, the repayment of principal on a $1 million five-year corporate bond will be worth $1 million if inflation is zero, $822,000 if inflation averages 4 percent a year over the five years, and $681,000 if inflation averages 8 percent. If no one knows what the average inflation rate will be, both the corporation and prospective bond buyers are taking a big gamble by entering into such a contract.

Rather than bear such risks, nervous investors may deem it wiser to put their money into something tangible—like real estate, precious metals, rare coins, or expensive works of art. Such investments, of course contribute nothing to productivity and economic growth. And so, it is argued, fears of inflation undermine the mainspring of economic prosperity. This charge, if true, would constitute a genuine and serious cost of inflation. But is it? On close examination, the argument founders on the same fallacy I mentioned earlier: failure to remember that every transaction has both a buyer and a seller.

Suppose I purchase a $25,000 painting rather than invest $25,000 in the bond market. The seller of the painting gets $25,000 in cash. What will he do with it? Surely he will not stuff it in his mattress. More likely, he will invest it in the bond market, or in the stock market, or deposit it in the bank. At that point, the funds are back in the financial system—where they can be channeled into productive investments. But what if the seller of the painting invests his money in, say, old coins? Then it may be the coin seller who puts the funds back into circulation. Eventually, however, *someone* must do so, for the supply of collectibles is fixed and every transaction has both a buyer and a seller. Society as a whole cannot buy more collectibles. Thus, though I may put my savings to an unproductive use, someone else will bail society out.

Nonetheless, the risks of inflation do pose a critical question: How much should society pay to avoid assuming such risks? People spend considerable sums on life insurance, fire insurance, and health insurance. Therefore, it is perhaps believable that the body politic knowingly and willingly pays the large premiums it does to insure itself against the risks of inflation. Millions of Americans, however, eagerly wager small sums in lotteries, at racetracks, and in casinos—suggesting a certain fondness for taking a chance. So, while the costs that stem from an uncertain future price level are genuine and potentially large, they are hard to translate into dollars and cents and may not amount to much.

More important, we could easily eliminate this risk if we really wanted to. All we need do is write long-term contracts with escalator clauses, as some businesses already do. In these so-called *indexed contracts,* the amount of money that will change hands in the future is not fixed in dollars, but is tied to the behavior of some price index, such as the Consumer Price Index. The number of dollar bills that will change hands is not known in advance, but the purchasing power of those dollars is.

This simple device would eliminate the risks that stem from an unpredictable future price level. Yet businesses and individuals acting in their own self-interest rarely choose to do so. The apparent reluctance to write indexed contracts suggest that people are willing to pay only small premiums to insure themselves against long-term inflation risks. Yet society pays huge premiums for anti-inflation insurance when it keeps millions of people unemployed. Something seems amiss here.

There is one further cost that a believer in the principle of efficiency should be aware of. In a market economy, the relative prices of different commodities guide the allocation of resources. If a severe frost reduces the Brazilian coffee crop, the price of coffee will rise relative to, say, the price of tea. Consumers pursuing their own best interests will buy less coffee and more tea. Similarly, more resources will be thrown into coffee production and less into tea. All this activity is as it should be, because nature has made coffee scarcer.

But variable and uncertain inflation makes relative prices hard to monitor because the dollar ceases to serve as a reliable measuring rod. A consumer goes to the store and finds that coffee costs 10 percent more than it did last week. Does that mean coffee has become 10 percent more expensive relative to tea? Or does it just mean that inflation has raised all prices by 10 percent? More information is needed to make an intelligent decision.

As with other costs of inflation, this cost can be colossal in a hyperinflation. If the price level rises 40 percent a week on average, but rises 70 percent in some weeks and 10 percent in others, the fact that coffee prices rise 10 percent in a week tells consumers little about the price of coffee relative to other commodities. But what is a mountain in a hyperinflation is only a molehill in a single-digit inflation. If the typical weekly price increase is only one-tenth of 1 percent (which is roughly what a 5 percent annual inflation rate means), then a 10 percent increase in the price of coffee strongly suggests that coffee has become 9.9 percent more expensive relative to most other goods. Dollar prices are almost as useful to shoppers under low inflation as under zero inflation.

Can that be all there is to the costs of inflation? The inefficiencies caused by hyperinflation are, of course, monumental, but the costs of moderate inflation that I have just enumerated seem meager at best.

I am forced to conclude that inflation's most devout enemies exhibit verbal hysteria. Inflation does indeed bring losses of efficiency. It also makes people feel unsure and unhappy. We would no doubt be better off without it. But, on close examination, the costs that attend the low and moderate inflation rates experienced in the United States and in other industrial countries appear to be quite modest—more like a bad cold than a cancer on society. And the myth that the inflationary demon, unless exorcised, will inevitably grow is exactly that—a myth. There is neither theoretical nor statistical support for the popular notion that inflation has a built-in tendency to accelerate.

As rational individuals, we do not volunteer for a lobotomy to cure a head cold. Yet, as a collectivity, we routinely prescribe the economic equivalent of lobotomy (high unemployment) as a cure for the inflationary cold. Why?

DISCUSSION

1. Blinder's main conclusion is that inflation is less harmful to the economy than most people think it is. Do you agree? Which of his arguments are convincing? With which do you disagree? Explain.

2. Economists generally agree that inflation has higher costs if it is variable (and cannot be predicted accurately) than if it is steady. If you knew exactly what next year's inflation rate was going to be, how could you protect yourself?

3. If Blinder is right, what implications do his conclusions have for the proper objective of government policy?

CHAPTER 9

An Introduction to Basic Macroeconomic Markets

TRUE OR FALSE

T F

☐ ☐ 1. The vertical LRAS curve indicates that by increasing the price level in the economy, technology will be improved so real output will increase as well.

☐ ☐ 2. When the economy is in long-run equilibrium, actual output will equal potential GDP.

☐ ☐ 3. A trade deficit is when a country's exports of goods and services are greater than its imports.

☐ ☐ 4. If interest rates rise, bond prices will increase.

☐ ☐ 5. Saving is disposable income that is not spent on consumption.

☐ ☐ 6. The aggregate demand curve shows the inverse relationship between the demand for goods and services and the money (or nominal) interest rate.

☐ ☐ 7. The real interest rate equals the money (or nominal) interest rate plus an inflationary premium.

☐ ☐ 8. When U.S. citizens make investments in foreign countries, this would be considered an "outflow of capital" from the United States.

☐ ☐ 9. The real balance effect is the increase in wealth that comes about when aggregate prices fall while the money supply remains constant.

☐ ☐ 10. When the U.S. dollar appreciates, it is less expensive for foreigners to buy U.S. goods and services.

☐ ☐ 11. In the loanable funds market, the true "price" paid by borrowers (demanders) and earned by lenders (suppliers) of money is the real interest rate.

☐ ☐ 12. When the foreign exchange market and loanable funds market are in equilibrium, injections will equal leakages in the circular flow of income.

☐ ☐ 13. The key markets in the circular flow of income are the goods and services market, the resource market, the loanable funds market, and the foreign exchange market.

☐ ☐ 14. The money available in an economy for investment loans comes from household savings.

☐ ☐ 15. The aggregate demand curve slopes downward for the same reason that all other demand curves slope downward.

PROBLEMS AND PROJECTS

EXHIBIT 1

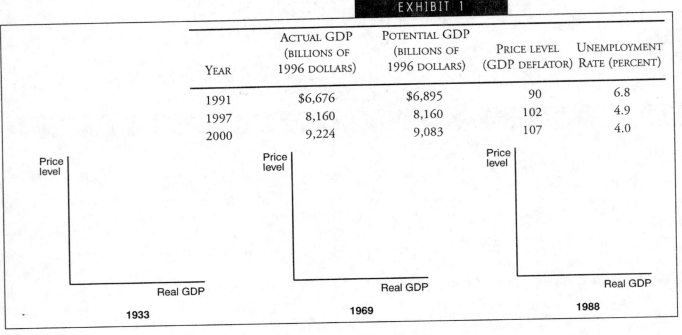

Year	Actual GDP (billions of 1996 dollars)	Potential GDP (billions of 1996 dollars)	Price Level (GDP deflator)	Unemployment Rate (percent)
1991	$6,676	$6,895	90	6.8
1997	8,160	8,160	102	4.9
2000	9,224	9,083	107	4.0

1. Consider the data in Exhibit 1.
   a. For each of these three years, draw an aggregate demand/aggregate supply diagram in which you show a short-run aggregate supply curve, a long-run aggregate supply curve, and an aggregate demand curve. Label the appropriate values for total output and the price level. (Hint: Remember that actual output occurs at the intersection between AD and SRAS.)
   b. Based upon this data, what is the economy's natural rate of unemployment?
   c. In which of these cases is the unemployment rate greater than the natural rate of unemployment? In which cases does actual output fall below potential GDP? Are they the same? In what part of the business cycle would you consider the economy?
   d. In which of these cases is the unemployment rate less than the natural rate of unemployment? In which cases does actual output exceed potential GDP? Are they the same? In what part of the business cycle would you consider the economy?
   e. In which of these cases is the unemployment rate equal to the natural rate of unemployment? In which cases does actual output equal potential GDP? Are they the same? In what part of the business cycle would you consider the economy?

2. Consider the information in Exhibit 2 at the top of the next page.
   a. Fill in the blanks by calculating the real interest rate for each of the years listed. Was the real interest rate constant, rising, or falling between 1979 and 1982? Was the real interest rate constant, rising, or falling between 1998 and 2001? (Hint: The prime interest rate is a well-publicized rate that banks charge some of their better customers and is a good measure of the money rate of interest. Also, since we do not know what rates of inflation were expected, assume that the actual inflation rates are good guesses for the inflationary premiums in those years.)
   b. Assuming all else constant, what effect would the change in real interest rate between 1979 and 1982 have had on the willingness of consumers and businesses to borrow money? Between 1998 and 2001?

EXHIBIT 2

	1979	1982	1998	2001
Prime interest rate	12.7%	14.9%	8.4%	6.9%
Inflation rate	11.3%	6.1%	1.6%	2.8%
Real interest rate	____	____	____	____

3. Exhibit 3 contains hypothetical information about the AD and SRAS curves giving the appropriate values for real GDP (in billions of dollars) at different price levels (P).

   a. Plot the data in an AD-AS diagram in the space provided. What is the current equilibrium level of real GDP? What is the price level?

   b. Suppose the level of full-employment real GDP is $330 billion. Add a LRAS curve to your diagram.

   c. Is this economy currently experiencing full employment, a recession, or a boom? Explain briefly.

EXHIBIT 3

AD	P	SRAS
$270	160	$350
290	140	330
310	120	310
330	100	290
350	80	270

4. Understanding the difference between real and nominal (or "money") interest rates is important but can sometimes be confusing. The easiest way to understand the difference is to consider loaning your friend $100 because he is having a party tonight and wants to buy ten large pizzas that cost $10 each. He will repay you in one year. The nominal (or money) interest rate is the percent difference in the *dollar amount* of money he repays you relative to what you loaned him. The real interest rate is the percent difference between the *quantity* of pizza that can be purchased now (at today's prices) with the money you loan him relative to the *quantity* of pizza that you will be able to buy when the money is repaid (at future prices). Use this analogy to answer the following questions.

   a. You tell your friend he can borrow the $100 today if he gives you back $100 one year from now. What money (or nominal) interest rate are you charging him?

   b. If inflation causes the price of a large pizza to increase from $10 to $20 by the time he repays you, how many pizzas will you be able to buy with the $100 when it is repaid? Is the real interest rate positive, negative, or zero?

   c. Suppose that instead of specifying the loan in dollars, you specify it in pizza. You will lend him enough for ten pizzas today if he returns enough money to buy ten pizzas next year. What real interest rate are you charging him? If the price of pizzas rises to $20, how much will he owe you?

   d.   Suppose that both you and your friend expect the price of pizzas to double from $10 to $20 between now and next year. You both agree to a written contract in which you loan him $100 today if he repays you $200 next year. If inflation turns out to be higher than you both expected, and the price of pizza rises to $25, are you (the lender) better or worse off when he repays you with $200? Is your friend (the borrower) better or worse off? What has changed relative to what you expected, the real or nominal interest rate, or both?

   e.   If both you and your friend had known in advance that the inflation rate would be higher (as in part d) and that pizza prices would rise to $25, how might the contract you agreed to in part d have changed? Would the real or nominal interest rate, or both, have been different?

5.   Exhibit 4 shows a simplified version of the circular flow diagram with the international sector omitted. Beside each arrow is a box with a letter corresponding to the question letter relating to that box. A few boxes are already done as examples. Follow the questions below to fill in the remaining boxes. [Hint: for every market or sector, the total of all the arrows coming in must equal the total of all flowing out.]

   a.   **The household sector**—At the lower right, national income is earned by households supplying their resources in the resource market (wage income from supplying labor, for example). Part of this income is taken by the government in taxes and the remaining disposable income must be either spent on consumption or saved. Of the $100 of income earned by households, $10 is paid out in taxes to the government and $70 is spent on consumption. How much is household saving? Note this amount in the box for net saving.

   b.   **The loanable funds market**—Household net saving is available to the economy for either business investment or government borrowing. If the government runs a budget deficit and borrows $5, how much is left to be borrowed by businesses for investment? Note these amounts in the boxes. Also, assume (for simplicity) that total business investment expenditures

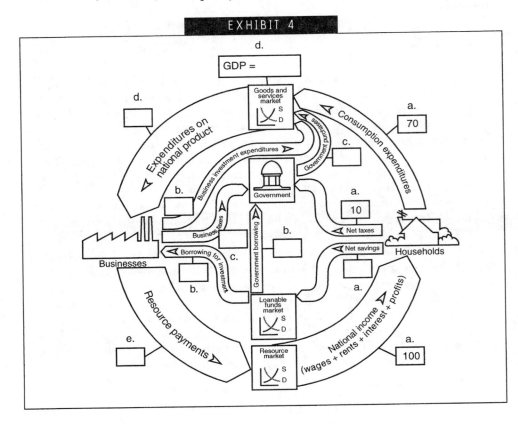

EXHIBIT 4

(going from the businesses into the goods and services market) is equal to the amount borrowed by businesses for investment and note this in the appropriate box as well.

c. **The government sector**—The government receives revenue from taxes (from both households and businesses) and also receives revenue from borrowing. This revenue is spent on government purchases in the goods and services market. If business taxes are $10, find total government purchases and note these amounts in the boxes.

d. **The goods and services market**—There are four sources of aggregate demand flowing into the goods and services market: consumption expenditures, business investment, government purchases, and net exports (which have been omitted here for simplicity). This total is the expenditure approach to measuring GDP. Write this total above the goods and services market for GDP. Also, put this value beside the arrow flowing from the goods and services market into the business sector as expenditures on national product.

e. **The business sector**—Businesses receive revenue from the expenditures on goods and services (top left arrow). They also have money flowing in from the loanable funds market that they have borrowed for investment. The money flowing out is in the form of taxes to the government, money spent on investment goods in the goods and services market, and resource payments to factors of production (workers, etc.). Find the remaining total resource payments flowing from businesses into the resource market.

f. **The resource market**—This is where we started by assuming that households received $100 of national income from supplying their resources. Does your total from part e above going into the resource market match the outflow that we began with? Given your answers above, what do you think is the primary determinant of household income?

6. Using your knowledge from working problem 5, answer the following questions. You might need to refer back to Exhibit 4 to answer these.

a. In a later chapter we will discuss several theories about how government borrowing affects the economy. Returning to the diagram, suppose government borrowing increases from $5 to $10. What must change to bring the loanable funds market back into equality so that the money coming in equals the money flowing out?

b. If households decide to spend more of their income on consumption, and save less, what will happen to the level of investment in the economy (assume government borrowing does not change)? Because economic growth requires investment, what does this tell you about the relationship between economic growth and household savings? If you were a politician in favor of increasing economic growth what would you propose?

MULTIPLE CHOICE

1. Within the aggregate demand/aggregate supply framework, the quantity on the horizontal axis in the aggregate goods and services market represents the
    a. total amount of government spending.
    b. total real output (real GDP) of the economy.
    c. total unemployment of the economy.
    d. price level of the economy.

2.   In the loanable funds market, the true burden of borrowers and the true yield to lenders is the
   a.   real (inflation adjusted) interest rate.
   b.   nominal (money) interest rate.
   c.   inflation rate.
   d.   inflation premium rate (in money terms).

3.   When AD is equal to SRAS at an output level equal to the LRAS curve,
   a.   we are at long-run macroeconomic equilibrium.
   b.   we are at the natural rate of unemployment.
   c.   both a and b are true.
   d.   neither a nor b are true.

4.   Your grandmother gives you a $100 savings bond that will mature in fifteen years. The bank tells you that they will buy it from you today at a price of $24. If interest rates rise in the near future, the value of your bond
   a.   will fall and it will be worth less than $24.
   b.   will rise and it will be worth more than $24.
   c.   will remain unchanged at $24.
   d.   This is a trick question, the value of a $100 bond is always $100.

5.   If the expected rate of inflation is zero, the
   a.   real interest rate must also equal zero.
   b.   money (nominal) interest rate must also equal zero.
   c.   real interest rate must equal the money interest rate.
   d.   economy is likely to experience high inflation in the near future.

6.   Which of the following is the primary factor that coordinates the actions of borrowers and lenders in the loanable funds market?
   a.   inflation rate
   b.   unemployment rate
   c.   the government
   d.   interest rate

7.   Which of the following statements about the circular flow diagram is *not* correct?
   a.   Households receive income from the resource market; they save some of it and spend the rest of it on domestic or foreign goods and services.
   b.   The loanable funds market takes net household savings and channels it in part to the government and in part to businesses for investment.
   c.   Expenditures on GDP are equal to consumption plus government purchases plus investment plus net exports (exports minus imports).
   d.   The net inflow of capital from foreign economies must always be positive and equal to the amount of business investment.

8.   The circular flow of income is coordinated by the
   a.   goods and services market, resources market, foreign exchange market, and loanable funds market.
   b.   consumption market, investment market, stock market, and government market.
   c.   government market, household goods market, bond market, and business market.
   d.   financial market, corporate market, stock market, and loanable funds market.

9. As prices rise, a fixed money supply will be able to buy fewer goods and services. This real balance effect is due to a(n)
   a. reduction in the interest rate.
   b. increase in aggregate demand.
   c. decline in the purchasing power of money.
   d. increase in income.

10. The aggregate demand curve slopes downward to the right because
    a. as prices decrease, the real value of the fixed quantity of money increases and thereby stimulates consumer spending (the real balance effect).
    b. a lower price level reduces the price of domestic goods relative to foreign goods, increasing net exports (the international substitution effect).
    c. a lower price level reduces the demand for money and lowers the real interest rate, stimulating consumption and investment spending (the interest rate effect).
    d. all of the above are correct.

11. Which of the following is true regarding an unanticipated increase in inflation?
    a. Both borrowers and lenders will be better off.
    b. Both borrowers and lenders will be worse off.
    c. Borrowers will be better off and lenders will be worse off.
    d. Borrowers will be worse off and lenders will be better off.

12. Suppose people anticipate that inflation will be 4 percent during the next several years. If the real rate of interest is 5 percent, the money rate of interest must be
    a. 1 percent.
    b. 4 percent.
    c. 5 percent.
    d. 9 percent.

13. Suppose you are earning 5 percent nominal interest on your savings account. If the rate of inflation is 3 percent, the real rate of interest your are earning is
    a. 2 percent.
    b. 3 percent.
    c. 5 percent.
    d. 8 percent.

14. In 1999, the nominal interest rate on a thirty-year bond was around 5.85 percent. Assuming that investors have set these contracts expecting a real interest rate of 3 percent, what is the average rate of inflation that investors in the market are expecting over the next thirty years?
    a. 2.85 percent
    b. 3 percent
    c. 5.85 percent
    d. 8.85 percent

15. Which of the following situations would you prefer if you planned to borrow money?
    a. The nominal interest rate is 5 percent, and future prices are expected to be stable.
    b. The nominal interest rate is 9 percent, and expected inflation is 7 percent.
    c. The nominal interest rate is 4 percent, and expected inflation is 1 percent.
    d. The nominal interest rate is 25 percent, and expected inflation is 22 percent.

16. If the dollar price of the English pound goes from $1.50 to $2.00, the dollar has
    a. appreciated and the English will find U.S. goods cheaper.
    b. appreciated and the English will find U.S. goods more expensive.
    c. depreciated and the English will find U.S. goods cheaper.
    d. depreciated and the English will find U.S. goods more expensive.

17. A depreciation of a nation's currency would cause
    a. the nation's imports to increase and exports to decline.
    b. the nation's exports to increase and imports to decline.
    c. both imports and exports to decline.
    d. both imports and exports to rise.

18. If the value of a nation's imports exceeds exports, the nation has a
    a. government budget deficit.
    b. trade surplus.
    c. trade deficit.
    d. negative net capital flow.

19. The long-run aggregate supply curve is vertical, reflecting the fact that
    a. changes in price have no effect on output in the long run. In the long run, the price of goods and the price of resources move together and firms have no incentive to change their output.
    b. fluctuations in inflation cannot be anticipated in the long run, so future prices have no effect on output.
    c. changes in price affect output a lot in the long run because in the long run firms can adjust factory sizes to meet changing demand conditions.
    d. changes in price have a large effect on output because they lead to highly variable interest rates, and business is hard to conduct under those circumstances.

20. Which of the following accurately indicates the relationship between the short-run and long-run aggregate supply curves?
    a. In the short run, aggregate supply is sloped upward to the right, and in the long run, it is vertical.
    b. In the short run, aggregate supply is vertical, and in the long run, it is sloped upward to the right.
    c. In the short run, aggregate supply is downward sloping, but in the long run, it is sloped upward to the right.
    d. In the short run, aggregate supply is sloped upward to the right, but in the long run, it is downward sloping.

21. If the current price level in the goods and services market is higher than what was expected, output will be
    a. at the economy's long-run capacity.
    b. below the economy's long-run capacity.
    c. above the economy's long-run capacity.
    d. equal to the expected rate of inflation minus net exports.

22. (I) If long-run equilibrium is present in the goods and services market, the current price level will equal the price level buyers and sellers anticipated.
    (II) When an economy is in long-run equilibrium, the actual rate of unemployment will equal the natural rate of unemployment.
    a. Both I and II are true.
    b. Both I and II are false.
    c. I is true; II is false.
    d. I is false; II is true.

23. A trade surplus is when
    a. imports are greater than exports of goods and services.
    b. exports are greater than imports of goods and services.
    c. imports are equal to exports of goods and services.
    d. there is a positive net inflow of foreign capital.

24. (I) Fiscal policy involves altering government tax and spending policies. (II) Monetary policy encompasses those actions that alter the money supply.
    a. Both I and II are true.
    b. Both I and II are false.
    c. I is true; II is false.
    d. I is false; II is true.

DISCUSSION QUESTIONS

1. Respond to the following statement: "It is impossible to produce more than what economists refer to as 'potential GDP.'" Use the aggregate supply/aggregate demand diagram to depict a situation where the economy is producing past potential GDP. How is it possible for the economy to produce at that point?

2. "The burden of inflation falls heavily on savers and creditors, for example, upon wealthy bondholders." (Campbell McConnell, *Economics*, 6th ed. [New York: McGraw-Hill, 1975], p. 380.) Under what circumstances is this statement likely to be correct? Incorrect?

3. Consider the natural rate of unemployment.
    a. What do economists mean by the natural rate of unemployment? Do you really believe there is such a thing as a natural rate of unemployment? Explain your answer.
    b. What reasons can you think of to explain why the natural rate of unemployment seems to have been higher in the United States than in Japan for most of the years since World War II?
    c. What ways can you think of to lower the natural rate of unemployment in the United States?
    d. If the natural rate of unemployment in the United States did fall, what would happen to the long-run aggregate supply curve?

4. Different loans have different interest rates. What are some of the types of interest rates that you know of? In considering how interest rates rise and fall, is it a major flaw in our model of the loanable funds market to consider just one interest rate for the economy?

5. In order to calculate the real rate of interest, we must somehow come up with an inflationary premium that is based on our expectation of inflation in the future. Do you have such an expectation? Do your friends? Would an inflation rate of 20 percent surprise you? If so, does that imply that you do or do not have some sort of expectation about future rates of inflation?

CHAPTER *10*

Working with Our Basic Aggregate Demand/Aggregate Supply Model

TRUE OR FALSE

T F

☐ ☐ 1. An anticipated change differs from an unanticipated change in that an anticipated change is foreseen by decision makers.

☐ ☐ 2. A decrease in real wealth, such as might be caused by a stock market crash, would decrease short-run aggregate supply.

☐ ☐ 3. A reduction in the real rate of interest would increase aggregate demand because it would increase business investment and consumer (consumption) spending.

☐ ☐ 4. Any factor, such as a technological advance, that shifts the long-run aggregate supply curve also similarly shifts the short-run aggregate supply curve.

☐ ☐ 5. Aggregate demand would fall if either the expected rate of inflation fell, foreign incomes fell, or the exchange rate value of the dollar fell (the dollar depreciated).

☐ ☐ 6. An unanticipated reduction in aggregate demand would cause the price level to fall and real output (real GDP) to fall as well.

☐ ☐ 7. An increase in resource prices (such as the price of oil) would cause a decrease in the long-run aggregate supply curve.

☐ ☐ 8. Adverse supply shocks that decrease short-run aggregate supply include major earthquakes, wars, and other natural disasters.

☐ ☐ 9. An unanticipated increase in short-run aggregate supply would cause the price level to fall and real output (real GDP) to fall as well.

☐ ☐ 10. During a recession, wages, resource prices, and the real interest rate will fall, helping to bring the economy back out of the recession.

☐ ☐ 11. When the economy is in a short-run equilibrium above the full employment level (an economic boom), rising resource prices will help the economy to "self-correct," redirecting it back to full employment at a higher price level.

☐ ☐ 12. Economic booms are sustainable in the long run because changes in aggregate demand are caused by changes in *permanent* income.

☐ ☐ 13. All economists agree that the self-correcting mechanism works very rapidly.

☐ ☐ 14. Once decision makers anticipate a given rate of inflation and build it into long-term contracts, an actual rate of inflation that is less than expected is essentially the equivalent of a reduction in the price level when price stability (zero inflation) is anticipated.

93

PROBLEMS AND PROJECTS

1. Use the aggregate demand/aggregate supply diagrams below to illustrate the changes in aggregate demand (AD), short-run aggregate supply (SRAS), long-run aggregate supply (LRAS), the price level (P), and real gross domestic product (RGDP) in response to the events described to the left of the diagrams. First show in the diagrams how AD, SRAS, and/or LRAS shift and then fill in the table to the right of the diagrams using + to indicate an increase (a shift to the right), − to indicate a decrease (a shift to the left), and 0 to indicate no change. [Hint: Only focus on the new short-run equilibrium and do not worry about any future long-run changes.]

EVENTS	DIAGRAMS	AD	SRAS	LRAS	P	RGDP
a. The government adopts economic policies that lower business optimism about the future direction of the economy.		—	—	—	—	—
b. A technological breakthrough in robotics significantly raises labor productivity.		—	—	—	—	—
c. Social Security reform leads to lower real interest rates.		—	—	—	—	—
d. Newly released economic indicators lead people to believe that the rate of inflation will increase in the near future.		—	—	—	—	—
e. A war disrupts oil supplies leading to temporarily higher oil prices.		—	—	—	—	—

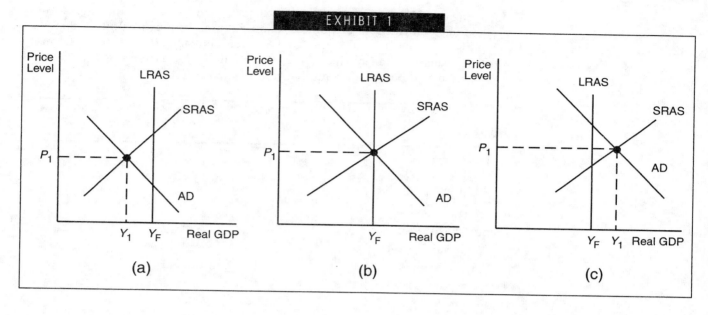

EXHIBIT 1

(a)   (b)   (c)

2. Use the aggregate demand/aggregate supply diagrams in Exhibit 1 to work the following questions.

   a. For each of the three cases shown above (a, b, and c), decide whether (1) the economy is currently in a short-run equilibrium or a long-run equilibrium or both; (2) whether the current level of GDP is above, below, or equal to the full-employment (or potential) level of GDP; (3) whether the current rate of unemployment is above, below, or equal to the natural rate of unemployment; and (4) whether the economy is in a boom, a recession, or at full employment.

   b. What would you expect to be happening to resource prices in the economy depicted in Exhibit 1a? Diagram the self-correcting process that would happen in the long run as a result of the changing resource prices. When the economy returns to long-run equilibrium, will the price level rise or fall relative to its current level?

   c. What would you expect to happen to the economy depicted in Exhibit 1b in the long run? Would there be a self-correction?

   d. What would you expect to be happening to resource prices in the economy depicted in Exhibit 1c? Diagram the self-correcting process that would happen in the long run as a result of the changing resource prices. When the economy returns to long-run equilibrium, will the price level rise or fall relative to its current level?

3. Using an AD/AS model, decide what happens to the price level, the output level, and unemployment in each of the following cases. Assume that the economy is initially in long-run equilibrium and the events initially catch people by surprise (the changes are unanticipated). Use + to indicate an increase, − to indicate a decrease, and 0 to indicate no change.

EVENT	PRICE LEVEL	OUTPUT (REAL GDP)	UNEMPLOYMENT RATE
a. Interest rates fall.	_____	_____	_____
b. The stock market crashes.	_____	_____	_____
c. The dollar depreciates.	_____	_____	_____
d. Severe flooding in agricultural areas.	_____	_____	_____
e. World oil prices fall (oil is a resource).	_____	_____	_____
f. A major technological advance occurs.	_____	_____	_____
g. The expected rate of inflation rises. (Hint: This shifts both AD and SRAS.)	_____	_____	_____
h. Consumers and businesses become pessimistic about the future direction of the economy.	_____	_____	_____
i. Foreign economies fall into recession.	_____	_____	_____

4   Use the diagrams in Exhibit 2 to label each of the statements below as (T) true or (F) false.

_____ a. B and G represent economic booms, while D and I represent recessions.

_____ b. A and F are points of long-run equilibrium.

_____ c. Beginning from A, a decline in the real interest rate would move the economy toward D.

_____ d. Beginning from F, an increase in resource prices would move the economy toward I.

_____ e. At B, there will be a tendency for resource prices to fall, moving the economy toward C.

_____ f. At I, there will be a tendency for resource prices to fall, moving the economy toward J.

_____ g. Beginning from A, if foreign economies (with whom this economy trades) went into recessions, the economy would move toward D.

_____ h. If a stock market crash moved the economy from A to D, the self-correcting mechanism of resource prices would tend to move the economy toward E in the long run.

_____ i. If the world price of oil rose, moving the economy from F to I, the self-correcting mechanism of resource prices would tend to move the economy toward J in the long run.

_____ j. A movement from F to G represents a decrease in short-run aggregate supply.

EXHIBIT 2

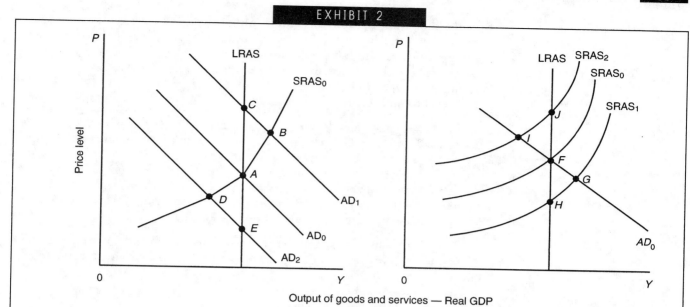

Output of goods and services — Real GDP

_____ k. A movement from *B* to *A* represents a decrease in short-run aggregate supply.

_____ l. If the economy was currently in a recession at *D*, a decrease in real interest rates could move the economy out of the recession and toward *A*.

MULTIPLE CHOICE

1. Which of the following will reduce aggregate demand?
   a. an increase in real wealth
   b. lower real incomes in foreign economies with whom an economy trades
   c. increased consumer and business optimism about the future
   d. an increase in the expected rate of inflation

2. An increase in the long-run aggregate supply curve shifts
   a. both LRAS and AD to the right.
   b. both LRAS and SRAS to the right.
   c. both LRAS and AD to the left.
   d. only LRAS to the right.

3. The permanent income hypothesis, developed by Milton Friedman, states that
   a. consumption spending depends more on a person's permanent (or lifetime) income than on their current level of income.
   b. consumption spending depends more on a person's current level of income than on their permanent (or lifetime) level of income.
   c. income levels remain permanent over long periods of time.
   d. any change in the economy will change income permanently.

4. During recessions, interest rates tend to fall because
   a. consumers attempt to borrow money to make up for their falling income.
   b. business borrowing for investment purposes tends to fall during recessions.
   c. lower real resource prices create profit opportunities for banks.
   d. recessions shift the economy's long-run aggregate supply curve to the left.

5. In the short run, equilibrium output in the goods and services market may be either above or below the full-employment level, but in the long run, it
   a. must be less than full-employment output.
   b. must be greater than full-employment output.
   c. must be equal to full-employment output.
   d. depends on aggregate demand, not just long-run aggregate supply.

6. In the aggregate-demand/aggregate-supply model, what market adjustments cause the economy to return to its long-run capacity when output is temporarily *greater than* the economy's long-run potential output?
   a. Lower wage rates and resource prices reduce short-run aggregate supply.
   b. Lower interest rates increase aggregate demand and thereby stimulate output.
   c. Higher wage rates and resource prices reduce short-run aggregate supply.
   d. A decrease in the price level reduces aggregate demand.

7. Which of the following is most likely to result from an unanticipated increase in short-run aggregate supply due to favorable weather conditions in agricultural areas?
   a. an increase in the inflation rate
   b. an increase in the unemployment rate
   c. a decrease in the price level
   d. a decrease in the natural rate of unemployment

8. Which of the following is most likely to accompany an unanticipated reduction in aggregate demand?
   a. an increase in the price level
   b. a decrease in unemployment
   c. an increase in real GDP
   d. an increase in the unemployment rate

9. Which of the following is most likely to accompany an unanticipated increase in short-run aggregate supply?
   a. an increase in real GDP
   b. a decrease in real GDP
   c. an increase in the price level
   d. an increase in the unemployment rate

10. In the aggregate demand/aggregate supply model, an economy operating below its long-run potential capacity will experience
    a. falling real wages and resource prices that will increase SRAS, moving the economy back toward full employment.
    b. rising interest rates that will increase SRAS, moving the economy back toward full employment.
    c. inflation that will stimulate additional spending and thereby restore full employment.
    d. a prolonged economic depression unless consumer optimism is increased.

For questions 11 through 14, assume that the economy is in long-run equilibrium in the aggregate demand/aggregate supply model and that some sort of event takes place. In each case, mark the most likely impact of the event on the aggregate demand/aggregate supply diagram given in Exhibit 3.

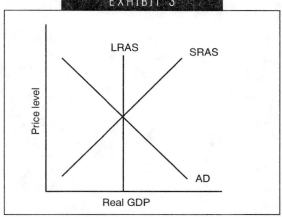

11. Good weather allows agricultural output to double.
    a. The aggregate demand curve would shift to the right.
    b. The aggregate demand curve would shift to the left.
    c. The short-run aggregate supply curve would shift to the right.
    d. The short-run aggregate supply curve would shift to the left.

12. There is an increase in the expected rate of inflation.
    a. The aggregate demand curve would shift to the right.
    b. The short-run aggregate supply curve would shift to the left.
    c. The price level would rise and real GDP would remain the same.
    d. All of the above are correct.

13. Consumers and businesses all suddenly decide that the future looks much better than it previously had.
    a. The aggregate demand curve would shift to the right.
    b. The aggregate demand curve would shift to the left.
    c. The short-run aggregate supply curve would shift to the right.
    d. The short-run aggregate supply curve would shift to the left.

14. A major technological advance occurs.
    a. The aggregate demand curve would shift to the right.
    b. The aggregate demand curve would shift to the left.
    c. Both the short-run and the long-run aggregate supply curves would shift to the right.
    d. Both the short-run and the long-run aggregate supply curves would shift to the left.

15. Which of the following would *not* cause a shift in the short-run aggregate supply curve?
    a. a major technological advance
    b. a decrease in the real interest rate
    c. a decrease in the expected rate of inflation
    d. an increase in resource prices

16. Which of the following would *not* cause a shift in the aggregate demand curve?
    a. a major technological advance
    b. a decrease in the real interest rate
    c. an increase in the expected rate of inflation
    d. a stock market crash

17. If an economy is in equilibrium at a given price level and a given output level, the aggregate-demand/aggregate-supply (AD/AS) model indicates that an unanticipated decrease in aggregate demand will cause
    a. real output to decline.
    b. the price level to fall.
    c. unemployment to increase.
    d. all of the above.

18. During the Gulf War, Iraq invaded Kuwait setting oil fields on fire, which caused the price of crude oil to increase sharply. Other things constant, how would such an increase in oil prices have influenced the short-run aggregate supply, growth rate of real GDP, and the inflation rate of the United States and other oil-importing nations who use oil as a resource in production?
    a. SRAS to fall, the growth rate of real GDP to increase, and the inflation rate to fall
    b. SRAS to fall, the growth rate of real GDP to decline, and the inflation rate to increase
    c. SRAS to rise, the growth rate of real GDP to decline, and the inflation rate to increase
    d. SRAS to rise, the growth rate of real GDP to increase, and the inflation rate to increase

19. Which of the following is most likely to accompany *a fully anticipated* reduction in short-run aggregate supply?
    a. an increase in the price level
    b. a decrease in the price level
    c. a decrease in real GDP
    d. both a and c

20. During the 1990s, a financial crisis spread throughout Asia causing those economies to drop into recessions. Other things constant, how would such a decrease in the income of foreign trading partners have influenced the price level and output of the United States?
    a. Both real output and the price level would have fallen.
    b. Both real output and the price level would have risen.
    c. Real output would have fallen, and the price level would have risen.
    d. Real output would have risen, and the price level would have fallen.

21. If an innovation in automation allows cars to be produced with fewer resources, buyers and sellers will plan for lower prices and larger supplies of cars. This is an example of
    a. unforeseeable change.
    b. anticipated change.
    c. supply shock.
    d. expansionary fiscal policy.

22. Which of the following will most likely occur in the United States as the result of an unexpected rapid growth in real income in Japan and Europe?
    a. a short-run increase in U.S. employment and output
    b. a short-run decrease in U.S. employment and output
    c. a short-run decline in prices in the United States
    d. a reduction in the natural rate of unemployment in the United States

23. If there is an unanticipated increase in aggregate demand, which of the following is most likely to occur?
    a. an increase in the price level (inflation)
    b. an increase in the rate of unemployment
    c. a reduction in the growth rate of real GDP
    d. a decrease in LRAS to restore full-employment

24. Which of the following will most likely increase the economy's long-run aggregate supply?
    a.   advances in technology
    b.   unfavorable weather conditions in agricultural areas
    c.   an increase in the expected inflation rate
    d.   a low rate of investment

25. If improvements in education and training programs increased the productivity of persons in the labor force,
    a.   aggregate demand would decrease.
    b.   short-run aggregate supply would increase, but long-run aggregate supply would not change.
    c.   long-run aggregate supply would increase, but short-run aggregate supply would not change.
    d.   Both short-run and long-run aggregate supply would increase.

DISCUSSION QUESTIONS

1. Recent improvements in the quality of South Korean goods have made Americans more willing to "buy Korean."
    a.   Use an AD/AS diagram to show the impact of this development on the U.S. economy.
    b.   What happens to the price level as the economy moves to its short-run equilibrium and then corrects to its new long-run equilibrium? What happens to inflation?
    c.   Can one-time shocks such as this cause persistent inflation? Why or why not?

2. The topic of tax rate changes will not be dealt with specifically until the following chapters, but you will not be surprised to hear that taxes have a profound effect on the economy. Could you analyze the impact of an income tax reduction on the economy with the AD/AS diagram? How?

3. Explain the self-correcting mechanisms present in a market economy. Specifically state how these work to bring an economy out of a recession. Do all economists agree on the speed with which the self-correcting mechanisms work? What implications does this debate have for government policy?

4. The economy is highly complex, and each of the main aggregate markets (the goods and services market, the resources market, and the loanable funds market) affect each other. Keeping that in mind, what should happen to real interest rates during a recession? Does it matter what caused the recession? Does it matter whether the drop in income was expected or unexpected? Whether the drop in income is expected to be temporary or permanent? What should happen to money interest rates? Will they always move with real interest rates? Why or why not?

5. Shifts in aggregate demand and short-run aggregate supply are usually given more attention than shifts in long-run aggregate supply. Do you think this emphasis is appropriate? Which is really more important to an economy? If you had a choice between a policy that would increase aggregate demand, one that would increase short-run aggregate supply, or one that would increase long-run aggregate supply, which one would you choose?

CHAPTER *11*

Keynesian Foundations of Modern Macroeconomics

T F

☐ ☐ 1. Keynes believed that during a recession people could induce more production by saving more.

☐ ☐ 2. Keynes believed that full employment would be automatically achieved because of flexible wages and prices.

☐ ☐ 3. Keynes' views about whether or not prices and wages are always flexible differed from the views of the classical economists who preceded him.

☐ ☐ 4. An increase in disposable income, other things being equal, will cause consumption to increase.

☐ ☐ 5. In a simple Keynesian model, the expenditure multiplier equals one divided by one minus the marginal propensity to consume.

☐ ☐ 6. According to Keynes, the main determinant of current consumption is current disposable income.

☐ ☐ 7. Keynes believed that changes in output, rather than in prices, direct the economy to equilibrium.

☐ ☐ 8. The marginal propensity to consume (MPC) is defined as the total amount of consumption in the economy divided by the change in disposable income.

☐ ☐ 9. Business pessimism can increase the severity of recessions by reducing investment.

☐ ☐ 10. The Keynesian model shows a positive relationship between income and net exports.

☐ ☐ 11. Since disposable income can only be consumed or saved, the knowledge of an economy's aggregate consumption function will permit one to calculate the economy's aggregate saving function with respect to disposable income.

☐ ☐ 12. In the Keynesian model, output would rise if planned aggregate expenditures were above output. In that situation, firms would find their inventories falling unexpectedly, and they would raise output in response.

☐ ☐ 13. The Keynesian model is often represented in the AD/AS framework with a SRAS curve that is horizontal below potential output and vertical at potential output.

PROBLEMS AND PROJECTS

1. Calculate the marginal propensity to consume for the following situations:
   a. Consumption increases by $2,000 when disposable income increases by $3,000.
   b. Consumption increases from $6,000 to $7,000 when disposable income increases from $8,000 to $9,500.
   c. Disposable income increases from $9,000 to $10,000, but consumption remains the same.
   d. Disposable income increases by $4,000 causing savings to increase by $1,000. [Hint: Disposable income must be either spent or saved.]

2. a. Calculate the simple multiplier for all four cases in question 1 above.
   b. What would happen to your answers in part *a* if the economies in question began to trade internationally, thus adding net exports to their planned aggregate expenditure.

3. Suppose that the economy's initial equilibrium is at $4,000 billion and the marginal propensity to consume is 1/2. Autonomous expenditure then rises by $200 billion.
   a. Complete the following table. [Hint: The subtotal row should be the sum of the numbers in rounds 1 to 5, while the grand total row should be obtained using the multiplier.]

EXHIBIT 1		
EXPENDITURE STAGE	ADDITIONAL INCOME ($ BILLION)	ADDITIONAL CONSUMPTION ($ BILLION)
Round 1	$200	$100
Round 2	____	____
Round 3	____	____
Round 4	____	____
Round 5	____	____
Subtotal	____	____
Grand Total	____	____

   b. Exhibit 2 illustrates the close relationship between the Keynesian aggregate expenditure model and the AD/AS model when the economy's short-run aggregate supply curve is flat. Each round of additional income in the upper panel pushes out the AD curve in the lower panel. The diagram illustrates the economy's movement during the first round of the multiplier process. Illustrate the rest of the multiplier process in the diagrams (RGDP denotes real GDP).

EXHIBIT 2

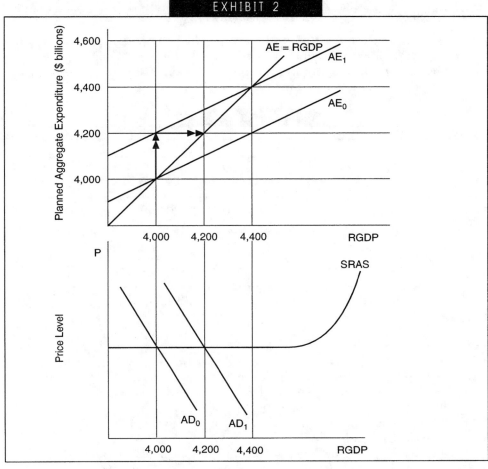

4. Consider Exhibit 3.
    a. What is the *equilibrium* real GDP in this economy?
    b. If current real GDP is presently 800 (in other words, different than equilibrium GDP), what is happening to firms' inventories? What will firms do in response?

EXHIBIT 3

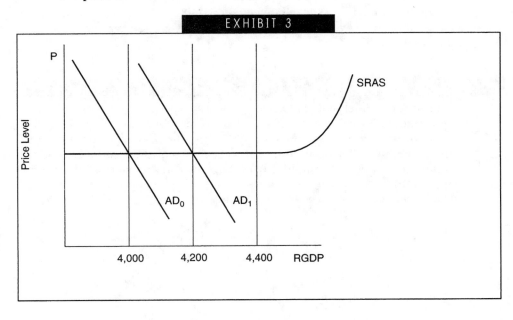

c. Assuming there are no net exports, what is the marginal propensity to consume in this economy?

5. Imagine two economies, Savit and Spendit, which are identical in all respects except that Savit has a marginal propensity to consume of 1/2, while Spendit has a MPC of 9/10. Exhibit 4 traces the impact of additional investment spending of $25 million in each economy.

EXHIBIT 4

| EXPENDITURE STAGE | SAVIT | | SPENDIT | |
	ADDITIONAL INCOME	ADDITIONAL CONSUMPTION	ADDITIONAL INCOME	ADDITIONAL CONSUMPTION
Round 1	$25.0	$12.5	$15.00	$22.5
Round 2				
Round 3				
Round 4				
Round 5				
All other rounds				
Total				

a. Fill in the missing entries for the expenditure stages in each of the two countries. [Hint: Use the multiplier to get the answer for the total row, and then get the all other rounds amount by subtracting what has happened in rounds 1 to 5 from the total.]
b. In which economy does the increased investment spending have the larger impact? Explain briefly.
c. From the "Total" row, calculate the ratio of total additional consumption to total additional income for each country. Are the magnitudes of these ratios surprising? Explain briefly.

6. Suppose that the current equilibrium level of aggregate income is $500 trillion, and the *full employment* level of income is $600 trillion. If the marginal propensity to consume is 4/5, how much would investment spending need to increase for the equilibrium level of income to equal the full employment level? Explain briefly. Attempt to show this situation on both AD/AS and aggregate expenditure diagrams.

MULTIPLE CHOICE

1. The expenditure multiplier is used to calculate the change in
    a. spending caused by a change in income.
    b. equilibrium income resulting from a change in interest rates.
    c. equilibrium income resulting from an independent change in spending.
    d. investment caused by a change in consumption.

2. Which of the following is a major insight of the Keynesian model?
   a. Changes in output, as well as changes in prices, play a role in the macroeconomic adjustment process, particularly in the long run.
   b. A general overproduction of goods relative to total demand is impossible since production creates its own demand.
   c. The responsiveness of aggregate demand to changes in supply will be directly related to the availability of unemployed resources.
   d. Fluctuations in aggregate demand are an important potential source of business instability.

3. In equation form, Keynesian macroeconomic equilibrium is attained when
   a. total output = real GDP.
   b. real GDP = planned consumption.
   c. planned aggregate expenditures = total output.
   d. $C + I + G + NX$ = planned aggregate expenditures.

4. Say's law of the market holds that supply creates its own demand because
   a. there is a buyer for each new product produced.
   b. the act of producing creates income equal to the value of the goods produced.
   c. prices are stable in the short run; thus, producers know how much to provide.
   d. supply prices are always equal to prices.

5. If the MPC is 3/4, the simple expenditure multiplier is
   a. 4.00.
   b. 1.33.
   c. 1.75.
   d. 0.75.

6. John Maynard Keynes
   a. was an American economist.
   b. did not believe Say's Law, that "supply creates its own demand."
   c. was the "father of microeconomics."
   d. did not believe that changes in private investment were an important source of economic stability.

7. The primary determinant of consumer spending is
   a. the interest rate.
   b. disposable income.
   c. expectations of inflation.
   d. the stage of the business cycle.

8. Which of the following is most likely to increase investment?
   a. an increase in the interest rate
   b. an increase in saving
   c. an increase in the expected quantity of future sales
   d. an increase in unemployment

9. The greater the MPC,
   a. the greater the expenditure multiplier.
   b. the larger the change in aggregate expenditure for a given change in spending.
   c. neither a nor b is correct.
   d. both a and b are correct.

10. Which of the following best describes a consumption function?
    a. a function that relates consumption to savings
    b. a function that relates investment to the interest rate
    c. a function that relates consumption to disposable income
    d. All of the above are correct; the consumption function includes all three relationships.

11. If consumption equals 800 when disposable income is 1,000, and then consumption increases to 1,000 when disposable income increases to 1,300, the marginal propensity to consume is
    a. 8/10.
    b. 10/13.
    c. 2/3.
    d. 3/4.

12. "If there is unemployment, the average wage rate will decline as the unemployed workers choose lower wages rather than going without a job. The demand curve for labor slopes downward and to the right so that more workers would be hired at the lower wage rate, restoring full employment." According to the Keynesian view, this quote is
    a. incorrect because widespread unemployment would cause wages to rise, not decline.
    b. incorrect because the demand for labor, other things constant, will not be negatively related to wages.
    c. incorrect because wages and prices tend to be highly inflexible downward.
    d. essentially correct.

13. Which of the following is most likely to lead to an increase in current consumption?
    a. an increase in personal income tax rates
    b. an increase in one's expected future income
    c. a decrease in one's marginal propensity to consume
    d. an increase in the interest rate

14. The Great Depression provided support for Keynes' declaration that
    a. government action was necessary to ensure that the saving rate remained at the equilibrium level.
    b. falling interest rates would induce consumers to increase their saving.
    c. the average propensity to consume will increase as disposable income rises.
    d. prolonged periods of unemployment were possible.

The following information is relevant to the next two questions.

Assume IBM decides, despite an ongoing recession, to build a new branch for computer analysis in Bozeman, Montana. The plant expects to spend $12 million to hire the necessary employees, all of whom move in from out of state to take the job.

15. If the marginal propensity to consume in Bozeman was 3/4, what would be the total change in income that would result from the operation of the plant for one year?
    a. $12 million
    b. $48 million
    c. $9 million
    d. $27 million

16. If Bozeman citizens decided to spend more than 3/4 of the additional income,
    a. the MPC would decrease.
    b. the expenditure multiplier would decrease.
    c. the expansion in income would be larger.
    d. aggregate expenditures would decline.

17. If an economy operating in the Keynesian range of its SRAS has a marginal propensity to consume of 4/5, and the government wants to boost real output by 400, by how much should it increase autonomous expenditure?
    a. 80
    b. 320
    c. 400
    d. 500

18. Which of the following is a correct implication of the Keynesian model for the shape of the aggregate supply curve in the goods and services market?
    a. The SRAS is horizontal because prices are assumed to be constant.
    b. The SRAS is vertical because it is impossible to increase real GDP past full employment.
    c. The SRAS is horizontal well below full employment and is vertical at full employment.
    d. The SRAS is vertical well below full employment and is horizontal at full employment.

19. The diminished popularity of the Keynesian AE model in recent years is due to
    a. the highly unstable business cycles over the past fifteen years.
    b. the fact that the model incorporates expectations and is therefore unreliable.
    c. the inability of the model to explain the presence of both inflation and high unemployment at the same time.
    d. scholars failing to remember the severity of the Great Depression.

20. If the economy is operating at a point where the aggregate expenditure line lies below the 45 degree line (AE = GDP),
    a. total spending is more than total output.
    b. unwanted business inventories will increase.
    c. businesses will reduce their future production.
    d. both b and c are correct.

21. According to Say's law, there cannot be overproduction of goods and services because
    a. planned aggregate expenditures sometimes fall short of total output.
    b. prices and wages are "sticky" or inflexible in the downward direction.
    c. demand creates its own supply.
    d. supply creates its own demand.

22. In the Keynesian aggregate expenditure model, the term "autonomous expenditures" is used when referring to those expenditures that do not depend on the
    a. difference between planned and actual.
    b. level of income.
    c. interest rate.
    d. price level.

23. If consumption expenditures are $180, total planned investment is $75, government purchases are $40, exports are $20, imports are $40, and taxes are $25, aggregate demand must be
    a. $225.
    b. $250.
    c. $275.
    d. $355.

24. Keynesian analysis suggests that if planned spending (aggregate demand) were $700 billion but GDP was $800 billion,
    a. businesses would accumulate inventories, and output would fall.
    b. output would rise, incomes would rise, and tax revenues would automatically increase.
    c. production would be stimulated, and output would increase, unless the full-capacity output was less than $950 billion.
    d. the Federal Reserve would eventually lower interest rates.

25. In the Keynesian aggregate expenditure model, the equilibrium level of income is achieved when
    a. the employment rate equals approximately 96 percent.
    b. actual saving equals actual investment.
    c. planned aggregate expenditures exceed actual output.
    d. actual output equals planned aggregate expenditures.

26. When the marginal propensity to consume is 3/4, and an economy operates well below its full-employment capacity, in the Keynesian model a $25 billion increase in investment expenditures will cause GDP to rise (assuming the full impact of the multiplier is instantaneous)
    a. $25 billion.
    b. $50 billion.
    c. $75 billion.
    d. $100 billion.

27. In the Keynesian model, if an economy *is operating at its full-employment capacity,* and the marginal propensity to consume is 3/4, an increase in government spending of $100 billion will cause real output to increase by
    a. $75 billion.
    b. $100 billion.
    c. $400 billion.
    d. zero; only inflation will occur.

DISCUSSION QUESTIONS

1. What is Say's Law? Explain why classical economists thought that a market economy would always return to full-employment equilibrium. Do Keynesians agree with Say's Law in the short run? the long run? Explain both answers.

2. Twice during the Reagan administration, income tax rates were cut. Indicate the effect you think such tax cuts have on each of the following: consumption, savings, the value of the multiplier, aggregate demand, and long-run aggregate supply. [Hint: Remember that consumption depends on disposable income, and that disposable income is the income remaining after taxes have been paid.]

3. What do you find most convincing about the economic theory of John Maynard Keynes? least convincing? On the whole, do you think the influence of Keynes has been good or bad?

4. How would each of the following influence the equilibrium level of output and employment? Explain your answer.
   a. an increase in planned saving
   b. the expectation of a recession in the near future
   c. the expectation of accelerating inflation during the next twelve months
   d. an increase in government spending
   e. a decline in the income tax

5. What are the reasons that wages might be inflexible downward? Do you think that such inflexibility is an empirically important feature of our economy? What sort of empirical evidence could you look for in order to answer this question?

CHAPTER 12

Fiscal Policy

TRUE OR FALSE

T F

☐ ☐ 1. The crowding-out effect refers to the hypothesis that high marginal tax rates crowd personal consumption out of the marketplace and therefore reduce the effectiveness of fiscal policy.

☐ ☐ 2. Fiscal policy is the use of government tax and expenditure policy to influence the economy.

☐ ☐ 3. A change in fiscal policy usually changes the full-employment level of output, allowing for a permanently higher level of real output.

☐ ☐ 4. Keynesians believe that wages and prices are inflexible—especially in the downward direction.

☐ ☐ 5. According to the new classical view, fiscal policy is generally impotent—it has little or no effect on the economy or aggregate demand.

☐ ☐ 6. After years of persistent budget deficits, the federal government began running a surplus in the late 1990s. This turnaround was primarily due to both faster revenue growth and slower expenditure growth in the area of national defense.

☐ ☐ 7. If government borrowing pushes up interest rates, private borrowing for consumption and investment will increase, further expanding the economy.

☐ ☐ 8. Automatic stabilizers are programs that tend to automatically carry out countercyclical fiscal policy—promoting a budget deficit during a recession and a budget surplus during a boom—without the need for discretionary government action.

☐ ☐ 9. The supply-side view is that higher marginal tax rates tend to decrease work effort reducing aggregate supply.

☐ ☐ 10. A budget surplus means that tax revenues exceed government expenditures.

☐ ☐ 11. Ricardian equivalence (the new classical view) holds that an increase in government spending financed by borrowing (debt) has an identical effect on the economy as if the spending were financed by an increase in current taxes instead.

☐ ☐ 12. Unlike monetary policy, fiscal policy is not subject to timing problems—it has an immediate effect on the economy.

☐ ☐ 13. Running a budget surplus would be considered restrictive fiscal policy, while a budget deficit is expansionary fiscal policy.

☐ ☐ 14. Modern theories suggest that fiscal policy is much more effective for stabilizing the economy than early Keynesian theories suggested.

PROBLEMS AND PROJECTS

1. Label each of the following statements as most likely to be made by a Keynesian (K), a believer in the crowding-out view (CO), a new classical economist (NC), or supply-sider (SS).

    ____ a. "Expansions in government spending financed by borrowing (debt) are a highly effective way to increase aggregate demand in the economy."

    ____ b. "Large budget deficits cause high real interest rates that reduce private spending and investment."

    ____ c. "There is no link between budget deficits and interest rates; higher deficits are simply matched by higher savings."

    ____ d. "The expansionary effect of increased government spending will be completely offset by reductions in private consumption; thus, fiscal policy has no effect on aggregate demand."

    ____ e. "The expansionary effect of increased government spending financed with debt will be at least partially offset by the negative effects of higher interest rates caused by government borrowing."

    ____ f. "Lower marginal tax rates stimulate people to work, save, and invest, resulting in more output and a larger tax base."

    ____ g. "The primary use of fiscal policy should not be to counter short-run business cycle fluctuations but rather to promote long-run growth in the economy."

    ____ h. "Whenever the economy is in a recession, expansionary fiscal policy should be employed to restore full employment."

EXHIBIT 1

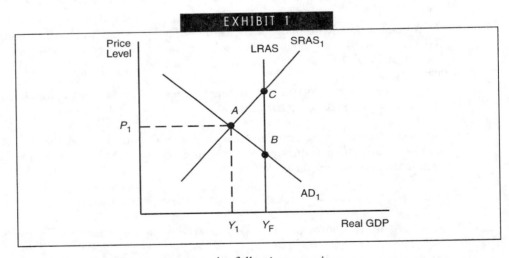

2. Refer to Exhibit 1 to answer the following questions.

    a. Is the economy depicted (at point *A*) in a recession, a boom, or at full employment?

    b. If no government action was taken, at which point would the economy return to long-run equilibrium with the self-correcting mechanism (changing resource prices affecting SRAS)? Show the curve shifting and note the new equilibrium point in the figure.

    c. What would a Keynesian suggest be done to government taxes or spending to help the economy out of the recession? Would this be consistent with running a budget deficit, budget surplus, or balanced budget?

    d. If the policies in part c were adopted, under the Keynesian view, at what point would the economy return to long-run equilibrium? Show the curve shifting and note the new equilibrium point in the figure.

e. How do your answers to parts b and d differ? That is, what is different when fiscal policy is used to restore full employment relative to when the economy restores full employment through a self correction?

f. Now, return to part d in which expansionary fiscal policy is enacted to increase aggregate demand. According to the new classical view, would aggregate demand still have shifted the same as under the Keynesian view?

g. What would a new classical economist suggest the government do with fiscal policy if the economy were in a recession?

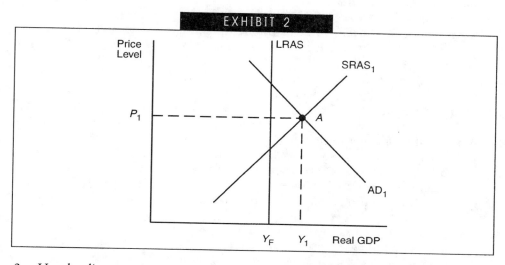

EXHIBIT 2

3. Use the diagram given in Exhibit 2 to answer the following questions.
   a. Is the economy depicted (at point A) in a recession or a boom or at full employment?
   b. According to the Keynesian view, what should be done with government taxes and/or spending to restore full employment? Is this consistent with running a budget deficit, a budget surplus, or a balanced budget?
   c. Suppose these policies are enacted, but during the time it takes for the impact of these policies to be felt, the economy has already self-corrected. First, show in the diagram where the economy would be if the self-correcting mechanism worked, then shift aggregate demand consistent with the impact of the policies enacted.
   d. What has been the effect of this policy? If these timing problems happen frequently, does it suggest that fiscal policy works to stabilize or destabilize the economy?

4. Decide whether an increase in government spending financed by a budget deficit (borrowing) would increase (+), decrease (−), or have no effect (0) on each of the following economic variables under the view given in the question.
   _____ a. the real interest rate under the crowding-out view
   _____ b. the real interest rate under the new classical view
   _____ c. private borrowing for investment under the crowding-out view
   _____ d. personal saving under the new classical view
   _____ e. foreign capital investment in the United States under the crowding-out view
   _____ f. U.S. net exports under the crowding-out view
   _____ g. aggregate demand under the Keynesian view
   _____ h. aggregate demand under the crowding-out view
   _____ i. aggregate demand under the new classical view

MULTIPLE CHOICE

1. Fiscal policy is defined as
   a. changes in government expenditure to influence the economy.
   b. changes in tax rates to influence the economy.
   c. changes in the money supply to influence the economy.
   d. both *a* and *b* but not *c*.

2. Expansionary fiscal policy financed by government borrowing can lead to
   a. higher interest rates and lower private investment under the crowding-out view.
   b. an increase in aggregate demand under the Keynesian view.
   c. no change in aggregate demand under the new classical view.
   d. all of the above.

3. A balanced budget means that
   a. aggregate consumption is in balance with aggregate saving.
   b. government spending is constant from year to year.
   c. public spending equals private spending.
   d. tax revenues during a period are equal to government expenditures.

4. The crowding-out effect implies that budget deficits will
   a. increase real interest rates and lower the future stock of private capital.
   b. decrease real interest rates and increase the future stock of private capital.
   c. increase the productivity of workers in the future.
   d. lead to higher levels of income for workers in the future.

5. The crowding-out effect suggests that
   a. expansionary fiscal policy causes inflation.
   b. high marginal tax rates crowd out tax deductions.
   c. fiscal policy will be less effective at shifting aggregate demand because the effects are at least partially offset by other factors that result.
   d. a budget surplus will cause the economy to slip into a major recession.

6. The new classical model implies that the effect of government increasing expenditures by debt financing
   a. has the same effect as if it was financed by raising current taxes.
   b. is highly expansionary on aggregate demand and the economy.
   c. will result in higher real interest rates.
   d. will result in lower personal savings.

7. Which of the following is *not* an example of an automatic stabilizer?
   a. unemployment payments that rise when unemployment increases
   b. a corporate profits tax whose revenues rise when the economy enters an economic boom
   c. an income tax whose revenues fall when economic activity declines
   d. a personal investment program in which the investor saves $50 per month regardless of the state of the economy

8. The timing problems associated with fiscal policy will be more severe to the extent that
    a. the self-adjustment mechanism of the market operates rapidly.
    b. the government can use the leading indicators of economic activity to reliably and quickly forecast swings in the business cycle.
    c. congressional responses to business cycles can be sped up through bipartisan cooperation.
    d. crowding out reduces the impact of fiscal policy.

9. When the federal government is running a budget surplus,
    a. government revenues exceed government expenditures.
    b. government expenditures exceed government revenues.
    c. the economy must be in a recession.
    d. the government will have to borrow money.

10. Consider an economy for which the government budget is in balance when the economy operates at long-run capacity. If policy makers do not alter either tax rates or expenditure programs, during a recession, automatic stabilizers will tend to cause
    a. the budget to remain automatically in balance.
    b. a budget deficit to occur.
    c. a budget surplus to occur.
    d. the recession to continue indefinitely.

11. An economy is in an inflationary boom, and unemployment is at a record low level. According to the Keynesian model, which of the following policies would be most appropriate?
    a. an increase in government expenditures
    b. an increase in the money supply
    c. a tax increase
    d. a tax cut

12. If policy makers believe a recession is coming, the Keynesian view indicates that they should
    a. increase government spending and/or decrease taxes.
    b. increase taxes while holding government spending constant.
    c. balance the budget.
    d. increase tax rates, reduce government spending, and shift toward a budget surplus.

13. If a budget surplus leads to a decrease in U.S. real interest rates, the lower rates will tend to cause
    a. the dollar to appreciate.
    b. the dollar to depreciate.
    c. a decrease in private investment.
    d. a decrease in net exports.

14. The new classical model implies that a shift to a more expansionary fiscal policy will
    a. stimulate aggregate demand and employment.
    b. retard aggregate demand and employment.
    c. increase the real rate of interest.
    d. exert little or no impact on the real interest rate, aggregate demand, and employment.

15. According to the new classical view, a $20 billion increase in government expenditures financed by a budget deficit will
    a. stimulate output by $20 billion.
    b. stimulate output more than $20 billion.
    c. stimulate output but by less than $20 billion.
    d. leave output unchanged.

16. Automatic stabilizers are government programs that tend to
    a. increase the ups and downs in aggregate demand without legislative action.
    b. bring expenditures and revenues automatically into balance without legislative action.
    c. move government spending and revenues in countercyclical directions without legislative action.
    d. increase tax collections automatically during a recession.

17. Other things constant, an increase in marginal tax rates will
    a. decrease the supply of labor and reduce its productive efficiency.
    b. decrease the supply of capital and decrease its productive efficiency.
    c. encourage individuals to buy goods that are tax deductible instead of those that are more desired but nondeductible.
    d. do all of the above.

18. Which of the following statements is true?
    a. The empirical evidence indicates that countries with higher marginal tax rates have higher economic growth rates.
    b. Unlike other policies, supply-side tax cuts have their full impact on an economy instantaneously.
    c. The supply-side effects of changes in marginal tax rates take place over lengthy time periods.
    d. In the 1960s and 1980s, when the marginal tax rates were reduced, the share of income taxes paid by high-income taxpayers fell.

19. Although the economy was entering the Great Depression, the Hoover administration followed a policy leading to a balanced budget. According to Keynesian theory, this balanced-budget fiscal policy was
    a. correct.
    b. incorrect; the government should have been running a surplus.
    c. incorrect; the government should have been running a deficit.
    d. correct if expenditures were cut, incorrect if taxes were increased.

20. The modern synthesis view of fiscal policy stresses
    a. the fact that changes in marginal tax rates have no effect on the economy.
    b. that offsetting factors make fiscal policy much less effective than the Keynesian view suggested.
    c. that proper timing of fiscal policy is very difficult to achieve, rendering fiscal policy less useful as a stabilization tool.
    d. that both b and c are true.

21. Which of the following is the best explanation of how expansionary fiscal policy can crowd out net exports?
    a. Expansionary fiscal policy leads to high budget deficits. Foreigners become concerned about the stability of the United States and stop buying American goods as a result.
    b. When the government spends more, some of its spending is on foreign goods. As imports rise, net exports fall.
    c. The higher interest rates associated with expansionary fiscal policy attract foreign investors. To buy U.S. financial assets, foreigners bid up the real exchange rate, which in turn causes net exports to fall.
    d. The cut in taxes associated with expansionary fiscal policy stimulates aggregate supply. As aggregate supply rises, consumers have a greater incentive to purchase domestic goods, causing imports to fall and net exports to drop.

22. Which of the following groups would be least likely to support a balanced budget amendment to the U.S. Constitution?
    a. Keynesians
    b. new classicals
    c. supply-siders
    d. believers in the crowding-out view

23. "Expansionary fiscal policy will tend to substantially increase current real output." Which of the following models would tend to support such a statement?
    a. the Keynesian model and the new classical model, but not the crowding-out model
    b. the Keynesian model and the crowding-out model, but not the new classical model
    c. the Keynesian model, but not the crowding-out and new classical models
    d. all three models

24. Unemployment compensation works as an automatic stabilizer because
    a. when it runs out during recessions, the unemployed are forced to find jobs, thus stimulating the economy to move back to long-run equilibrium.
    b. during recessions, unemployment compensation lowers disposable income, thus stabilizing consumption.
    c. changes in unemployment compensation laws change the natural rate of unemployment, thus helping the economy return rapidly to its long-run equilibrium following shocks.
    d. the unemployment compensation program helps to stabilize income (and thus consumption) by paying out more during recessions and falling during booms.

DISCUSSION QUESTIONS

1. "A reduction in tax rates will lead to a decline in tax revenues and an increase in the size of the budget deficit. The deficit spending will be inflationary. Thus, there is little reason to believe that a tax cut will be able to alter the real output rate of an economy." Evaluate each of these three sentences.

2. Explain the New Classical position on the effect of tax cuts in your own words. What are the main criticisms of the New Classical position? Think of some empirical work that you could do that would help you decide whether to accept or reject the New Classical position. Some economists in this debate have done

research on the extent to which people leave bequests to their children and their reasons for leaving these bequests. How could such research have any bearing on the debate on the New Classical position?

3. The large reductions in marginal tax rates enacted during the Reagan administration were followed by a long boom. How would a Keynesian explain this result? a supply-sider? Use the AS/AD diagram to illustrate their explanations. Is there any way we could tell whose explanation is correct?

4. A leading politician once said, "The government budget should always be balanced, so a tax cut does not make sense without a cut in spending." Would you favor a balanced budget amendment? Why or why not?

5. "Government spending financed by budget deficits pushes up real interest rates. The higher real interest rates cause private borrowing for consumption and investment to fall. In addition, the inflow of foreign capital will cause an appreciation of the U.S. dollar, reducing net exports. Thus, in the aggregate demand equation (AD = $C + I + G + NX$), whenever G is increased the other three variables fall." Evaluate and discuss each of these sentences using diagrams where possible to explain your answer. What views are consistent with this statement, and which are not?

CHAPTER 13

Money and the Banking System

TRUE OR FALSE

T F

☐ ☐ 1. M1 is the broadest definition of the money supply because it includes all currency and checkable deposits.

☐ ☐ 2. Liquidity refers to how easily an asset can be converted into purchasing power, thus money is the most liquid of all assets.

☐ ☐ 3. Money serves three basic functions: It is a medium of exchange, a store of value, and a unit of account.

☐ ☐ 4. Fiat money is money that is backed by gold or some other valuable commodity.

☐ ☐ 5. All money that is deposited in a bank must be kept by the bank in its vault in case the customer wants to withdraw the money.

☐ ☐ 6. If the reserve requirement was 5 percent, and you deposited $100 in your bank account, the bank would have to keep $95 in required reserves.

☐ ☐ 7. A reserve requirement of 25 percent implies a potential deposit expansion multiplier of 4.

☐ ☐ 8. If the reserve requirement was 25 percent, and the Federal Reserve System (Fed) wanted to expand the money supply by $800 using open market operations, it would buy $200 worth of bonds.

☐ ☐ 9. Because money is defined in specific units ($5 and $20 bills for example), the value of money never changes.

☐ ☐ 10. The purchasing power of money falls when the price level rises.

☐ ☐ 11. Raising the reserve requirement is one way in which the Fed can reduce the money supply.

☐ ☐ 12. An increase in the discount rate would encourage loans and thereby expand the supply of money.

☐ ☐ 13. When the Fed sells bonds on the open market, it results in an increase in the money supply.

☐ ☐ 14. When the U.S. Treasury issues and sells new bonds to the general public, it results in a decrease in the money supply.

PROBLEMS AND PROJECTS

1. For each of the following, write *M1* to indicate that the item is included in the M1 money supply and *M2* to indicate that it is included only when the definition is expanded to M2. Write *neither* to indicate that the item is not a part of either the M1 or M2 money supply.
   _____ a. a $100 bill
   _____ b. a $10,000 six-month certificate of deposit with your bank
   _____ c. a $10,000 retirement account invested in stocks
   _____ d. a $50 traveler's check
   _____ e. a $5,000 credit line on an American Express credit card
   _____ f. a quarter
   _____ g. a $1 off coupon clipped from the Sunday newspaper
   _____ h. a $100 balance in a noninterest-earning checking account
   _____ i. a $200 balance in an interest-earning savings account
   _____ j. a $10,000 U.S. Treasury bill

2. Suppose the Fed wished to increase the money supply by $50 billion to head off a coming recession. Also assume that the reserve requirement is 20 percent and banks hold no excess reserves.
   a. What is the deposit expansion multiplier?
   b. If the Fed wanted to use open market operations, should it buy or sell bonds?
   c. How many dollars worth of bonds should it buy or sell?
   d. Rework parts a, b, and c using a value for the reserve requirement of 10 percent. Does the multiplier rise or fall? To accomplish the same increase, will the Fed now have to buy/sell more or less bonds?

3. For each of the following, indicate whether the result will create an increase (+), decrease (–), or have no change (0) in the money supply and the national debt.

	MONEY SUPPLY	NATIONAL DEBT
a. The Fed sell $100 million of government securities (bonds) to the general public.	_____	_____
b. Government spending exceeds tax revenue, so the U.S. Treasury responds by issuing $100 million of new bonds and sells them to the general public.	_____	_____
c. Government spending exceeds tax revenue, so the U.S. Treasury responds by issuing $100 million of new bonds and sells them to the Fed.	_____	_____
d. Jim sells his five-year $100 U.S. savings bond to his friend Sarah for $80.	_____	_____
e. Worried about terrorist attacks, bank customers withdraw their money from their accounts and store the cash in their houses.	_____	_____
f. The Fed buys $20 million of government securities from the general public.	_____	_____
g. The federal government runs a $100 billion surplus and uses the money to pay off the national debt by buying (retiring) bonds.	_____	_____

4. Assume the required reserve ratio for the U.S. banking system is 20 percent and that banks keep no excess reserves. Suppose the Fed buys a $10,000 U.S. government security from the public.
   a.   Will the action by the Fed increase or decrease the money supply?
   b.   Complete the following table to track the change in the money supply resulting from the Fed's action through the first four rounds of the multiplier process. [Hint: Find the totals using the multiplier, not by adding up the numbers.]

	BANK (DEMAND) DEPOSITS	REQUIRED RESERVES	EXCESS RESERVES (NEW LOANS)
Round 1	_____	_____	_____
Round 2	_____	_____	_____
Round 3	_____	_____	_____
Round 4	_____	_____	_____
Remaining rounds	. . .	. . .	. . .
Total	_____	_____	_____

MULTIPLE CHOICE

1. If the Fed used "open market operations" to decrease the money supply, it
   a.   increased the federal funds rate.
   b.   issued more federal government debt.
   c.   sold U.S. government securities (bonds) to the general public.
   d.   increased the required reserve ratio.

2. Suppose the Fed buys $10 million of U.S. securities from the public. Assume a reserve requirement of 5 percent and that all banks hold no excess reserves. The total impact of this action on the money supply will be
   a.   an increase of $200 million.
   b.   a decrease of $200 million.
   c.   a decrease of $10 million.
   d.   an increase of $10 million.

3. In the United States, the control of the money supply is the responsibility of the
   a.   Federal Reserve System (the Fed).
   b.   the president.
   c.   the U.S. Treasury.
   d.   the U.S. Congress.

4. Further difficulties in measuring the money supply can be expected in the future as
   a.   the penny is likely to be discontinued from circulation.
   b.   the U.S. Congress continues the process of decreasing the independence of the Fed.
   c.   the volume of transactions conducted with credit cards continues to escalate.
   d.   debit cards and electronic money come into widespread use.

5. Suppose a bank receives a new deposit of $500. The bank extends a new loan of $400 because it is required to hold the other $100 on reserve. What is the legal required reserve ratio?
   a.   10 percent
   b.   15 percent
   c.   20 percent
   d.   25 percent

6. Fiat money is defined as
   a. the money of U.S. citizens deposited at banks and other financial institutions outside the United States.
   b. money spent on Italian sports cars.
   c. money that has little intrinsic value; it is neither backed by nor convertible to a commodity of value.
   d. vault cash plus deposits at the Fed.

7. The most frequently used tool of the Fed to control the money supply in recent years has been
   a. changes in the premiums charged for FDIC deposit insurance.
   b. open market operations.
   c. changes in the discount rate.
   d. changes in reserve requirements.

8. The federal funds rate is the interest rate
   a. banks pay when they borrow money from each other.
   b. the federal government pays on the national debt.
   c. the Fed charges banks when banks need to borrow from the Fed.
   d. the federal government charges foreign banks.

9. The three basic functions of money are
   a. fiat, seigniorage, and debt.
   b. a medium of exchange, a store of value, and a unit of account.
   c. a standard of pay, a coincidence of wants, and a measure of the value of time.
   d. demand deposits, other checkable deposits, and time deposits.

10. If the Federal Reserve wanted to expand the supply of money to head off a recession, it could
    a. decrease the reserve requirements.
    b. lower taxes.
    c. sell U.S. securities in the open market.
    d. increase the discount rate.

11. The larger the reserve requirement, the
    a. larger the potential deposit multiplier.
    b. smaller the potential deposit multiplier.
    c. more profitable the banks will be.
    d. larger the proportion of an additional deposit that is available to the bank for the extension of additional loans.

12. The total expansion in the money supply can be less than is predicted by the deposit expansion multiplier if
    a. banks choose to hold some excess reserves rather than lending all excess reserves.
    b. some individuals prefer to hold cash instead of depositing their money in banks.
    c. instead of a monopoly banking system, there are many banks.
    d. both a and b are correct.

13. If the Fed wanted to use all three of its tools to decrease the money supply, it would
    a. decrease the discount rate, decrease reserve requirements, and buy bonds.
    b. decrease the discount rate, decrease reserve requirements, and sell bonds.
    c. increase the discount rate, increase reserve requirements, and buy bonds.
    d. increase the discount rate, increase reserve requirements, and sell bonds.

14. When economists say that money serves as a unit of account, they mean that money
    a. allows people to avoid barter (trading goods for other goods) by using money.
    b. is always issued in fixed denominations (for example $1, $5, $10, $20 bills).
    c. allows people to value all goods and services in terms of one commodity (money), rather than in terms of several commodities.
    d. makes it easier for people to maintain value across time by letting them save it in the form of money, rather than in the form of physical goods that might depreciate over time.

15. The value (purchasing power) of each unit of money
    a. does not depend on the amount of money in circulation.
    b. tends to increase as the money supply expands.
    c. increases as prices rise.
    d. is inversely related to prices (in other words, money's value falls as prices rise and vice versa).

16. Which of the following is **not** a component of the M1 money supply?
    a. demand deposits
    b. large-denomination (more than $100) bills
    c. interest-earning checking deposits
    d. outstanding balances on credit cards

17. Which of the following compose the M2 money supply?
    a. currency only
    b. currency, demand deposits, other checkable deposits, and traveler's checks
    c. M1 plus large denomination time deposits
    d. M1 plus savings deposits, small-denomination time deposits, and money market mutual funds (retail)

18. The difference between the total reserves that a bank holds and the amount that is required by law are called
    a. excess reserves.
    b. nonborrowed reserves.
    c. borrowed reserves.
    d. actual reserves.

19. A reserve requirement of 20 percent implies a potential money deposit multiplier of
    a. 1.
    b. 5.
    c. 20.
    d. 80.

20. Suppose the Fed sells $100 million of U.S. government securities (bonds) to the public. How will this affect the money supply and the national debt?
    a. The money supply will increase; the national debt will decrease.
    b. The money supply will decrease; the national debt will increase.
    c. The money supply will increase; the national debt will be unaffected.
    d. The money supply will decrease; the national debt will be unaffected.

21. Suppose the U.S. Treasury issues and sells $100 million of U.S. government securities (bonds) to the public. How will this affect the money supply and the national debt?
    a. The money supply will increase; the national debt will decrease.
    b. The money supply will decrease; the national debt will increase.
    c. The money supply will be unaffected; the national debt will increase.
    d. The money supply will be unaffected; the national debt will decrease.

22. Which of the following is **not** part of the M1 money supply?
    a. paper bills (currency)
    b. travelers' checks
    c. savings deposits
    d. coins

23. Saying that the Fed is an "independent" central bank means
    a. members of the Fed are not allowed to register with a political party.
    b. the Fed is insulated from the political pressures of voters and politicians seeking reelection.
    c. the Fed is a private bank that has no links to the government.
    d. the Fed has control over the money supply of foreign nations.

DISCUSSION QUESTIONS

1. Would you be better off if the amount of
   a. food and clothing *you* have suddenly doubles?
   b. food and clothing *everyone* has suddenly doubles?
   c. money *you* have suddenly doubles?
   d. money *everyone* has suddenly doubles?
   Explain the difference in your answers to parts b and d.

2. "Since our currency can no longer be exchanged for gold, it is only a matter of time until people realize that a dollar bill is worthless. Exchanging pieces of paper that are not backed by valuable minerals cannot go on forever." Do you agree or disagree? Explain.

3. Consider the following paradoxes:
   a. Paradox 1: When the Treasury sells government securities to the public, the money supply does not change, but when the Fed sells government securities to the public, the money supply falls.
   b. Paradox 2: When the Treasury buys government securities from the public, the national debt falls, but when the Fed buys government securities from the public, the national debt does not change.
   Since both the Federal Reserve Board and the Treasury Department are part of the government, how can you explain these paradoxes?

4. Consider the following questions about fractional reserve banking.
   a. Why do banks need to hold only a fraction of the demand deposits of their customers on reserve?
   b. If the Fed stopped setting required reserve ratios, would bank reserves drop to zero? Why or why not?
   c. Why don't banks keep all of their customer deposits on reserve?
   d. If fractional reserve banking were outlawed and banks had to keep all customer deposits on reserve, would depositors pay more or less for the banking services they receive? Explain.

5. How free do you think the Federal Reserve is from political pressure? What are the advantages of having an independent central bank? What are the disadvantages? Why do countries with less independent central banks tend to have more inflation? Why would government officials "want" more inflation than the authorities of the central bank "want"?

6. So far we have presented two "multipliers," the deposit expansion multiplier in this chapter and the expenditure multiplier in Chapter 11. What is the difference between the two? Explain.

PERSPECTIVES IN ECONOMICS

HOW THE FEDERAL RESERVE DECIDES HOW MUCH MONEY TO PUT INTO THE ECONOMY

By Edwin L. Dale Jr. Special to The New York Times

[From *The New York Times,* May 6, 1976. Copyright © by The New York Times Co. Reprinted by permission.]

WASHINGTON, May 4—Only one thing is entirely agreed, accepted and understood about the somewhat mysterious and often controversial subject of the Government's monetary policy, which is conducted by the semi-independent Federal Reserve Board.

This is that the Fed, as it is commonly known, can create money out of thin air by writing a check on itself without any deposits to back that check. It can do so in unlimited amounts. And only it can do so—the Treasury cannot.

Yesterday, Arthur F. Burns, chairman of the Federal Reserve Board, disclosed to Congress the Fed's intentions and targets for the creation of money in the year ahead. But he gave his targets in the form of range, not a precise number, and he is the first to admit that he and his colleagues are not at all certain what exactly is the "right" amount of money to create for the good of the nation's economy.

The Government's "printing press" is literally in the Bureau of Engraving and Printing, which turns out currency notes in amounts that depend on the public's demand for them. But the true printing press is a little known man named Alan R. Holmes who sits in an office every day, under instructions and guidelines, from a powerful body of the Federal Reserve known as the Open Market Committee, on how much money to create.

Orders Securities. Mr. Holmes creates money by placing an order in the money market for Treasury bills or other Government securities. He pays for them by writing a check on the Federal Reserve Bank of New York. If the order is for $100 million, an additional $100 million in cash suddenly flows into the economy, possessed originally by the people who sold the Government securities to the Fed.

Mr. Holmes can "extinguish" money, too. If he places a sell order in the market, the Fed sells securities to a money market dealer or bank and gets a check in payment. The amount of money in that check essentially vanishes. The buyer of the securities from the Fed has less cash, but the Fed, in effect, tears up the check.

How much money Mr. Holmes creates makes a good deal of difference to the performance of the economy—the rate of inflation, the expansion of production and jobs, interest rates and indeed general well-being—because the amount of money affects how rapidly the wheels of the economy turn.

But what Mr. Holmes does is cause of controversy because the creation of additional money is also linked by economists to inflation. Friedrich Hayek, the Pulitzer Prize-winning Austrian economist, asserts unequivocally that "inflation is an all monetary phenomenon." Mr.

Hayek has innumerable followers. While other economists think his view is a little oversimplified, nearly all of them agree that "money matters."

What is more, the check that Mr. Holmes writes is only the beginning of the process of creating money. That initial $100 million starts a process by which the nation's money supply—currency plus deposits in banks—will grow not by $100 million but by some multiple of that amount.

It is at this point that things begin to get a little more complicated. In brief, the "multiplier" effect arises from the way the nation's—any advanced nation's—banking system works. It is called a "fractional reserve" system and it works this way:

Suppose that Salomon Brothers receives Mr. Holmes's check on the Federal Reserve Bank of New York and deposits it in Citibank, where deposits are now higher than $100 million.

Under the Fed's "reserve requirement" regulations, which are crucial to the multiplier process, Citibank must deposit about $15 million of this in its "reserve" account at the Fed. But then it can, and does, lend the remaining $85 million to, say, the United States Steel Corporation, which needs money to pay wages while it waits for its inventories of steel to be bought.

U.S. Steel gets the money from Citibank and deposits it at the Pittsburgh National Bank, and the multiplying process goes on. Pittsburgh National puts about $13 million in its reserve account at the Fed and uses the remaining $72 million to buy notes of the city of Boston, which deposits this income in the First National Bank of Boston.

At this point Mr. Holmes's original $100 million has already become $257 million, as follows:
- Salomon Brothers has $100 million more cash (but correspondingly less in Treasury bills).
- U.S. Steel has $85 million more cash (but a debt to Citibank).
- Boston has $72 million more cash (but a debt to Pittsburgh National).

The process continues until, with a 15 percent reserve requirement, Mr. Holmes's original check for $100 million eventually adds more than $600 million to the total of bank deposits in the nation, the nation's money supply. And that money, obviously, can be and is spent. Sometimes more spending is desirable to bring forth production and add to jobs, but by no means always.

The more money there is in circulation, the easier it is for sellers to raise prices, whether to cover higher wages and other costs or to increase profits, because customers around the nation have more to spend. When prices go up all over, this is inflation. But it is impossible to know precisely just how much money is enough or how much is too much at any given time. But there is obviously a point of "too much," as all of history teaches.

For policy makers, there are the two following questions:
- What targets for Mr. Holmes should the Open Market Committee, which consists of seven members of the Federal Reserve Board and the presidents of five of the twelve regional

Federal Reserve banks, establish? The relationship of the money supply to the economy at large, including inflation, is by no means clear, even to the experts.

- Because Mr. Holmes's buying and selling affects short-term interest rates as well as the money supply, which should he concentrate on?

At the bottom, the nation's central bank is controversial, and frequently unpopular, because it is a "naysayer." Whenever inflation rears its head, the job of the Fed is to slow the creation of money and, for a while at least, that often means higher interest rates and sometimes a cutback in production and a loss of jobs.

Switching of Funds. The right policy will always be a matter of judgement. But at the moment the problem of setting the target for Mr. Holmes is complicated by what Mr. Burns calls the "new financial technology," such as those little electronic "tellers" that many banks now make available to their depositors. Among other services, they permit immediate switching of funds from savings to checking accounts by the push of a button and even payment of some bills, such as utilities bills, directly out of savings.

The "money supply" as long defined means currency plus checking accounts (known in the jargon as M1). There were fairly well-established relationships between the growth of M1 and the overall courage of the economy, including the rate of inflation, but now that people, and business, too, have learned to use savings accounts as almost the equivalent of checking accounts, those relationships have gone awry.

"Our equations are all fouled up," a high Federal Reserve official concedes.

The report of the Open Market Committee on its meeting of last January disclosed that the panel, puzzled by a slow growth in money but a rapid growth in the economy, threw up its hands and simply gave Mr. Holmes an unusually wide "target range" for money growth in the period immediately ahead. This meant that he was not to take any special action to create or extinguish money as long as M1 growth stayed within a very wide band.

The Fed also keeps track of and sets targets for M2, which includes savings accounts. But Mr. Holmes cannot tell when he writes one of his checks how much of the ultimate deposits will be in checking or savings accounts. Thus his art will always be imprecise and his results subject to criticism. At present, the Fed does not know whether M1 or M2 is the more important measure, though in the end it controls the growth of both.

The interest rate problem is a different one.

When Mr. Holmes intervenes in the market to buy or sell Government securities, he not only changes the amount of money in the economy but, unavoidably, also affects what are called "money market interest rates" —the rates on very short-term instruments such as Treasury bills.

Rate on Bank Loans. The impact of his intervention decisions shows up first in the most sensitive and closely watched of all rates, called the "Federal funds" rate, which is the interest rate charged on loans from one bank to another. In daily operations some banks wind up short of their required reserve deposits with the Federal Reserve and some have an excess, and this gives rise to overnight loans from one bank to another.

Eventually, a rising prime rate brings along with it higher interest rates to ordinary consumers and other borrowers.

Sometimes, as occurred last week, Mr. Holmes is instructed to intervene in such a way as to "nudge up" the Federal funds rate himself, as a signal that the Federal Reserve feels the money supply is growing too rapidly. In either case, whether he "lets" the rate go up or pushes it up himself, the result is higher interest rates. And these days that often means a quick drop in the stock market, as happened in the last few days.

Every time Mr. Holmes writes a check, he adds to bank reserves and makes the Federal funds interest rates "easier" —that is, lower or less likely to rise.

DISCUSSION

1. Explain how the Federal Reserve System is actually creating money when Alan Holmes places an order in the money market for Treasury bills or other government securities. How will this money supply change affect employment and output?

2. The article refers to "the multiplier." Is this the deposit expansion multiplier that we talked about in this chapter or the multiplier we covered in Chapter 11?

3. Who actually decides to expand the money supply—the Treasury, Alan Holmes, the Open Market Committee, or the Board of Governors of the Federal Reserve Board?

CHAPTER 14

Modern Macroeconomics: Monetary Policy

TRUE OR FALSE

T   F

☐ ☐ 1. The money (nominal) interest rate is the opportunity cost of holding money balances.

☐ ☐ 2. If the demand for money does not shift, an increase in the money supply would lower the interest rate in the short run.

☐ ☐ 3. If other factors remain unchanged, lower real interest rates make more investment projects worthwhile.

☐ ☐ 4. In the long run, a higher rate of growth in the money supply will generally cause a higher rate of inflation and an increase in money (nominal) interest rates.

☐ ☐ 5. Based on the equation of exchange (MV = PY), the quantity theory of money states that an increase in the money supply (M) will cause a proportional increase in output, or real GDP(Y).

☐ ☐ 6. The supply curve of money is vertical because the quantity of money supplied is strongly influenced by changes in the interest rate.

☐ ☐ 7. Anticipated and unanticipated changes in the money supply have the same impact on the economy.

☐ ☐ 8. Monetarists believe that instability in the supply of money is the major cause of fluctuations in real GDP.

☐ ☐ 9. Because the Federal Reserve can make decisions much more quickly than can Congress, monetary policy, unlike fiscal policy, is not subject to timing problems.

☐ ☐ 10. If the velocity of money is constant and an economy's real output tends to grow at 3 percent, a stable 5 percent growth rate for the money supply would be consistent with an inflation rate of 8 percent.

☐ ☐ 11. If the Fed expands the supply of money by buying bonds, this action would be considered restrictive monetary policy.

☐ ☐ 12. If an expansion in the money supply is fully anticipated, it will cause an increase in the price level (inflation) but no change in real GDP even in the short run.

☐ ☐ 13. Unanticipated changes in the money supply can affect real output in the short run, but in the long run the effect is the same as if the policy had been anticipated.

☐ ☐ 14. The effect of monetary policy is the same in the short run regardless of whether it is unanticipated or anticipated, the only difference will be in the long-run impact.

PROBLEMS AND PROJECTS

1. The modern consensus view of monetary policy depends not on whether your views are monetarist or Keynesian but instead on whether the policies are anticipated and on the length of time between the policy and the impact. Attempt to organize each of these views by filling in Exhibit 1, which analyzes the impact of a sudden increase in the money supply caused by open market purchases of bonds by the Fed.

EXHIBIT 1

	SHORT RUN	LONG RUN
Unanticipated increase in money supply	Real interest rates fall Real GDP rises Unemployment falls Price level (inflation) increases	
Anticipated increase in money supply		

2. The equation of exchange (MV = PY) is a useful formula for understanding the relationships between the money supply (M), the velocity of money (V), the price level (P), and real GDP(Y). In addition, because P × Y is equal to nominal GDP, the formula can be written as MV = GDP, where GDP is nominal GDP. Further, sometimes we use the "growth rate version" of this equation which is %ΔM + %ΔV = %ΔP + %ΔY, where %Δ stands for "percent change." This final version relates the growth rate of the money supply [%ΔM] to the growth rate of velocity [%ΔV], the inflation rate [%ΔP], and the growth rate of real output [%ΔY]. To summarize, we have three versions of this equation:

(I)   MV = PY
(II)   MV = GDP
(III) %ΔM + %ΔV = %ΔP + %ΔY

Answer each of the following questions, and indicate which version of the equation you used.
   a. In 2000, nominal GDP in the United States was $9,963 billion and the M2 money supply was $4,945 billion. What was the velocity of the M2 money supply in 2000?
   b. If the money supply is 600, velocity is 5, and the price index is 100, what is real GDP?
   c. If the velocity of money remains constant [so, %ΔV = 0], real output grows at 3 percent, and the money supply grows at 7 percent, what is the inflation rate?
   d. If the velocity of money remains constant, real output grows at 3 percent, and the money supply grows at 1 percent, what is the inflation rate?
   e. If the velocity of money remains constant, real output grows at 3 percent, what rate of growth in the money supply would be consistent with a policy of zero inflation?
   f. Suppose currently, the money supply is 20, the velocity of money is 4, the price level is 8, and real GDP is 10. If the Fed doubles the money supply and both velocity and real output remain unchanged, what will be the new price level?

g. Suppose the money supply is 100, the velocity of money is 3, the price level is 5, and real GDP is 60. An unanticipated increase in the money supply to 200 increases real GDP to 100 in the short run, but then real GDP returns to 60 in the long run. Assuming the velocity of money remains constant, what will happen to prices in the short run? in the long run?

3. Exhibit 2 below illustrates the macroeconomy initially in equilibrium at the real GDP level of Y_1, price level of P_1, and nominal and real interest rates of i_1 and r_1 respectively.

EXHIBIT 2

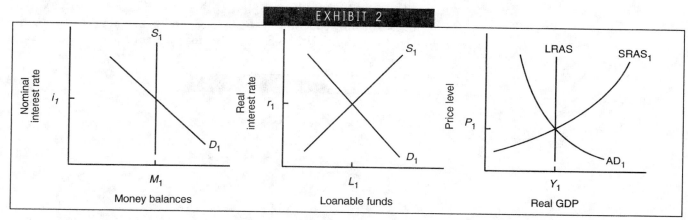

a. Suppose the Fed conducts an open market sale of bonds. Show the short-run impact of this sale in the money balances and loanable funds markets. Briefly explain the changes you make in the diagrams. Assume the policy is unanticipated.

b. Now show the short-run impact of these changes on real GDP and the price level in the AD/AS model at the far right. Again, explain briefly the changes you make in the diagram.

4. Exhibit 3 illustrates the macroeconomy in equilibrium initially at real GDP level Y_f (the full-employment level) and price level P_1. Suppose the Fed increases the money supply.

EXHIBIT 3

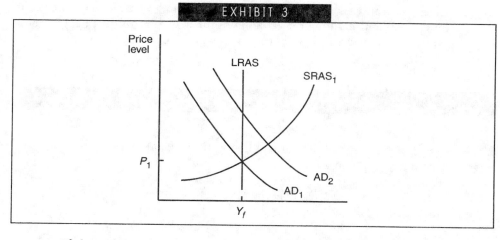

a. If the policy is unanticipated, and the increase in the money supply raises aggregate demand in the second period to AD_2, what will be the short-run impact on real GDP and the price level? Explain briefly.

    b. Will the change in real GDP you described in part a above be sustainable in the long run? Explain, modifying the diagram as necessary to reflect the long-run impact of this policy.

    c. What would have been different in parts a and b above had the Fed announced their policy in advance so that decision makers anticipated the increase in the money supply?

5. In an effort to combat high inflation, suppose the Fed decides to decrease the money supply by selling bonds on the open market.

    a. Using the space provided in Exhibit 4, graph both the short-run and long-run impacts of this reduction in the money supply, assuming the policy is announced in advance by the Fed and is thus fully anticipated by decision makers.

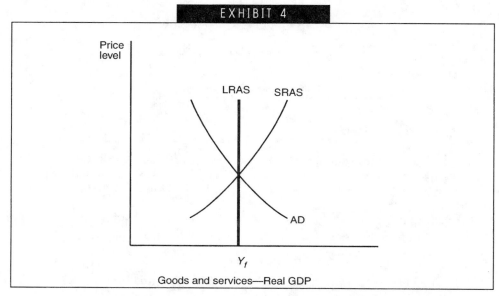

EXHIBIT 4

    b. How would the impact have differed had the Fed decided to keep its actions secret so that the policy was unanticipated?

    c. Given your answers to parts a and b and assuming that reducing inflation (prices) without harming the economy is the main goal of the policy, would you suggest that the Fed announce the policy in advance or attempt to do it secretly?

MULTIPLE CHOICE

1. A decrease in the nominal (or money) interest rate would
    a. encourage people to hold smaller money balances.
    b. encourage people to hold larger money balances.
    c. force the Fed to increase the money supply.
    d. cause the real interest rate to rise.

2. According to monetarists, which of the following would most likely eliminate inflation?
    a. a steady increase in federal expenditures at an annual rate of approximately 3 percent
    b. indexing of wages, taxes, and pensions to the rate of inflation
    c. a steady expansion in the money supply at a rate no greater than the long-run growth of real output
    d. a steady 3 percent increase in the size of the budget deficit

3. Given the strict quantity theory of money, if the quantity of money doubled, prices would
    a. fall by half.
    b. double.
    c. remain constant.
    d. increase somewhat but less than double.

4. The velocity of money is 6, the amount of money in circulation is $200 million, prices are 120, and real GDP is $10 million. According to the strict quantity theory of money, if the money supply increased to $400 million,
    a. velocity of money would fall to 3.
    b. prices would increase to 240.
    c. real GDP would increase to $20 million.
    d. it is unclear what would happen to GDP, prices, and the money velocity.

5. If the amount of money in circulation is $200 million and *nominal* GDP is $400 million, the velocity of money is
    a. 0.5.
    b. 2.
    c. 200.
    d. 400.

6. If the growth rate of real GDP is 3 percent, velocity is constant, and the money supply grows at 9 percent, the rate of inflation will be approximately
    a. 3 percent.
    b. 6 percent.
    c. 9 percent.
    d. 12 percent.

7. When the Fed unexpectedly increases the money supply, it will cause an increase in aggregate demand because
    a. real interest rates will fall, stimulating business investment and consumer purchases.
    b. the dollar will appreciate on the foreign exchange market, leading to a decrease in net exports.
    c. lower interest rates will tend to decrease asset prices (such as the prices of homes), which decreases wealth and thereby decreases current consumption.
    d. all of the above are true.

8. The most likely short-run impact of an unanticipated decrease in the money supply is a(n)
    a. decrease in the real interest rate, which in turn reduces investment and real GDP.
    b. increase in the real interest rate, which in turn reduces investment and real GDP.
    c. increase in real output, which causes the interest rate to rise and in turn reduces investment and real GDP.
    d. decrease in real output, which causes the real interest rate to rise.

9. An unanticipated increase in the money supply will **initially** exert its primary impact on
   a. output and employment rather than on prices.
   b. prices; output and employment will be largely unaffected.
   c. interest rates; rising interest rates will stimulate additional saving.
   d. prices, if the economy operates at an output level below its long-run supply constraint.

10. If decision makers fully anticipate the effects of a shift to a more expansionary monetary policy, the policy will
    a. decrease the real rate of interest.
    b. increase real GDP in the short run.
    c. increase prices (or the inflation rate) and leave real output unchanged.
    d. do all of the above.

11. Which of the following is true?
    a. An unanticipated shift to a more expansionary monetary policy will temporarily stimulate output and employment.
    b. Persistent growth of the money supply at a rapid rate will cause inflation.
    c. Both a and b are true.
    d. None of the above are true.

12. In the short run, an unanticipated increase in the money supply will
    a. increase interest rates and shift the aggregate demand curve to the left.
    b. increase interest rates and shift the aggregate demand curve to the right.
    c. lower interest rates and shift the aggregate demand curve to the left.
    d. lower interest rates and shift the aggregate demand curve to the right.

13. Suppose the economy is experiencing full employment. An unanticipated increase in the money supply will
    a. raise real GDP and the price level in the short run, but in the long run will cause no change in real GDP and only a higher price level.
    b. lower real GDP and the price level in the short run, but in the long run will cause no change in real GDP and only a lower price level.
    c. cause no change in real GDP in either the short run or long run but will increase the price level.
    d. cause the price level to rise in the short run but will increase real GDP in the long run.

14. In the equation of exchange, V stands for
    a. velocity, or the annual rate at which money changes hands in the purchase of final products.
    b. the investment component of aggregate demand.
    c. the amount of money in circulation.
    d. a constant equal to 3.1416, discovered by classical economists.

15. The demand curve for money
    a. would shift if the interest rate changed.
    b. shifts with an increase in the reserve requirement.
    c. shows the relationship between the quantity of money demanded and the interest rate.
    d. is a relationship between the quantity of investment demanded and the interest rate.

16. If velocity was constant, real GDP was growing at 5 percent, and the money supply was allowed to grow at 3 percent, inflation would be
    a. 8 percent.
    b. 2 percent.
    c. −2 percent.
    d. 4 percent.

17. Classical economists, who adhered to the quantity theory of money, believed that an increase in the money supply would cause
    a. a proportional change in velocity.
    b. a proportional change in real GDP.
    c. a proportional change in prices.
    d. no effect on velocity, prices, or real GDP.

18. "Inept government monetary policy is the major source of economic instability. Monetary expansion has been the source of every major inflation. Every major recession was perpetuated by monetary contraction. We would have less instability if we simply required the monetary authorities to stabilize the growth rate of the money supply." This quote is indicative of the views of
    a. the classical economists.
    b. both Keynesians and monetarists.
    c. the monetarists.
    d. the Keynesians.

19. Under conditions of very high inflation but full employment, a new chairperson is appointed to the Federal Reserve. To bring the rate of inflation down, he decides to cut the growth rate of the money supply substantially.
    a. If the policy is announced and is fully anticipated, it will bring the inflation down without affecting real GDP.
    b. If the policy is unanticipated, it will cause the economy to go through a short-run recession.
    c. He has followed the wrong policy; the money supply growth should have been increased to lower the inflation rate.
    d. Both a and b are correct.

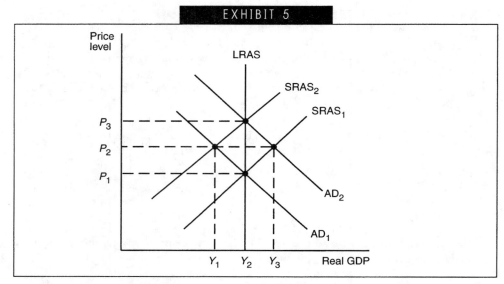

Use Exhibit 5 to answer questions 20 through 24.

20. AD$_1$ and SRAS$_1$ indicate the initial conditions in an economy, with the current level of output, Y_2, being the full employment level, and the current price level is P_1. If the Fed unexpectedly increases the money supply, the short-run impact of this policy will be a movement to
    a. P_1 and Y_2.
    b. P_2 and Y_1.
    c. P_2 and Y_3.
    d. P_3 and Y_2.

21. Continuing with the change in question 20, in the long run, the impact of the unanticipated expansionary policy will be a movement to
    a. P_1 and Y_2.
    b. P_2 and Y_1.
    c. P_2 and Y_3.
    d. P_3 and Y_2.

22. Return to the original initial conditions at AD$_1$ and SRAS$_1$, shown by output of Y_2 and a price level of P_1. Suppose the increase in the money supply had instead been fully anticipated. The short-run impact of this policy will be a movement to
    a. P_1 and Y_2.
    b. P_2 and Y_1.
    c. P_2 and Y_3.
    d. P_3 and Y_2.

23. Continuing with the change in question 22, in the long run, the impact of the anticipated expansionary policy will be a movement to
    a. P_1 and Y_2.
    b. P_2 and Y_1.
    c. P_2 and Y_3.
    d. P_3 and Y_2.

24. Based upon your answers to questions 20 through 23, which of the following is a true statement?
    a. Expansionary monetary policy has the same effect in the long run regardless of whether it is originally anticipated or unanticipated.
    b. Expansionary monetary policy increases real output only when it is unanticipated, and the increase is only in the short run.
    c. The primary long-run impact of expansionary monetary policy is a higher price level (or inflation).
    d. All of the above are true.

DISCUSSION QUESTIONS

1. In the previous chapter, we discussed the emergence of two new forms of money: debit cards and electronic money. How might these new forms of money affect the demand for money? How might they affect velocity? As these new money forms emerge, what impact might they have on the effectiveness of monetary policy?

2. Susan, who always likes to be prepared for the unexpected, keeps $200 in cash in a drawer at her house in case of emergency. If the money, or nominal, interest rate is 10 percent, how much does it cost Susan to hold this money balance each year? How much would it cost her if the interest rate was 50 percent? Do you think she would be likely to hold a smaller money balance if the interest rate was that much higher?

3. "I've read this chapter three times, and I still can't figure out why monetary policy has an effect on output sometimes and not others. It seems to me that monetary policy *either* should or should not have an effect on output. Why doesn't it?" Consider each of the following statements and relate them to the ideas of why the impact of monetary policy differs when it is anticipated versus unanticipated, and why it differs in the short run and the long run.
    a. Bob: "Boy, I just didn't know what to expect on Dr. Smith's first exam, and I really studied wrong for it. I'll adjust my studying techniques from now on."
       Jim: "Well, Bob, I had Dr. Smith last semester and knew what to expect, so I was prepared."
    b. Sarah: "My boyfriend gave me a surprise birthday party yesterday. Had I known, I would have dressed up better last night."
       Betty: "When my boyfriend gave me a surprise birthday party, one of my friends warned me in advance, so I was prepared for it."

4. The monetarists believe that changes in the money supply can, and do, have large effects on real GDP. However, they also are very "nonactivist" in believing that the Fed should not actively try to direct the economy with monetary policy. Explain the reasoning behind this apparent contradiction. Be sure to address the problem of proper timing in your answer.

5. An expansion in the money supply eventually results in an increase in aggregate demand. Discuss the possible means by which the increase in the money supply is transmitted to the economy in this manner.

CHAPTER *15*

Stabilization Policy, Output, and Employment

T F

☐ ☐ 1. At least three kinds of lags seriously undermine the potential of discretionary policy; these lags are the recognition lag, the administrative lag, and the impact lag.

☐ ☐ 2. A major difference between activists and nonactivists is that activists think that the economy is inherently unstable, while nonactivists think that the economy is inherently self-correcting.

☐ ☐ 3. Nonactivists believe that errors in the conduct of active macropolicy have contributed to economic instability in the economy.

☐ ☐ 4. The constant growth rate rule for the money supply is an activist strategy for monetary policy.

☐ ☐ 5. The high accuracy of complex economic forecasting models allows us to predict every recession and expansion of the economy in advance.

☐ ☐ 6. The administrative lag for fiscal policy is much longer than for monetary policy.

☐ ☐ 7. Allowing policy makers the freedom to conduct discretionary macroeconomic policy is disadvantageous because the policy can be used to pursue political objectives as well as stabilization objectives.

☐ ☐ 8. Recent evidence from Japan and the United States suggests that fiscal policy is far less effective than was thought to be the case in the 1960s

☐ ☐ 9. A balanced budget amendment is an activist strategy for fiscal policy.

☐ ☐ 10. Nonactivists favor rules over discretion in the operation of both fiscal and monetary policy.

☐ ☐ 11. Activists as well as nonactivists are aware of the difficulties involved in the proper timing of macropolicy.

☐ ☐ 12. Under rational expectations, the impact of macropolicy change is unpredictable.

☐ ☐ 13. People with rational expectations base their expectations on more information than do people with adaptive expectations.

☐ ☐ 14. People with adaptive expectations base their expectations for the future on whatever has happened in the recent past.

PROBLEMS AND PROJECTS

1. Tammy is a great believer in adaptive expectations. Last year, when the inflation rate was 10 percent, she bought a new car with a loan that carried a nominal interest rate of 13 percent. Unfortunately, at least for her, this year's inflation rate is only 4 percent. For Tammy, calculate the following. [Hint: Remember the real interest rate is the nominal interest rate minus the inflation rate.]
   a. the rate of inflation she expected
   b. the real interest rate she expected to pay
   c. the real interest rate she actually paid this year
   d. Has the fall in the inflation rate made her happy or unhappy (at least with respect to the interest rate she is paying on her car)?

2. Using Exhibit 1 below, indicate the appropriate equilibrium for each of the following situations. Throughout the question, assume that the self-correcting mechanism operates through changes in resource prices (shifts in the short-run aggregate supply curve) only.

EXHIBIT 1

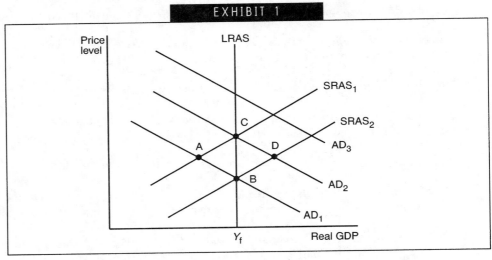

   a. If the economy is in recession at point A, the economy, if left to itself, would eventually adjust to a long-run equilibrium at which point?
   b. If the economy is in recession at point A, what policy recommendations might an activist make?
   c. If the policy recommendations of the activist in part b are adopted quickly and impact the economy long before the self-correcting mechanism starts working, where would the economy end up? [Hint: Assume people have adaptive expectations, so the policy is unanticipated.]
   d. If the policy recommendations of the activist in part b are adopted but do not impact the economy until after the self-correcting mechanism has taken place, where would the economy end up?

3. Assume the economy depicted in Exhibit 2 is in equilibrium at point A (AD_1 and $SRAS_1$).
   a. Would an expansionary monetary policy designed to increase aggregate demand from AD_1 to AD_2 and move the economy to point B be effective *in the long run?*
   b. Is there any way the economy could be moved to point B on a sustainable basis? [Hint: Think about ways of shifting LRAS.]

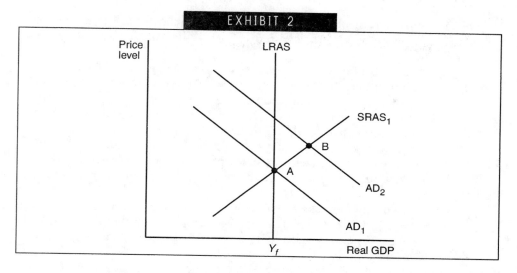

EXHIBIT 2

4. The economy depicted in Exhibit 3 is originally in equilibrium at point A (AD_1 and $SRAS_1$), and expansionary monetary and fiscal policy are conducted that increase aggregate demand from AD_1 to AD_2. For this question, assume no lags in policy (the effects are immediate).

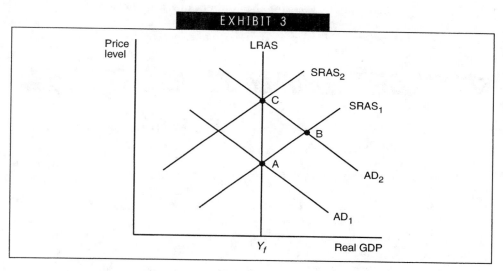

EXHIBIT 3

a. Where would the economy move in the short run if people form their expectations adaptively?

b. Where would the economy move in the long run if people form their expectations adaptively?

c. Where would the economy move in the short run if people form their expectations rationally and had correctly anticipated the policy?

d. Where would the economy move in the long run if people form their expectations rationally and had correctly anticipated the policy?

e. In light of your answers, assess the following statement: "In the long run, the effects of the policy are the same regardless of how expectations are formed, or whether the policy is anticipated or unanticipated. There is only a difference in the short-run effects."

5. For each of the statements below, decide whether the statement is likely the view of a (NA) nonactivist, an (A) activist, or is part of the emerging consensus view shared by (B) both.

_____ a. "The primary focus of monetary policy in the long run should be price stability."

_____ b. "Policy is subject to long and variable time lags. These lags have resulted in a misguided policy that has worked to create more instability in our economy than would normally have been present."

_____ c. "Equipped with forecasts and tools such as the Index of Leading Indicators, policy makers can forecast the economy accurately enough to conduct policy far enough in advance to overcome problems with time lags."

_____ d. "Allowing policy makers to have discretion over monetary and fiscal policy jeopardizes the stability of the economy because the politicians will use these policies to get reelected rather than using them to properly stabilize the economy."

_____ e. "Expansionary policy cannot reduce the rate of unemployment or stimulate the economy in the long run."

_____ f. "The economy's self-correcting mechanism works fairly rapidly and effectively to restore full employment after an economic shock."

_____ g. "The longer time lags involved in fiscal policy make it a more impractical stabilization tool than monetary policy."

_____ h. "We should adopt rules for the conduct of fiscal and monetary policy, such as a balanced budget amendment and a constant growth rate rule, rather than allowing for discretionary macropolicy."

MULTIPLE CHOICE

1. The strategy of using discretionary monetary and fiscal policy to counteract economic fluctuations is called a(n)
    a. nonactivist strategy.
    b. monetarist strategy.
    c. activist strategy.
    d. rational expectations strategy.

2. A typical activist policy during a recession would be to
    a. increase the rate of growth of the money supply.
    b. decrease tax rates.
    c. increase government spending.
    d. do all of the above.

3. A typical nonactivist policy during a recession would be to
    a. increase the rate of growth of the money supply.
    b. decrease tax rates.
    c. increase government spending.
    d. do none of the above.

4. The index of leading indicators is
   a. an alphabetical listing of all the most popular indicators in the economy for a given month.
   b. a composite index of indicators that provides information on the future direction of the economy.
   c. an alphabetical listing of the most important indicators of the current economic well-being of the U.S. economy.
   d. a composite index of the most important indicators of the current economic well-being of the U.S. economy.

5. Which of the following did **not** contribute to the severity of the Great Depression?
   a. a sharp reduction in the money supply during the early 1930s
   b. a large tax increase (to balance the budget) in the early 1930s
   c. substantial increases in the tariff rates on imported goods
   d. All of the above were contributing factors to the severity of the Great Depression.

6. The policy ineffectiveness theorem offers the possibility that policy is ineffective because
   a. of lags.
   b. it is anticipated by decision makers.
   c. macroeconomic conditions really do not have much of an effect on the lives of individual decision makers.
   d. politicians choose policies that are best for their reelection.

7. Which of the following is **not** one of the emerging consensus views about economic policy?
   a. The primary focus of monetary policy in the long run should be price stability.
   b. Wide swings in both monetary and fiscal policy should be avoided.
   c. Discretionary fiscal policy is an effective stabilization tool, particularly in countries like the United States.
   d. Policy is unable to permanently reduce unemployment below the natural rate or to stimulate real GDP beyond the full-employment level in the long run.

8. Analysis of the Great Depression indicates that
   a. even though monetary and fiscal policies were highly expansionary, they were unable to offset the economic plunge.
   b. even though monetary policy was expansionary, restrictive fiscal policy dominated during the 1930s.
   c. a reduction in tax rates could not prevent the economic downturn from spiraling into a depression.
   d. the depth of the economic plunge, if not its onset, was the result of perverse monetary and fiscal policies.

9. Policy A: A decrease in money supply growth and a movement toward a budget surplus during an economic boom; Policy B: Allow the money supply to grow at 3 percent per year
   a. Policy A is an activist policy; Policy B is a nonactivist policy.
   b. Policy A is an nonactivist policy; Policy B is an activist policy.
   c. Both are nonactivist policies.
   d. Both are activist policies.

10. Since there is a lag between when a policy change is instituted and when it exerts its major impact, nonactivists fear that
    a. fiscal policy will become a more effective stabilization tool than monetary policy.
    b. policy changes will often exert their primary impact on aggregate demand at the wrong time.
    c. monetary rule is ineffective as a stabilization tool.
    d. restrictive monetary policy will be unable to control inflation.

11. The interval between the recognition of a need for a policy change and when the policy change is instituted is called the
    a. recognition lag.
    b. impact lag.
    c. policy lag.
    d. administrative lag.

12. If expansionary fiscal policy initially stimulates output growth, according to the shortsightedness effect,
    a. macrostimulus before a major election will generally be unattractive to political entrepreneurs.
    b. macrostimulus will be attractive only if the economy is in a recession.
    c. political entrepreneurs will have a strong incentive to shift to a more expansionary policy before major elections.
    d. political entrepreneurs will generally gain more by fighting inflation at election time, even if the anti-inflation policy causes a recession.

13. Use the table below to choose the correct answer.

TIME PERIOD	ACTUAL INFLATION
1	4 percent
2	4 percent
3	6 percent
4	8 percent

    According to the adaptive expectations hypothesis, at the beginning of period 3, decision makers would expect inflation during period 3 to be
    a. 4 percent.
    b. 5 percent.
    c. 6 percent.
    d. 8 percent.

14. The theory according to which individuals weigh all available evidence when they formulate their expectations about economic events (including information concerning the probable effects of current and future economic policy) is called
    a. the adaptive expectations hypothesis.
    b. the permanent income theory.
    c. the rational expectations hypothesis.
    d. Laffer curve analysis.

15. The rational expectations hypothesis implies that discretionary macropolicy may be
    a. relatively ineffective, even in the short run.
    b. relatively effective in the short run but ineffective in the long run.
    c. effective both in the short run and long run.
    d. effective in the long run since decision makers will continually make systematic, predictable errors.

16. Under *adaptive* expectations, which of the following will likely be an initial effect of an unanticipated shift to a more restrictive macroeconomic policy?
    a. a short-run decrease in output and a long-run decrease in inflation
    b. no change in output even in the short run, only a permanent decrease in inflation
    c. a short-run decrease in inflation and a long-run decrease in output
    d. lower inflation and lower output in the long run

17. Under *rational* expectations, which of the following will likely be an initial effect of an unanticipated shift to a more restrictive macroeconomic policy?
    a. a short-run decrease in output and a long-run decrease in inflation
    b. no change in output even in the short run, only a permanent decrease in inflation
    c. a short-run decrease in inflation and a long-run decrease in output
    d. lower inflation and lower output in the long run

18. Which of the following is true regarding the impact of expectations on the actions of decision makers?
    a. If expectations are formed adaptively, decision makers will adapt to future policies, rendering those policies ineffective.
    b. If expectations are formed rationally, decision makers will anticipate future policies, rendering those policies ineffective.
    c. If expectations are formed rationally, decision makers will rationally ignore future policies since they are known to be ineffective.
    d. If expectations are formed adaptively, decision makers will be able to perfectly predict future policies, making them ineffective.

19. Use statements I and II to answer this question. (I) Discretionary macroeconomic policy can effectively combat business instability by injecting demand stimulus during a recession and demand restraint during an inflationary boom. (II) Given our inability to forecast the future accurately and our limited knowledge as to when a policy change will exert its major impact, discretionary policy is often a source of economic instability.
    a. I represents the views of activists, while II represents the views of nonactivists.
    b. I represents the views of nonactivists, while II represents the views of activists.
    c. Both activists and nonactivists would agree with the two statements.
    d. Neither activists nor nonactivists would agree with the two statements.

20. Which of the following is an argument **against** a monetary rule (growth of the money supply at a constant rate such as 3 percent)?
    a. Since the time lag between when a change in monetary policy is instituted and when the change exerts its major effect is unpredictable, changes in monetary policy are difficult to time properly.
    b. Inability to forecast the future direction of the economy makes it difficult to time monetary policy properly.
    c. A monetary rule would prevent the monetary authorities from taking action to offset abrupt changes in the economy.
    d. A monetary rule would reduce uncertainty in the economy and thus would increase the efficiency of private decision making.

21. According to the adaptive expectations hypothesis,
    a. people will adapt to whatever income they are earning.
    b. the more people save, the less total savings will be available to the economy.
    c. the anticipated rate of inflation is based on the actual rates of inflation experienced during the recent past.
    d. the expected rate of inflation is adapted to macropolicy changes.

22. An individual who had rational expectations would be most likely to
    a. ignore information about all current policies of both the government and the Fed.
    b. always disagree with the expectations of someone who believed in adaptive expectations.
    c. use all pertinent information when formulating views about the future.
    d. never anticipate stable prices because monetary authorities continually expand the supply of money rapidly.

23. If the economy were currently operating at point A in Exhibit 4 and expansionary policy was enacted that would shift AD_1 to AD_2,
    a. if people have adaptive expectations, the economy would move to point B in the short run.
    b. if people have rational expectations, the economy would move to point C in the short run.
    c. in the long run, the economy would move to point C regardless of how expectations are formed.
    d. all of the above are true.

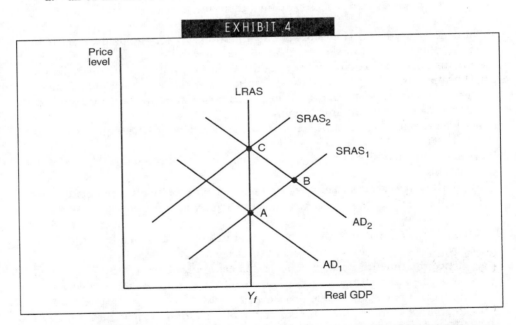

EXHIBIT 4

DISCUSSION QUESTIONS

1. A few years ago, MIT economist Robert Solow gave a public lecture titled, "What Do Economists Know, If Anything?" Following the lecture, a member of the audience asked Professor Solow, "I'm a meteorologist and what I want to know is, how come you guys get paid more than I do?"
    a. Is economic forecasting useful? Why or why not?
    b. If there were no administrative and impact lags, would forecasting be more or less useful? Explain.

c. Is it realistic to expect to *ever* be able to forecast unexpected events? If so, how? If not, how, if at all, can forecasting still be useful?

d. If we made more use of centralized planning instead of markets, would forecasting be easier or harder? more or less useful?

2. It appears that persons marketing economic forecasts have sometimes oversold the ability of economists in this area. Why do you think that competition between forecasters hasn't driven bad forecasters out of the business?

3. There is a distinct psychological side to the argument between activism and non-activism. In particular, which side seems to be almost "fatalistic" in its acceptance of the economic future? Which side wants to intervene and "do something," even if that something can potentially make things worse? Do you think it possible that some economists choose sides on this issue because of their personalities rather than on the basis of economic theory?

4. Suppose you were president of the United States and were faced with the activist/nonactivist debate. How would you go about making up your mind? Would the lack of a clear unified message from the economics profession make you more or less likely to make decisions based on political rather than economic grounds? Does this seem to be happening in the real world?

5. What are some of the methods currently used to shorten the various time lags of macroeconomic policy making? What other methods can you think of that might help? What are the odds that your ideas would be passed by Congress or approved by the Federal bureaucrats?

6. "The Great Contraction (1929–1939) is a tragic testimony to the power of money—not as Keynes and so many of his contemporaries believed, evidence of its unimportance." —Milton Friedman.
a. Do you agree or disagree? Explain why.
b. What other factors contributed to the Great Depression?
c. Do you think the monetarist or Keynesian view of the business cycle better explains the Great Depression? Why?
d. What are some of the safeguards we have today against another Great Depression? Do you think there will ever be another Great Depression? Why or why not?

CURRENT DEBATES IN ECONOMICS

DEBATE NUMBER TWO: SHOULD WE USE ACTIVIST MACROPOLICY?

Yes, We Should Use Activist Macropolicy:
Activist Government: Key to Growth
By Walter H. Heller
[Reprinted from *Challenge*, March/April 1986. Copyright © 1986. Reprinted with permission of M. E. Sharpe, Inc., Armonk, New York 10504. Abridged.]

In a period when government activism, especially in economic affairs, is under attack—indeed, when President Reagan, charming, disarming,

and sometimes alarming, tells the country that the government's impact on the economy is somewhere between baneful and baleful and that the greatest contribution he can make is to get government's clammy hands out of our pockets and government monkeys off our backs—against that background, the Joint Economic Committee's 40th anniversary is an especially appropriate time to take stock of the role government has played and should play in the economy.

Down Memory Lane . . . The early postwar years were really vintage years in our fiscal policy annals. We ran appropriate surpluses (that alone shows I'm dealing in ancient history) in 1947 and 1948. Then, in mid-1950, the Joint Economic Committee, in one of its finest hours, recognized the inflationary potential of the Korean War and led the charge to reverse gears, i.e., to take a tax cut that was halfway through the congressional mill and help convert it to a tax increase. As has been true so often, it was providing the intellectual leadership in Congress on economic policy. . . .

But the 1953–1960 period, with three recessions in seven years, was hardly activist policy at its best, especially during the 1950–1960 period of overly tight fiscal-monetary policy.

The Good Times. Then came the Golden Sixties, truly watershed years with a revitalizing of the Employment Act of 1946. President Kennedy asked us to return to the letter and spirit of that Act. He ended equivocation about the intent of the Act by translating its rather mushy mandate into a concrete call for meeting the goals of full employment, price stability, faster growth, and external balance—all within the constraints of preserving economic freedom and choice and promoting greater equality of opportunity. He went on to foster a rather weak-kneed antirecession program in 1961 and a powerful growth-promoting tax-cut program in 1962–1964. In that process, I counted six firsts for presidential economics:

- He was the first president to commit himself to numerical targets for full employment, namely 4 percent unemployment, and growth, namely 4.5 percent per year.
- He was the first to adopt an incomes policy in the form of wage-price guideposts developed by his Council of Economic Advisers. The guideposts, flanked by sensible supply-side tax measures to stimulate business investment, by training and retraining programs, and the like, helped maintain a remarkable record of price stability 1961–1965, namely, only 1.2 inflation per year.
- He was the first president to shift economic policy focus from moderating the swings of the business cycle to achieving the rising full-employment potential of the economy.
- In that process, he moved from the goal of a balanced budget over the business cycle to a balanced budget at full employment.
- He was the first president to say, as he did in January 1963, that budget deficits could be a positive force to help move a slack or recession-ridden economy toward full employment.
- As a capstone, he was the first president to say that a tax cut was needed, not to cope with recession (there was none), but to make full use of the economy's full-employment potential.
    . . .

Those were the halcyon days of economic policy. Aided and abetted by the Fed, the 1964 tax cut worked like a charm. In mid-1965, just before the July escalation in Vietnam, we saw the happy combination of an inflation rate of only 1.5 percent; unemployment coming down steadily, to 4.4 percent; defense expenditures continuing their four-year decline from 9 percent of GNP in 1960 to 7 percent of GNP in 1965; and the cash budget running $3 billion in the black.

The Downturn Begins. Then came the dark years of Vietnam, in economics as well as foreign policy. Unlike 1950–1951, we did not reverse gears in spite of the timely warnings of the Joint Economic Committee and of most of the economists, both inside and outside the government, who were advising President Johnson. . . . He did not propose a tax increase until early 1967, and no tax action was completed until 1968, long after the inflation horse was out of the barn. . . .

As I put it in testimony before the JEC in July 1970, "There are no magic formulas, no pat solutions, no easy ways to reconcile full employment and price stability. No modern, free economy has yet found the combination of policies that can deliver sustained high employment and high growth side by side with sustained price stability." That was all well and good, as far as it went, but in light of the experience of the 1970s, it did not go nearly far enough.

The policy travails of the seventies are too well known to require lengthy review:

- First, there was the Nixon fiasco of freezes and phases serving as a facade for pumping up the economy with tax cuts, spending increases, and a rapid run-up in the money supply, with surefire consequences of an over-heated economy.
- Superimposed on that were the supply shocks in 1973–1974—oil prices quadrupling, food prices jumping 40 percent in two years, other world raw-material prices doubling in about the same time—that served to consolidate stagflation.

The shocks, of course, were not just to the price level, but the economics profession, led by Keynesians. We learned the sad lesson that as to wages and prices, what goes up, propelled by overstimulative monetary-fiscal policy and a series of external shocks, does not necessarily come down when the fiscal-monetary stimulus and supply shocks subside. We have since learned a lot about sticky wages and prices that stay in high orbit even without visible means of fiscal-monetary support. At least they stayed there until we administered a dose of sadomasochism, better known as the double-dip recession of the eighties, the deepest since the Great Depression.

One should not recite the economic sins of the seventies without acknowledging one bright fiscal episode, namely, the tax rebate and tax cut enacted in the second quarter of 1975. Granted, it was a bit late to blunt the recession, but it provided a welcome boost to an economy that had fallen into what, until topped by the recession of the early eighties, was the deepest postwar recession. The 1975 tax cut was a winner in both size and timing.

As one surveys the whole postwar period, activist economics and New Deal intrusions into the marketplace can surely take credit not only for building in strong defenses against depression but also for 25 years (1948–1973) of high-octane operation of the economy and sharply reduced instability. Within the framework, one can criticize antirecession fiscal policy as often too little and too late, monetary policy as sometimes too easy and other times overstaying tightness. The far-too-late and considerably-too-little tax increase to finance the war in Vietnam, coupled with excessive monetary ease in 1967–1968, has to go down in the annals as one of the flat failures of postwar fiscal-monetary policy. And the stagflation experience of the 1970s still hangs like a pall over expansionary policy today.

Still, it is worth reminding ourselves that even in the face of high performance of the economy, inflation in the 1949–1972 rose above 6 percent only once (during the Korean War), and averaged only 2.3 percent. If inflation was the price of activism in public economics, it was a long time in coming.

No, We Should Not Use Activist Macropolicy: Economic Policy: The Old Tools Won't Work

By Marc Levinson

[Reprinted with permission from *Business Monthly*, January 1987. Copyright © 1987 by Goldhirsch Group, Inc. Abridged.]

Since the advent of the New Deal more than half a century ago, the federal government has actively helped shape the course of the economy. Its ability, at least in the short run, to pump up the economy in hard times and slow it down when inflation began to boil up has been unquestioned. As recently as 1981, when a sharp cutback in money supply growth pushed the country into recession, or 1983, when the

stimulative effects of a tax cut brought the economy back to health, the old elixirs worked as they had in the past.

But in 1986, things were different. Heady growth in the money supply, repeated cuts in the Federal Reserve Board's discount rate and record federal budget deficits all failed to juice the lackluster economy. The old linkages between the government's actions and the economy's responses have changed in ways economists do not fully understand. As a result, the government's economic tools have been partially blunted. Contends Lawrence Chimerine, chairman of Chase Econometrics, "The ability of policy changes to improve the economy is much smaller than ever."

The reason: the growing internationalization of the U.S. economy. Flexible exchange rates and the resulting mushrooming of international capital markets have made traditional economic policies act in unexpected ways. "No one has a reliable theory of exchange rates," says Paul Krugman, a professor of international economics at the Massachusetts Institute of Technology. "That makes it very difficult to be sure of the effects of macroeconomic policy."

These international connections make it increasingly difficult to aim economic weapons at purely domestic targets. Even thinking of "domestic" in terms of economic problems is misleading. "The problem is global overcapacity and global underconsumption," contends Steve Quick, an economist with the Joint Economic Committee of Congress. "But we have no tools. We have no global fiscal policy. We have no global monetary policy." Adds Harold Rose, chief economist of Britain's Barclays Bank: "It's very hard to see how we can get out of these problems by macroeconomic policy alone."

Certainly, the assumption that the government can "fine tune" the economy has been in disrepute since the early 1970s, when policy makers were helpless as they faced high unemployment and high inflation at the same time. But faith in the government's ability to deal with one of these problems at a time has remained strong. Now, however, the government's very ability to achieve some domestic goals—3 percent growth in output, 4 percent unemployment—appears increasingly limited. The jury is still out on whether these limitations are a temporary phenomenon or a permanent fact of life.

Take monetary policy, the Federal Reserve Board's method of influencing the economy's performance by manipulating the money supply. Financial deregulation, of course, has blurred the meaning of the money supply figures. But international capital flows have also made it much more difficult for the central bank to plot the nation's monetary course.

Suppose, for example, that the Fed wants to boost the economy's growth rate. When international capital flows were small, the central bank could stimulate borrowing by pumping up the money supply or cutting the discount rate. But now, lower interest rates will spur investors to move their capital out of dollar-denominated investments. Economists can't even begin to estimate the likely extent of those capital flows. If little capital moves abroad, the lower interest rates will powerfully stimulate the U.S. economy. If, on the other hand, lower rates trigger a massive flight from the dollar, higher import prices will inject a strong dose of inflation into the economy, which would discourage the very business spending the Fed wanted to stimulate. Would faster money growth cut the U.S. trade deficit? Nobody knows.

The direction of the overall change remains undisputed: Increasing the rate of money supply growth will stimulate the economy, and reducing it will retard growth. But the magnitude of the change is now almost unpredictable. There is no doubt that a $108 billion budget slash will cut domestic demand. It will also lower deficits and reduce the government's borrowing from abroad, driving down the dollar. But whether a more favorable exchange rate for exports will boost the economy more than lower government spending retards it is an open question. "We don't know the responsiveness of the economy to a changed deficit," contends economist Mickey D. Levy of Philadelphia's Fidelity Bank. "We don't know the lags." Concurs Rudolph Penner, director of the Congressional Budget Office, "If we had been analyzing that big a change twenty years ago, there wouldn't have been much debate that it would cause a recession." The venerable Keynesian multiplier, which links changes in government spending to predictably larger changes in economic output, can, for all practical purposes, be tossed out the window. Using fiscal policy to reach some desired target in terms of, say, unemployment or Gross National Product is thus far more difficult than in the past.

The use of both fiscal and monetary policy has become even more treacherous as government officials have come to realize that they are not operating in an isolated economy. Indeed, the reactions of other governments can blunt or reverse Washington's initiatives, making economic policy a strategic game, according to a brand new line of economic research. The United States must figure out how other countries will respond to its moves, and determine the degree to which those responses will counteract the effects that American policy makers seek to achieve. "We can't make policy without taking into account what our competitor overseas is doing," contends University of Illinois economist Stephen J. Turnovsky.

One way to deal with diminishing effectiveness of monetary and fiscal policies, says the Joint Economic Committee's Quick, is to examine the economic impact of policies long considered unrelated, such as foreign aid or regulation of international lending. Increasing the industrial nations' contributions to the International Monetary Fund, for example, could help stimulate growth in the developing countries, which in turn would step up their purchases of U.S. exports. This viewpoint is catching on in Washington, where Congress has finally come to understand that the debts of developing countries are a major drag on U.S. growth.

Holding a Debate

Many students will enjoy participating in a debate on this topic either in class or in an informal study group. After completing both readings and possibly doing some additional research, get three to four volunteers for each side of the debate, choose a moderator if your instructor is not available, and devote about half an hour to opening statements, rebuttals, and summaries.

Discussion

1. If you read both articles, it is time to make a judgment. Do the difficulties of accurate policy making make it better to do nothing? Are there times when even Levinson would agree to an activist policy? Explain your answers.

2. If you read the Heller article, it is important to note that Professor Heller was the chairman of the Council of Economic Advisers under Presidents Kennedy and

Johnson and played a major role in shaping the fairly activist macropolicy of that era. Do you think his participation in the policy making made him a better or worse judge of the effectiveness of activist policy? Why?

3. If you read the Levinson article, into what economic "camp" would you group him? Reread the article for evidence that he is a monetarist or a supply-sider or a new classical. Why is it unlikely that he is Keynesian?

CHAPTER 16

Economic Growth

TRUE OR FALSE

T F

☐ ☐ 1. Growth in a country's output is necessary for growth in a country's income.

☐ ☐ 2. When output grows at a faster rate than population, per capita GDP will fall.

☐ ☐ 3. Higher levels of per capita GDP are generally associated with better living standards and improvements in life expectancy, literacy, and health.

☐ ☐ 4. A less-developed country (LDC) is a low-income country generally characterized by rapid population growth and a large agriculture-household sector.

☐ ☐ 5. Because it is so small, an economic reform that increases growth by only one percent will have no long-term impact on an economy.

☐ ☐ 6. Less-developed countries (LDCs) have not been able to achieve long-term growth rates comparable to the major industrialized nations.

☐ ☐ 7. The key sources of economic growth are investment in human and physical capital, technological advances, and institutions and policies consistent with efficient economic organization.

☐ ☐ 8. A country that protects and enforces the private property rights of its citizens, follows policies of free international trade, and maintains low marginal income tax rates will generally grow faster than a country that does not.

☐ ☐ 9. A country that regulates its capital markets and has very unstable monetary policy (and thus high price instability) will generally grow faster than a country that does not.

☐ ☐ 10. When the size of a country's government grows to a large share of GDP, it will result in slower economic growth.

☐ ☐ 11. Most industrial countries, such as the United States, could achieve higher rates of economic growth by reducing the size of their governments.

☐ ☐ 12. In Ireland, reductions in the size of government, a more stable monetary policy, reductions in marginal tax rates, and lower tariffs have substantially increased the rate of economic growth.

☐ ☐ 13. Economic growth can be depicted as an outward shift (increase) in a country's production possibilities curve or in the aggregate demand/aggregate supply model by an increase in LRAS (shift to the right).

T F

☐ ☐ 14. If an economy sustains a 3.5 percent rate of growth, the size of the economy will double approximately every twenty years.

PROBLEMS AND PROJECTS

1. For each of the following pairs of countries, decide which would tend to have the higher rate of economic growth.

    ___ a. Country A has a large government accounting for 50 percent of GDP, while Country B has a smaller government accounting for 25 percent of GDP.

    ___ b. Country C has pursued stable monetary policy that has led to a fairly stable inflation rate of 3 percent, while Country D's inflation rate has averaged 15 percent but has been extremely variable from year to year.

    ___ c. Country E devotes most of its resources to producing current consumption goods, while Country F devotes more resources toward investment in physical capital.

    ___ d. Country G's government devotes most of its resources toward transfer programs, while Country H's government devotes most of its resources toward the enforcement of laws, the construction of infrastructure, and education.

    ___ e. Because of differences in tax laws, the businesses in Country I devote substantially fewer resources toward research and development than the businesses in Country J.

2. Exhibit 1 is a compound growth table in which each entry shows the amount to which $1 will accumulate at various rates of growth after *n* years. For example, if $30 were to grow at 2 percent for twenty-five years, it would grow to a value of $49.23 (30 × 1.641). Use the data in the table to compute the answers to the following questions regarding economic growth.

    a. The Smiths are a typical U.S. family with two children and in 2000 had income of $50,000. If the real rate of growth in the United States remains around its recent average of 3 percent, what level of family income can their children expect to have in twenty-five years (assume they will also earn the new median income with their families)? How about the Smith's grandchildren who will have families in about fifty years?

    b. Cross-country evidence suggests that if the size of government were to be reduced by 10 percent of GDP, economic growth would increase by 1 percent. If this were to happen today and as a result growth increased to 4 percent, on average how much more will their children have in family income relative to if the growth rate had been 3 percent? their grandchildren?

    c. Suppose bad economic policies in the United States result in the growth rate falling to 2 percent over the next fifty years. On average, how much less will their children have in family income relative to if the growth rate had been 3 percent like in part a? their grandchildren?

    d. Generally, the laws, rules, and form of economic organization set forth in a country's constitution remain for many years. Suppose two identical countries both gained their independence exactly one hundred years ago, but because of a better structured constitution, Country 1 has been able to sustain a growth rate of 4 percent while Country 2 has only been able to sustain a growth rate of 1 percent. Assume both countries began with levels of GDP equal to $300. By how much would Country 1's level of GDP exceed Country 2's today after one hundred years of growing at these different rates?

    e. The growth rate of per capital real GDP in most major industrialized countries has recently been around 2 percent. Several lesser-developed countries

EXHIBIT 1

COMPOUND GROWTH TABLE

YEARS	1 PERCENT	2 PERCENT	3 PERCENT	4 PERCENT	5 PERCENT	6 PERCENT	7 PERCENT
			RATE OF GROWTH				
5	1.051	1.104	1.159	1.217	1.276	1.338	1.403
10	1.105	1.219	1.344	1.480	1.629	1.791	1.967
15	1.161	1.346	1.558	1.801	2.079	2.397	2.759
20	1.220	1.486	1.806	2.191	2.653	3.207	3.870
25	1.282	1.641	2.094	2.666	3.386	4.292	5.427
30	1.348	1.811	2.427	3.243	4.322	5.743	7.612
40	1.489	2.208	3.262	4.801	7.040	10.286	14.974
50	1.645	2.692	4.384	7.107	11.467	18.420	29.457
75	2.109	4.416	9.179	18.945	38.833	79.057	159.876
100	2.705	7.245	19.219	50.505	131.501	339.302	867.716

have adopted sound economic policies and are experiencing rates of growth of 5 percent or more. Assume that the real per capita GDP is currently $20,000 in the major industrialized countries and $10,000 in the LDCs. How many years will it take for these LDCs to attain levels of income comparable to the major industrialized countries? [Hint: For both sets of countries, find income in ten years, twenty years, thirty years, etc., at their respective growth rates and compare your answers.]

MULTIPLE CHOICE

1. Which of the following is true?
   a. Countries with high marginal tax rates have generally had similar rates of economic growth as those with lower tax rates.
   b. Countries with high marginal tax rates have generally had higher rates of economic growth than those with lower tax rates.
   c. Countries with low marginal tax rates have generally had higher rates of economic growth than those with high tax rates.
   d. For LDCs, lower marginal tax rates increase growth, but for developed countries high marginal tax rates increase growth.

2. If population is rising more rapidly than real GDP,
   a. per capita real GDP will be decreasing.
   b. per capita real GDP will be increasing.
   c. per capita real GDP will stay constant.
   d. none of the above would occur.

3. Which of the following will be required for a country to move up the income ladder and achieve high-income status?
   a. rapid growth of the money supply to increase inflation and prices
   b. restrictions limiting the import of goods from other nations
   c. high tax rates to support a government sector that is at least 35 percent of GDP
   d. a high rate of sustained economic growth

4. Which of the following will most likely contribute to the growth of a less-developed country?
    a. secure property rights and low marginal tax rates
    b. price controls that keep the cost of agricultural products low
    c. rapid monetary growth
    d. exchange rate controls and export restrictions

5. An open capital market affects a nation's economic growth by
    a. channeling capital into productive projects and away from wasteful projects.
    b. rewarding investors who find the most productive projects and invest in them.
    c. making the lowest-cost capital available from around the world.
    d. all of the above.

6. Compared to *no* government, a small government can enhance economic growth by
    a. helping to secure and enforce property rights.
    b. providing a monetary environment that includes stable prices.
    c. requiring only low tax rates to support its activities.
    d. all of the above.

7. Which of the following correctly expresses the relationship between the size of government and economic growth?
    a. Because it is the private sector in which growth occurs, the size of government is generally unrelated to the rate of economic growth.
    b. When government is small, an increase in its size may increase economic growth, but beyond some point, further increases in the size of government will reduce economic growth.
    c. When government is small, an increase in its size may initially lower economic growth, but when it becomes large enough, expansions in government generally increase the rate of economic growth.
    d. The rate of economic growth appears to be increasing with the size of government for the levels of government that we observe in most major industrialized countries.

8. Countries with less economic freedom, as described in the text, have levels of economic growth that
    a. are higher than nations with more economic freedom.
    b. are similar to those of nations with more economic freedom.
    c. cannot continue at high levels because too little government planning is being done.
    d. are lower than nations with more economic freedom.

9. Which of the following has contributed to Ireland's significantly higher rate of economic growth in the last half of the 1990s?
    a. a substantial reduction in government size as a share of GDP
    b. a more stable monetary policy and lower tariffs on international trade
    c. lower marginal income tax rates
    d. All of the above are correct.

10. Which of the following is **not** one of the major sources of economic growth?
    a. a large government sector
    b. investment in physical and human capital
    c. advancements in technology
    d. institutions and policies that improve economic efficiency

11. How do high tariffs and other restraints on international trade affect the prosperity of a nation?
    a. They increase employment and thereby promote the growth of real GDP.
    b. They prevent the nation from fully realizing the potential gains from specialization, exchange, and competition, thereby reducing economic growth.
    c. They encourage rent-seeking and lobbying by producers and thus promote economic growth.
    d. Both a and c are correct.

12. If the political leaders of a country wanted to promote economic growth, which of the following policy alternatives would be most effective?
    a. price controls on agricultural products in order to keep the price of food low
    b. expansionary monetary policies designed to increase the rate of inflation
    c. increasing marginal tax rates in order to increase the size of government to a large share of GDP
    d. elimination of price controls and trade restraints and establishment of a monetary policy consistent with long-run price stability (a low rate of inflation)

13. Which of the following is **not** a government policy that can enhance economic growth?
    a. having free international trade
    b. keeping marginal tax rates low
    c. adopting regulations fixing interest rates at low levels
    d. protecting and enforcing private property rights and contracts

14. A 3.5 percent growth rate in GDP will bring about a doubling of GDP in about how many years?
    a. 3.5
    b. 20
    c. 35
    d. 70

15. Which of the following best characterizes the relationship between the developed nations and the less-developed nations?
    a. The developed nations are growing, and the less-developed nations are stagnating.
    b. The less-developed nations are growing, but the developed nations are growing even faster.
    c. Population is growing faster in developed nations.
    d. Some developing countries are growing faster than developed nations, while others are stagnating.

16. A country with _____ marginal tax rates and a relatively _____ government sector as a share of GDP is likely to have faster economic growth. (Fill in the blanks.)
    a. low; small
    b. low; large
    c. high; large
    d. high; small

17. A "stable monetary environment" is used to describe monetary policy consistent with
    a. keeping the money income of citizens constant while population grows.
    b. keeping the rate of inflation low.
    c. minimizing the year-to-year fluctuations in the inflation rate.
    d. both b and c.

DISCUSSION QUESTIONS

1. What are the major sources of economic growth? Give examples of government policy changes that could increase the rate of economic growth in a country.

2. How does the size of a country's government influence its growth rate? Does it matter whether the government sector is small or large? Does the evidence indicate that reducing the size of government would increase or reduce economic growth in the United States?

3. Why is the structure of a country's capital market a factor in economic growth? Which is important to growth, a higher level of physical capital, human capital, or both?

4. How do you think the less-developed countries can best help themselves attain more rapid growth rates? How do you think the developed countries can best help them?

5. The book discusses the concept of "economic freedom." How would you define economic freedom? Give some examples of government policies that promote economic freedom. Which current policies do you believe are the most restricting on economic freedom?

CHAPTER 17

Gaining from International Trade

TRUE OR FALSE

T   F

☐ ☐ 1. Economic theory suggests that free trade between two countries generally benefits only one country, the other is harmed.

☐ ☐ 2. Economic analysis shows that *every* individual within an economy gains from international free trade whenever it takes place.

☐ ☐ 3. The joint output of countries would be maximized if each country specialized in production of those commodities for which it is the low opportunity-cost producer, exchanging them for other commodities for which it is a high opportunity-cost producer.

☐ ☐ 4. In a sense, tariffs and quotas are identical in that they can be designed to produce the same exact outcome in terms of price and quantity of imports.

☐ ☐ 5. A secondary effect of policies that restrict imports is that they lower the demand for the nation's export products.

☐ ☐ 6. An import quota places a maximum limit on the amount of a product that can be imported during a specific time period.

☐ ☐ 7. A country that is rich in resources and an efficient producer will gain if it refuses to trade, although this action hurts the rest of the world.

☐ ☐ 8. Three popular arguments for imposing trade restrictions are to protect infant industries, to prevent dumping of goods below cost, and to keep in place certain industries essential for a country's national defense.

☐ ☐ 9. If all tariffs were removed in the United States, fewer jobs would be available to U.S. workers since wage rates are high in the United States.

☐ ☐ 10. The North American Free Trade Agreement (NAFTA) has caused widespread job losses in the United States and a large movement of U.S. companies to Mexico.

☐ ☐ 11. Canada, Japan, and Mexico are the major trading partners of the United States.

☐ ☐ 12. U.S. tariffs, in general, are much lower now than they were in 1930.

☐ ☐ 13. Because trade restrictions generate concentrated benefits to special interest groups at the expense of the general public, politicians find them attractive to implement.

PROBLEMS AND PROJECTS

1. Use Exhibit 1 when answering the following questions.
    a. In the space provided, plot the production possibilities curves for Lebos and Egap from the data given. Label the points in the graph with the corresponding letters and connect the points.
    b. Lebos is currently producing at point C (80 units of food and 80 units of clothing) but wishes to expand its production of food to 120 units. What point would Lebos move to? How many units of food has Lebos gained? How many units of clothing has Lebos had to give up to free the extra resources to produce this additional food? Write your answers in equation form such as $xx\,F = xx\,C$ where $xx\,F$ represents the number of units of food gained and $xx\,C$ represents the number of units of clothing given up in your answers above.
    c. Pick any two points (such as points A and B) for Egap. Between these two points, how many units of food are gained? How many units of clothing are given up? Write this in equation form similar to what you did in part b.
    d. Take the equations you found above for each country and simplify them in terms of *one* unit of food. [Hint: As an example, for Lebos divide both sides by 40 to get $1F = 1C$.] These equations now represent the opportunity cost

EXHIBIT 1

Production Possibilities for Lebos and Egap

	LEBOS FOOD	CLOTHING		EGAP FOOD	CLOTHING
A	0	160	A	0	120
B	40	120	B	10	90
C	80	80	C	20	60
D	120	40	D	30	30
E	160	0	E	40	0

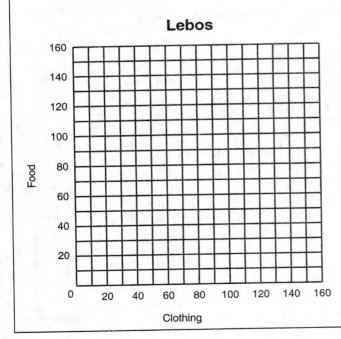

Lebos

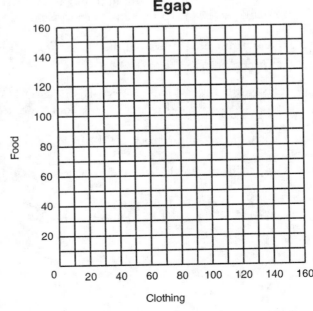

Egap

of producing one unit of food in each country in terms of how much clothing must be given up. From these new equations, which country has to give up the *least* amount of clothing to produce one unit of food? Note that this country has the comparative advantage in food (because it has the lowest opportunity cost of producing food). Now, rewrite and simplify each equation in terms of one unit of *clothing*. Using this, which country has the comparative advantage in clothing?

e. For survival, Lebos needs to have 120 units of food and Egap needs 40. If these countries do not trade, how much clothing will the people of Lebos be able to produce and consume given the resources remaining after the required food is produced? Egap? Circle these points in the diagrams.

f. Suppose that Lebos and Egap agree to trade with each other at the rate of 1 unit of food for 2 units of clothing (1F = 2C). Lebos will specialize in producing all food and Egap all clothing. If Lebos produces only food, how much food can it produce? How many units of food will Lebos have left to trade after keeping 120 units for itself? Given the rate of exchange above, how many units of clothing will they acquire in trade from Egap for these extra units of food?

g. Carefully compare the amount of food and clothing Lebos has after specializing and trading with the amount it had when it was self sufficient in part e. Is Lebos better off?

h. After Egap specializes in clothing and trades with Lebos, how much food will it have acquired in trade? How much clothing will it have left after trading for this food? Compare the amount of food and clothing Egap has after trade with the amount it had when it was self sufficient in part e. Is Egap better off?

2. The country of Arcadia produces and consumes unique computers. Exhibit 2 shows Arcadia's demand and supply curves for their computers along with the demand for Arcadian computers from the rest of the world (ROW). The final column in the table is the total demand for Arcadia's computers from both domestic citizens and foreigners combined.

a. In the space provided, graph Arcadia's domestic supply and Arcadia's domestic demand for computers in the absence of trade. What is the equilibrium price and quantity with no international trade?

b. With trade there will be additional demand for Arcadian computers. Fill in the missing values for the total demand column in the table. Now, graph the *total* demand with foreign trade in the diagram. What is the equilibrium price and quantity with trade?

c. What has happened to the price of Arcadian computers when they begin to trade? the quantity produced? What happened to Arcadia's productions of *other* goods and services as a result of international trade?

EXHIBIT 2

PRICE	ARCADIA'S QUANTITY SUPPLIED	ARCADIA'S QUANTITY DEMANDED	ROW'S QUANTITY DEMANDED	TOTAL QUANTITY DEMANDED
$3,000	14,000	5,000	1,000	6,000
$2,500	12,000	6,000	2,000	_____
$2,000	10,000	7,000	3,000	_____
$1,500	8,000	8,000	4,000	_____
$1,000	6,000	9,000	5,000	_____
$500	4,000	10,000	6,000	_____

d. With trade (and the new higher price), what is the new quantity of computers demanded only by the citizens of Arcadia? [Hint: not the total, just the amount demanded by Arcadia.] Compare the quantity of computers demanded in Arcadia without trade. What quantity of computers is exported by Arcadia?

e. Given your answers above, what can you say about how exporting a product affects a country's citizens? Does it benefit domestic producers?

3. Exhibit 3 depicts the domestic supply and demand for a product that the United States can import from the rest of the world at a fixed price of $500 per unit.

a. In the absence of international trade, what would be the price of this product in the United States? What quantities would be demanded and supplied?

b. Suppose this product can be imported into the United States without restriction at a price of $500. Draw a world supply curve in the diagram [Hint: It is a horizontal line at the world price.] Show in the diagram the new price, quantity demanded, the total quantity supplied, the quantity domestically supplied, and the quantity imported with trade.

c. If a 20 percent tariff is imposed on the importation of the product, the price of the imported products will rise to $600. Show this new world supply with tariff in the diagram as a horizontal line at the new price with the tariff included. How will the price, amount demanded, the amount domestically produced, and the amount imported change as a result of the tariff?

d. Suppose that *instead* of the tariff of part c, government imposed a quota on imports of twenty units per year. How would the effects of this quota differ from the effects of the tariff on the price, quantity demanded, amount domestically supplied, and amount imported?

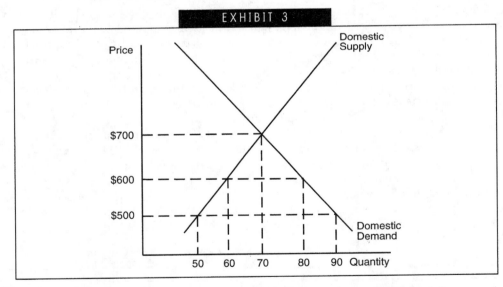

EXHIBIT 3

4. Consider the following hypothetical information about the United States and South Korea shown in Exhibit 4.

a. Which country has the
absolute advantage in steel production? _____
absolute advantage in wheat production? _____
comparative advantage in steel production? _____
comparative advantage in wheat production? _____

b. If these countries trade steel and wheat with each other, which country will export steel and import wheat?
c. Suppose that the United States and South Korea agree to a daily trade of ten tons of steel for fifty bushels of wheat. One worker in the United States then switches from steel production to wheat production. At the same time, four workers in South Korea switch from wheat production to steel. Complete the following table to show that both countries end up with more steel and more wheat than they had initially.

EXHIBIT 4		
OUTPUT PER WORKER PER DAY		
	UNITED STATES	SOUTH KOREA
Tons of steel	8	4
Bushels of wheat	80	8

UNITED STATES	TONS OF STEEL	BUSHELS OF WHEAT
Change in production	−8	+80
Trade	+10	−50
Change in consumption	_____	_____

SOUTH KOREA	TONS OF STEEL	BUSHELS OF WHEAT
Change in production	_____	_____
Trade	_____	_____
Change in consumption	_____	_____

MULTIPLE CHOICE

1. A tariff or quota that limits the entry of foreign goods to the U.S. market will
    a. benefit domestic producers in the protected industries and harm domestic consumers.
    b. increase the nation's real income by protecting domestic jobs from foreign competition.
    c. reduce the demand for U.S. export goods, lowering employment in export industries.
    d. do both a and c.

2. According to the law of comparative advantage, a nation will benefit from international trade when it
    a. imports more than it exports.
    b. exports more than it imports.
    c. imports goods for which it is a high opportunity-cost producer, while exporting goods for which it is a low opportunity-cost producer.
    d. exports goods for which it is a high opportunity-cost producer, while importing those goods for which it is a low opportunity-cost producer.

EXHIBIT 5							
ITALIA		SLAVIA	
FOOD	CLOTHING	FOOD	CLOTHING
0	16	0	8
2	12	2	6
4	8	4	4
6	4	6	2
8	0	8	0

Exhibit 5 outlines the production possibilities of Italia and Slavia for food and clothing. Use it to answer questions 3 through 6.

3. Italia is currently producing 4 units of food and 8 units of clothing. If it increases its production of food by 2 units (up to a total of 6 units of food), its clothing production will
    a. fall by 2 units.
    b. fall by 4 units.
    c. increase by 2 units.
    d. increase by 4 units.

4. What is the opportunity cost of producing *1* unit of food in Italia?
    a. one-half of a unit of clothing
    b. 1 unit of clothing
    c. 2 units of clothing
    d. 5 units of clothing

5. Which of the following is true?
    a. Italia has the comparative advantage in producing food.
    b. Italia has the comparative advantage in producing clothing.
    c. Slavia has the comparative advantage in producing clothing.
    d. Slavia is the low opportunity cost producer of clothing.

6. The law of comparative advantage suggests that
    a. neither country would gain from trade.
    b. only Slavia would gain from trade, Italia would be harmed.
    c. both countries could gain if Italia traded food for Slavia's clothing.
    d. both countries could gain if Slavia traded food for Italia's clothing.

7. If the United States were to adopt a policy of free trade with European countries and Japan, this policy would
    a. help the United States and hurt the other countries because the United States has a larger population.
    b. help all of the countries involved because every country would have a comparative advantage in the production of some good.
    c. hurt the United States and help the other countries involved because job opportunities in the United States would fall while they rose in other countries.
    d. help the United States and hurt the other countries because the United States has more natural resources than the other countries.

8. The theory of comparative advantage suggests that nations should produce a good if they
    a. have the lowest opportunity cost.
    b. have the lowest wages.
    c. have the most resources.
    d. can produce more of the good than any other nation.

9. A tariff differs from a quota in that a tariff is
    a. levied on imports, whereas a quota is imposed on exports.
    b. levied on exports, whereas a quota is imposed on imports.
    c. a tax levied on exports, whereas a quota is a limit on the number of units of a good that can be exported.
    d. a tax imposed on imports, whereas a quota is an absolute limit to the number of units of a good that can be imported.

10. An import quota on a product protects domestic industries by
    a. reducing the foreign supply to the domestic market and thereby raising the domestic price.
    b. increasing the foreign supply to the domestic market and thereby lowering the domestic price.
    c. increasing the domestic demand for the product and thereby increasing its price.
    d. providing the incentive for domestic producers to improve the efficiency of their operation and thereby reduce their per-unit costs of production.

11. Which of the following would be the most likely long-run effect if the United States increased its tariff rates and adopted stricter import quotas?
    a. a decrease in both U.S. imports and exports
    b. an increase in both U.S. imports and exports
    c. a decrease in U.S. imports and an increase in U.S. exports
    d. an increase in U.S. imports and a decrease in U.S. exports

12. Trade restrictions that limit the sale of low-price foreign goods in the U.S. market
    a. increase the real income of Americans.
    b. benefit domestic producers in the protected industries at the expense of consumers and domestic producers in export industries.
    c. help channel more of our resources into producing goods for which we are a low-cost producer.
    d. reduce unemployment and increase the productivity of American workers.

13. A basic flaw in the infant-industry argument is that
    a. most industries need protection when they are mature, not when they are first established.
    b. the amount of the tariff is unlikely to have much impact on the success of an infant industry.
    c. once a tariff is granted, political pressure will likely prevent the withdrawal of the tariff even when the industry matures.
    d. domestic consumers will continue to buy the foreign products anyway, regardless of the tariff.

14. Countries that impose high tariffs, exchange rate controls, and other barriers that restrict international trade have, on average,
    a. high rates of economic growth.
    b. low rates of economic growth.
    c. a large export sector.
    d. a large import sector.

15. If the United States imports low-cost goods produced in low-wage countries instead of producing the goods domestically,
    a. the United States will lose jobs.
    b. the United States will gain and domestic resources will be employed more productively.
    c. dollars that leave the United States will not return to buy goods produced by high-wage American workers.
    d. the availability consumption of goods in the United States will be reduced.

16. Suppose that the United States eliminated its tariff on automobiles, granting foreign-produced automobiles free entry into the U.S. market. Which of the following would be most likely to occur?
    a. The price of automobiles to U.S. consumers would decline, and the demand for U.S. export products would increase.
    b. The price of automobiles to U.S. consumers would increase, and the demand for U.S. export products would decline.
    c. The price of automobiles to U.S. consumers would decline, and the demand for U.S. export products would decline.
    d. The price of automobiles to U.S. consumers would increase, and the demand for U.S. export products would increase.

17. If Japan offered every U.S. citizen a new automobile for a price of only $1,
    a. the action would be considered "dumping."
    b. domestic automobile manufacturers and workers would likely favor imposing tariffs or quotas to restrict this action.
    c. domestic citizens would benefit from this action by Japan.
    d. all of the above are true.

18. Relative to a no-trade situation, what effect will importing a good from foreign nations have on the domestic market for the good?
    a. Equilibrium price will rise and total domestically produced output will fall.
    b. Equilibrium price will rise and total domestically produced output will rise.
    c. Equilibrium price will fall and total domestically produced output will fall.
    d. Equilibrium price will fall and total domestically produced output will rise.

19. Relative to a no-trade situation, what effect will exporting a good to foreign nations have on the domestic market for the good?
    a. Equilibrium price will rise, domestic production will fall, and domestic consumption will fall.
    b. Equilibrium price will rise, domestic production will rise, and domestic consumption will fall.
    c. Equilibrium price will fall, domestic production will fall, and domestic consumption will increase.
    d. Equilibrium price will fall, domestic production will rise, and domestic consumption will increase.

20. If all tariffs (and quotas) between countries on the North American continent were eliminated,
    a. small Central American countries would be hurt since they would be unable to compete with larger nations.
    b. the United States would gain at the expense of the less-developed North American countries.
    c. the combined wealth of the countries would increase since elimination of trade restrictions would permit greater gains from specialization.
    d. wage rates in the United States would decline to the average for the North American continent.

21. Which of the following is **not** an argument for adopting trade restrictions on imported goods?
    a. antidumping argument
    b. national-defense argument
    c. consumer-protection argument
    d. infant-industry argument

Questions 22 through 25 refer to Exhibit 6, which shows the effect of a country imposing a tariff on an imported product.

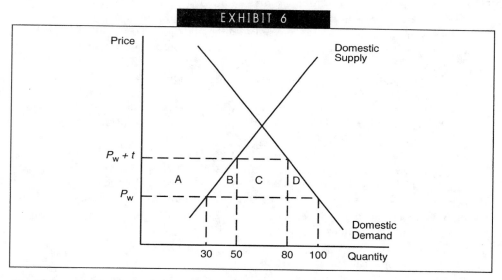

EXHIBIT 6

22. If the world price of this good is P_W and there are no restrictions on imports, domestic suppliers will produce _____ units, domestic demanders will consume _____ units, and total imports will be _____ units. (Fill in the blanks.)
    a. 30; 100; 70
    b. 50; 100; 50
    c. 30; 80; 80
    d. 100; 70; 30

23. Suppose that a tariff of t is imposed upon this good, raising the price to $P_W + t$. As a result,
    a. imports will fall to 30.
    b. domestic production will increase to 50.
    c. domestic consumption will fall to 80.
    d. all of the above are true.

24. Given the tariff described in the question above,
    a. the combined areas A + B + C + D represent the losses to domestic consumers from the tariff.
    b. area C represents the government's revenue from the tariff.
    c. area A represents the gain to domestic suppliers from the tariff.
    d. all of the above are true.

25. The same price and quantity outcomes under the tariff above could have also been produced by the imposition of a quota of
    a. 30 units.
    b. 50 units.
    c. 80 units.
    d. No quota can produce the same price and quantity outcomes.

DISCUSSION QUESTIONS

1. "We are not opposed to competition when it does not destroy jobs. But last year, while many American auto workers were idle, we exported a million jobs to foreigners by importing automobiles that could have been produced by domestic workers. An increase in the tariff on automobiles would strengthen our economy, provide jobs, and improve our standard of living." [Auto Workers' Union official]
   a. Do you agree that higher automobile tariffs would "provide jobs"? Why or why not?
   b. Do you agree that higher automobile tariffs would "improve our standard of living"? Why or why not?
   c. Prior to the 1970s, the United Auto Workers were an advocate of free trade. What do you think accounts for the reversal in their position?

2. All else constant, if the cost of Japanese laser printers is $1,000 in Japan, would you expect the cost of Japanese laser printers in the United States to be $1,000? more than $1,000? less than $1,000? If the Japanese are, in fact, selling laser printers in the United States for $800, what arguments for protection might U.S. manufacturers of laser printers make? Does selling the printers at prices lower than the cost of production benefit or harm U.S. consumers?

3. Describe each of the major, "partially valid," reasons for adopting trade restrictions. Discuss the pros and cons of each argument.

4. a. Montana encourages a local liquor-bottling industry by taxing bulk imports into the state at lower rates than bottled liquors. Does this make economic sense? Why or why not?
   b. Should Connecticut ban imports of bananas to promote a local banana industry? Explain.
   c. Should state governments adopt trade restrictions to target specific industries for promotions? If not, why not? If so, why and under what circumstances?

5. In the United States, the price of labor is relatively high and the price of capital is relatively low. In developing countries, the reverse is true.
   a. Based on these resource market conditions, what types of products would you expect the United States to import from developing countries? to export to them?
   b. Most U.S. trade is with other industrial high-wage nations. In light of the law of comparative advantage, is this surprising? If not, why not? If so, why and how can you account for this aspect of U.S. trade?

PERSPECTIVES IN ECONOMICS

THE ECONOMIC CASE FOR FREE TRADE

By Milton and Rose Friedman

[Reprinted with permission from Chapter 2 of *Free to Choose* (New York: Harcourt Brace Jovanovich, 1980) Abridged.]

Today, as always, there is much support for tariffs—euphemistically labeled "protection," a good label for a bad cause. Producers of steel and steelworkers' unions press for restrictions on steel imports from Japan. Producers of TV sets and their workers lobby for "voluntary agreements" to limit imports of TV sets or components from Japan, Taiwan, or Hong Kong. Producers of textiles, shoes, cattle, sugar—they and myriad others complain about "unfair" competition from abroad and demand that government do something to "protect" them. Of course, no group makes its claim on the basis of naked self-interest. Every group speaks of the "general interest," of the need to preserve jobs or to promote national security.

One voice that is hardly ever raised is the consumer's. The individual consumer's voice is drowned out in the cacophony of the "interested sophistry of merchants and manufacturers" and their employees. The result is a serious distortion of the issue. For example, the supporters of tariffs treat it as self-evident that the creation of jobs is a desirable end, in and of itself, regardless of what the persons employed do. That is clearly wrong. If all we want are jobs, we can create any number—for example, have people dig holes and then fill them up again, or perform other useless tasks. Work is sometimes its own reward. Mostly, however, it is the price we pay to get the things we want. Our real objective is not just jobs but productive jobs—jobs that will mean more goods and services to consume.

Another fallacy seldom contradicted is that exports are good, imports bad. The truth is very different. We cannot eat, wear, or enjoy the goods we send abroad. We eat bananas from Central America, wear Italian shoes, drive German automobiles, and enjoy programs we see on our Japanese TV sets. Our gain from foreign trade is what we import. Exports are the price we pay to get imports. As Adam Smith saw so clearly, the citizens of a nation benefit from getting as large a volume of imports as possible in return for its exports, or equivalently, from exporting as little as possible to pay for its imports.

The misleading terminology we use reflects these erroneous ideas. "Protection" really means exploiting the consumer. A "favorable balance of trade" really means exporting more than we import, sending abroad goods of greater total value than the goods we get from abroad. In your private household, you would surely prefer to pay less for more rather than the other way around, yet that would be termed an "unfavorable balance of payments" in foreign trade.

The argument in favor of tariffs that has the greatest emotional appeal to the public at large is the alleged need to protect the high standard of living of American workers from the "unfair" competition of workers in Japan or Korea or Hong Kong who are willing to work for a much lower wage. What is wrong with this argument? Don't we want to protect the high standard of living of our people?

The fallacy in this argument is the loose use of the terms "high" wage and "low" wage. What do high and low wages mean? American workers are paid in dollars; Japanese workers are paid in yen. How do we compare wages in dollars with wages in yen? How many yen equal a dollar? What determines that exchange rate?

It is simply not true that high-wage American workers are, as a group, threatened by "unfair" competition from low-wage foreign workers. Of course, particular workers may be harmed if a new or improved product is developed abroad, or if foreign producers become able to produce such products more cheaply. But that is no different from the effect on a particular group of workers of other American firms, developing new or improved products or discovering how to produce at lower costs. That is simply market competition in practice, the major source of the high standard of life of the American worker. If we want to benefit from a vital, dynamic, innovative economic system, we must accept the need for mobility and adjustment. It may be desirable to ease these adjustments, and we have adopted many arrangements, such as unemployment insurance, to do so, but we should try to achieve that objective without destroying the flexibility of the system—that would be to kill the goose that has been laying the golden eggs. In any event, whatever we do should be evenhanded with respect to foreign and domestic trade.

What determines the items it pays us to import and to export? An American worker is currently more productive than a Japanese worker. It is hard to determine just how much more productive—estimates differ. But suppose he is one and a half times as productive. Then, on average, the American's wages would buy about one and half times as much as a Japanese worker's wages. It is wasteful to use American workers to do anything at which they are less than one and a half times as efficient as their Japanese counterparts. In the economic jargon coined more than 150 years ago, that is the *principle of comparative advantage.* Even if we were more efficient than the Japanese at producing everything, it would not pay us to produce everything. We should concentrate on doing those things we do best, those things where our superiority is the greatest.

Another source of "unfair competition" is said to be subsidies by foreign governments to their producers that enable them to sell in the United States below cost. Suppose a foreign government gives such subsidies, as no doubt some do. Who is hurt and who benefits? To pay for the subsidies the foreign government must tax its citizens. They are the ones who pay for the subsidies. U.S. consumers benefit. They get cheap TV sets or automobiles or whatever it is that is subsidized. Should we complain about such a program of reverse foreign aid? Was it noble of the United States to send goods and services as gifts to other countries in the form of Marshall Plan aid or, later, foreign aid, but ignoble for foreign countries to send us gifts in the indirect form of goods and services sold to us below cost? The citizens of the foreign government might well complain. They must suffer a lower standard of living for the benefit of American consumers and of some of their fellow citizens who own or work in the industries that are subsidized. No doubt, if such subsidies are introduced suddenly or erratically, that will adversely affect owners and workers in U.S. industries producing the same products. However, that is one of the ordinary risks of doing business. Enterprises never complain about unusual or accidental events that confer windfall gains. The free enterprise system is a *profit* and *loss* system. As already noted, any measures to ease the adjustment to sudden changes should be applied evenhandedly to domestic and foreign trade.

We are a great nation, the leader of the free world. It ill behooves us to require Hong Kong and Taiwan to impose export quotas on textiles to "protect" our textile industry at the expense of U.S. consumers and of Chinese workers in Hong Kong and Taiwan. We speak glowingly of the virtues of free trade, while we use our political and economic power to induce Japan to restrict exports of steel and TV sets. We should move unilaterally to free trade, not instantaneously, but over a period of, say, five years, at a pace announced in advance.

Few measures that we could take would do more to promote the cause of freedom at home and abroad than complete free trade. Instead of making grants to foreign governments in the name of economic aid—thereby promoting socialism—while at the same time imposing restrictions on the products they produce—thereby hindering free enterprise—we could assume a consistent and principled stance. We could say to the rest of the world: we believe in freedom and intend to practice it. We cannot force you to be free. But we can offer full cooperation on equal terms to all. Our market is open to you without tariffs or other restrictions. Sell here what you can and wish to. Buy whatever you can and wish to. In that way cooperation among individuals can be worldwide and free.

DISCUSSION

1. When a politician speaks out in favor of protectionism against imports, how do you react? Is this debate a question of economic theory against political reality, or are there political and economic arguments on both sides? Explain.

2. As you read the article, you were probably impressed with the superb logic and internal consistency with which the Friedmans write. If you were going to attempt to refute their arguments, where would you start? Are there any major assumptions you could question? Are there secondary effects that they neglect to analyze? Explain.

3. The article points out that the harm done to consumers by restricting trade is usually ignored. Why do you think this is the case? Generally, even people who are "pro-consumer/antibusiness" are in favor of restricting imports, when economic theory tells us that it only helps producers while harming individual consumers. Can you explain this apparent contradiction?

CHAPTER 18

International Finance and the Foreign Exchange Market

TRUE OR FALSE

T F

☐ ☐ 1. Foreign exchange markets enable individuals to exchange the currency of one nation for the currency of another nation.

☐ ☐ 2. A nation's exports generate a demand for the currency of the exporting nation on the foreign exchange market.

☐ ☐ 3. Under a system of fixed exchange rates, a balance-of-payments equilibrium is automatic.

☐ ☐ 4. Under a system of flexible exchange rates, the government must use monetary policy to ensure a balance-of-payments equilibrium.

☐ ☐ 5. The economic analysis of foreign trade is unique in that supply-and-demand relationships do not usually determine equilibrium.

☐ ☐ 6. One problem with a system of flexible exchange rates is that black markets in foreign currencies are more likely to develop than with controlled rates of exchange.

☐ ☐ 7. When a country's balance of trade registers a deficit, both its current and capital accounts will also be in deficit.

☐ ☐ 8. If foreigners suddenly began investing more in the United States, causing the capital account to run a larger surplus, the current account deficit would rise.

☐ ☐ 9. If imports consistently exceeded exports, U.S. consumers would be hurt as a result of an unfavorable balance of trade implied by such a situation.

☐ ☐ 10. If expansionary fiscal policy (a budget deficit) leads to higher interest rates, it will cause a nation's currency to appreciate and the current account to move toward a trade deficit.

☐ ☐ 11. A rapid U.S. monetary expansion would tend to reduce the number of euros it takes to buy a U.S. dollar, other things constant.

☐ ☐ 12. For a common currency, such as the euro, to be successful, each country must give up the independence of their monetary policy.

☐ ☐ 13. Bilateral trade between countries should be balanced. If other countries are treating us fairly, our exports to them should be approximately equal to our imports from them.

PROBLEMS AND PROJECTS

1. Exhibit 1 shows the exchange rate values of several major world currencies relative to the U.S. dollar as they were on March 26, 2002. The first column shows the number of units of the foreign currency that could be obtained by trading in one U.S. dollar. The second column shows the number of U.S. dollars that could be obtained by trading in one unit of the foreign currency. (Note: These are simply the reciprocals of the data in the first column.)

EXHIBIT 1

FOREIGN CURRENCY	UNITS OF FOREIGN CURRENCY PER U.S. DOLLAR	U.S. DOLLARS PER UNIT OF FOREIGN CURRENCY
English pound	0.701	1.4263
European euro	1.141	0.8764
Canadian dollar	1.589	0.6293
Mexican peso	9.025	0.1108
Japanese yen	132.700	0.0075

  a. If a Mexican citizen wished to purchase a Ford automobile costing 30,000 U.S. dollars, how much would it cost in Mexican pesos?

  b. If a U.S. citizen wished to purchase a bottle of French wine costing 80 euros, how much would it cost in U.S. dollars?

  c. If a Canadian citizen wished to purchase a Japanese automobile costing 2,500,000 Japanese yen, how much would it cost in Canadian dollars? [Hint: With the data given, you must first convert from Japanese yen to U.S. dollars, then convert U.S. dollars to Canadian dollars.]

  d. To carry out the transaction in part c, a Canadian citizen could either convert Canadian dollars to U.S. dollars, then U.S. dollars to yen, or she could simply convert Canadian dollars directly to yen. From the data above, what would you expect the exchange rate to be between the Canadian dollar and the yen?

  e. In March 2000, one euro was equal to 0.9645 U.S. dollars, one Japanese yen was equal to 0.0093 U.S. dollars, and one Mexican peso was equal to 0.1089 U.S. dollars. Compare these values to the ones in Exhibit 1 and decide whether each of these currencies has either appreciated or depreciated over this period relative to the U.S. dollar.

2. Each of the diagrams below represents the U.S. demand for and supply of foreign exchange, here the English pound. For each of the events described below, diagram how the demand and/or supply of English pounds changes (use +, −, or 0 to show no change). Then fill in the blanks to the right of the diagram, indicating in the last blank whether the *English pound* has appreciated, depreciated, or undergone an indeterminate change as a result of the event(s). The first question has been answered as an example, and in the diagrams, price (P) is in dollars per English pound.

EVENTS	DIAGRAMS	D	S	CHANGE

a. As a result of recovering from a depression, U.S. incomes rise significantly.

 __+__   __0__ depreciated

b. The United Kingdom experiences a serious recession, causing a decline in income.

____ ____ _____

c. Restrictive monetary policy in the United States causes U.S. interest rates to rise relative to United Kingdom rates.

____ ____ _____

d. The Chairman of the Fed is quoted as saying, "If the high value of the dollar is not soon corrected by market forces, the Fed will take corrective action."

____ ____ _____

e. While the United States experiences stable price, prices in the United Kingdom rise by 15 percent.

____ ____ _____

f. In an effort to stimulate the economy, the United States embarks on an expansionary fiscal policy.

____ ____ _____

EVENTS	DIAGRAMS	D	S	CHANGE
g. Both the United States and the United Kingdom experience inflation rates of 20 percent		—	—	—

EXHIBIT 2

DEBIT		CREDIT	
	(BILLIONS OF DOLLARS)		
CURRENT ACCOUNT			
Merchandise imports	249.3	Merchandise exports	224.0
Service imports	84.6	Service exports	120.7
Net unilateral transfers	7.1		
CAPITAL ACCOUNT			
U.S. investment abroad	18.5	Foreign investment	
Loans to foreigners	58.1	in the United States	10.9
		Loans from foreigners	70.2

3. Exhibit 2 presents balance-of-payment data for the United States for 1980.
    a. Use the data in Exhibit 2 to calculate the balance on the (1) merchandise trade account, (2) services account, (3) current account, and (4) capital account.
    b. Compare these balances to the ones for 2000 in Exhibit 5 in the text. What happened to U.S. international balances between those years?

MULTIPLE CHOICE

1. If the exchange rate value of one U.S. dollar changes from 120 Japanese yen to 140 yen,
    a. the U.S. dollar has appreciated relative to the yen.
    b. the Japanese yen has depreciated relative to the dollar.
    c. the U.S. dollar has depreciated relative to the yen.
    d. both a and b have occurred.

2. Under a flexible exchange rate system, which of the following will be most likely to cause a depreciation in the exchange rate value of the dollar (relative to the English pound)?
    a. An economic boom occurs in England, inducing English consumers to buy more American-made automobiles, trucks, and computer products.
    b. Real interest rates in the United States fall lower than real interest rates in England.
    c. Restrictive monetary policy in the United States causes inflation to be lower than in England.
    d. Attractive investment opportunities in the United States induce English investors to buy stock in U.S. firms.

3. If the exchange rate between the U.S. dollar and the Japanese yen were such that one U.S. dollar equals 100 yen, what would be the price in dollars of a Japanese automobile that cost 2,000,000 yen?
    a. $100
    b. $20,000
    c. $120,000
    d. $2,000,000

4. Other things constant, which of the following will most likely cause the dollar to appreciate on the exchange rate market?
    a. higher interest rates in the U.S.
    b. the U.S. Fed pursuing restrictive monetary policy
    c. high rates of income growth in Europe
    d. all of the above

5. If the U.S. dollar depreciates, then U.S. exports become _____ expensive to foreigners and foreign goods become _____ expensive to U.S. citizens. (Fill in the blanks.)
    a. less; less
    b. less; more
    c. more; less
    d. more; more

6. An unanticipated shift to a more expansionary monetary policy will most likely cause the nation's currency to _____ and its current account to move toward a _____. (Fill in the blanks.)
    a. depreciate; deficit
    b. depreciate; surplus
    c. appreciate; deficit
    d. appreciate; surplus

7. Under a pure flexible exchange rate system, the rate that equates demand and supply in the exchange rate market will also lead to a balance of
    a. merchandise exports and merchandise imports.
    b. current account transactions.
    c. capital account transactions.
    d. current and capital account transactions.

8. If the value of a nation's merchandise imports exceeds merchandise exports, the nation is running a
    a. balance of payments deficit.
    b. balance of payments surplus.
    c. merchandise trade deficit.
    d. merchandise trade surplus.

9. Which one of the following would supply dollars to the foreign exchange market?
    a. the spending of U.S. tourists in Europe
    b. the purchase of U.S. automobiles by Japanese consumers
    c. the sale of U.S. automobiles to European consumers
    d. the purchase of an American electronics factory by a Japanese investor

10. During the 1990s, the United States ran a trade deficit (our exports of goods and services were less than our imports of goods and services). Which of the following is true regarding these trade deficits?
    a. They were primarily caused by rapid economic growth in the United States stimulating imports and also the attractiveness of the United States as a place to invest causing a capital inflow.
    b. These trade deficits put the United States in debt to foreign economies and thus weaken future economic conditions in the United States.
    c. These trade deficits are evidence that other countries practice unfair trade against the United States because under fair trade exports equal imports to another country.
    d. None of the above are true regarding the trade deficits of the United States.

11. (I) The U.S. trade deficit is a financial obligation of the federal government, and if it is not paid off, foreigners will be reluctant to loan money to the U.S. government. (II) When a nation runs a current account deficit due to a merchandise trade deficit, it must also be true that the nation has a surplus on its capital account due to an inflow of foreign capital.
    a. I is true; II is false.
    b. I is false; II is true.
    c. Both I and II are true.
    d. Both I and II are false.

12. For a country to successfully maintain a fixed exchange rate value of its currency relative to another currency (for example, as is done when currencies are unified or pegged), it must
    a. maintain a relatively high rate of inflation.
    b. balance the government budget each year.
    c. give up the independence of its monetary policy.
    d. run a trade deficit.

13. An appreciation in the value of the U.S. dollar would
    a. encourage foreigners to make more investments in the United States.
    b. encourage U.S. consumers to purchase more foreign-produced goods.
    c. increase the number of dollars that could be purchased with the euro.
    d. discourage U.S. consumers from traveling abroad.

14. Which of the following would be likely to cause a nation's currency to depreciate?
    a. an increase in foreign demand for the nation's products
    b. a lower domestic rate of inflation than that of the nation's trading partners
    c. higher domestic interest rates
    d. higher foreign interest rates

15. Under a system of flexible exchange rates, transactions that increase the supply of the nation's currency to the foreign exchange market will cause the nation's
    a. currency to depreciate in value.
    b. currency to appreciate in value.
    c. trade deficit to increase.
    d. products to become more expensive to foreigners.

16. With time, a depreciation in the value of a nation's currency in the foreign market will cause the nation's
    a. imports to increase and exports to decline.
    b. exports to increase and imports to decline.
    c. imports and exports to decline.
    d. imports and exports to rise.

17. "Wine experts are discovering that California wines of several varieties and vintages are comparable to many of the best French wines. The result is an increased demand, here and abroad, for California wines." With regard to the U.S. balance on current account, this trend will
    a. increase the U.S. deficit because of the rise in the price of California wine.
    b. decrease the U.S. deficit because of increased shipments of California wines abroad.
    c. decrease the demand for U.S. dollars.
    d. increase the U.S. demand for euros.

18. The major impact of a restrictive monetary policy on the domestic exchange rate would be
    a. an increase in the foreign exchange value of the domestic currency.
    b. a decrease in the foreign exchange value of the domestic currency.
    c. no change in the foreign exchange value of the domestic currency.
    d. It is impossible to predict the impact on the foreign exchange value of the domestic currency.

19. Under a system of flexible exchange rates, which of the following will cause the nation's currency to depreciate in the exchange market?
    a. an increase in foreign incomes
    b. a domestic inflation rate of 10 percent while the nation's trading partners are experiencing stable prices
    c. an increase in domestic interest rates
    d. a reduction in interest rates abroad

20. Expansionary fiscal policy exerts upward pressure on prices, output, and interest rates. As a result, expansionary fiscal policy tends to cause
    a. an appreciation of the exchange rate and a deficit in the current account.
    b. a depreciation of the exchange rate and a surplus in the current account.
    c. an uncertain effect on the exchange rate and a deficit in the current account.
    d. uncertain effects on both the exchange rate and the current account.

DISCUSSION QUESTIONS

1. "Exports pay for a nation's imports. Other countries will not continue shipping us their goods if they lose interest in the goods, services, and financial assets we export to them in exchange." Do you agree? Explain.

2. "No patriotic American wants the value of the dollar to fall on the foreign exchange market." Whether or not this quote is true, it is fair to say that Americans seem to like a strong dollar and a trade surplus.
   a. What are the advantages of a strong dollar? the disadvantages?
   b. What are the advantages of a trade surplus? the disadvantages?
   c. Why is it difficult to have both a strong dollar and a trade surplus at the same time?

3. In today's world of flexible exchange rates and mobile financial assets, a country's domestic macroeconomic policies and its foreign sector are closely interrelated. Economists focus especially on the interaction between domestic policies, interest rates, exchange rates, and international capital flows.
   a. How can a budget deficit contribute to capital inflows and an offsetting current account deficit?
   b. With flexible exchange rates, why does trade protection tend to be ineffective as a cure for a current account deficit?
   c. Some economists have recommended that a tax be imposed on international capital flows to reduce their volume. Would you favor such a tax? Why or why not?

4. "A nation's balance of payments must always be in balance." In what sense is this true? What is a "balance-of-payments deficit"? Under a flexible exchange system, will a balance-of-payments deficit automatically be corrected? Explain.

5. "A system of flexible exchange rates is advantageous because it enables a nation to stabilize domestic employment and prices without regard to the foreign sector and insulates a country from the effects of foreign macroeconomic policies." Do you agree or not? Explain.

6. Discuss the role of time in balance-of-payments adjustments. Why might the current account of a country with a depreciating currency deteriorate in the short run and improve in the long run? Why would the opposite scenario for the capital account be surprising?

PERSPECTIVES IN ECONOMICS

DON'T WORRY ABOUT THE TRADE DEFICIT

By Herbert Stein

[From *The Wall Street Journal*, May 16, 1989. Reprinted with permission from *The Wall Street Journal*. Copyright © Dow Jones & Co., Inc. All Rights Reserved.]

There seems to be a conspiracy against telling even the simplest truth.

This somber thought was brought home to me by an experience on a recent Tuesday afternoon. I'm goofing off, staying at home and watching daytime TV. I have a choice of 16 channels. On 15 of them beautiful women and handsome men are working out the complications of their love-lives, mostly in hospital rooms. I know that at my age I cannot expect any of these complications to be resolved during my lifetime, so I settle for C-SPAN and the U.S. Senate at "work."

I'm hearing a senator carrying on about how terrible it is that other countries insist on selling us more stuff than they buy from us. He demands that we let these countries know in no uncertain terms that we are not going to put up with that kind of thing any longer.

Excuses for Economists. At first I am shocked. Is there no limit to what can be put over the air, even in the daytime when children may be listening? But then I get over it and become more philosophical. I know that this senator has an undergraduate degree from one of our leading liberal arts colleges and another degree from one of our most eminent law schools. He is, however, a senator and may be forgiven for committing nonsense on the public airwaves.

But what about the trained staffs of international financial institutions who write serious reports about the need to correct "imbalances"—which is polite language for eliminating or reducing the U.S. trade deficit? What about the finance ministers from the industrial countries who meet every six months or so to cook up plans for correcting these "imbalances"—again meaning the U.S. trade deficit? And what about my sophisticated economist friends who talk about the need to eliminate the trade deficit? What are they all talking about?

I say to my economist friends that the trade deficit is not hurting the U.S., but, on the contrary, is helping us, and I ask them why we should be concerned about reducing the trade deficit. The more candid among them answer as follows: "We know that the trade deficit is not hurting us. But there are a lot of people out there—including presidents, senators, and congressmen—who think that the trade deficit is a bad thing and as long as it persists they will feel driven to protectionist measures, which would be very bad. In order to restrain the protectionist movement the trade deficit must be reduced."

What this comes down to is an argument for reducing the budget deficit as a way to reduce the trade deficit and thereby head off protectionism, even though we all know that the trade deficit is not hurting us and does not constitute a valid reason for protectionism.

Readers of this page may know that I am more willing than most people to pay more taxes and give up some of my Social Security and Medicare benefits in order to balance the federal budget and run a surplus. There are good reasons for wanting to do that. But I would hate to pay anything in the hope of thereby heading off protectionism.

Some people have good reason to be protectionist; they have immediate interests at stake. No economist, however much devoted to free trade, ever denied that. These "knowing" protectionists will not be dissuaded by seeing the trade deficit disappear. But most people have no good reason to be protectionist. They support or tolerate protectionism out of ignorance. There should be a more efficient way to convert them to the virtues of free trade than by eliminating the trade deficit. Or, to put the case more modestly, it is worth trying to convert them by telling the truth. That is what economists are for. If some more "devious" ways of avoiding protectionism have to be found, let some one else do it.

Let's remember a few simple propositions.

1. The U.S. has a trade deficit because people in the rest of the world invest their savings here. This inflow of capital is voluntary on both sides—foreigners are seeking the best place to put their money and American governments and companies are seeking the best place to obtain money. Foreigners seeking to invest here have to obtain dollars. Their demand for dollars keep the exchange rate of the dollar at a level where U.S. imports exceed U.S. exports.

2. As a result of the capital inflow—and the accompanying trade deficit—over the past eight years, the stock of productive capital in the U.S. is now about $700 billion higher than it would otherwise have been. This fact is commonly misunderstood because people think the capital inflow is financing the budget deficit. It is true that foreigners have bought a large amount of U.S. Treasury securities. But if foreigners had not bought them they would have had to be bought by Americans, who would have had less of their own savings to invest in productive assets.

3. This inflow of capital has been mainly of benefit to American workers, who as a result of it, work with a larger capital stock and have higher productivity and real incomes. It has also increased the U.S. tax base.

4. Large and persistent trade deficits have not prevented an unusually long recovery and the achievement of an unusually high level of total output.

5. Continuation of the capital inflow-trade deficit combination will increase the amount of interest and dividends that American governments and corporations have to pay to foreigners. But it will also increase the amount of capital in this country that would not otherwise be here, and that additional capital will generate the income to pay for foreigners. That income will not come out of income that Americans would otherwise have earned.

6. The inflow of capital and ownership of assets in the U.S. by foreigners is not a cause of dangerous dependence that is a political or security danger to us. What may be politically dangerous is the effort of governments to manipulate this relationship—an effort to which we are the leaders, unfortunately.

7. The inflow of goods and capital may not go on forever, but it is unlikely to stop so abruptly as to create difficulties for us. The two-sided inflow is an adaptation to basic conditions—propensities to save and investment opportunities at home and abroad—that will change only gradually. The most serious qualification is that government efforts to manage exchange rates may cause such great uncertainties about the future of those rates that international capital flows dry up for a time.

Exchange Rates Everything

8. Protectionist measures imposed by government, ours and others, impair efficiency but do not cause the trade deficit. Trying to eliminate these measures would be worthwhile whether we have a deficit or a surplus, but success would not change the deficit.

9. Having a trade deficit is not a sign of low productivity or economy weakness. Poor, weak countries—like Brazil—can have trade surpluses. Rich, strong countries like us can have trade deficits. Everything depends on prices and exchange rates.

10. Let's forget about the trade deficit. We have plenty of real deficits to worry about—including the education deficit, the defense deficit, the poverty deficit and the investment deficit.

DISCUSSION

1. Do you agree with Stein? Should we worry about the trade deficit? Why or why not?

2. If Stein is right that "rich, strong countries like us can have trade deficits," then why are Congress and the media so concerned with avoiding the current U.S. trade deficit?

3. If the trade deficit isn't hurting the United States but policy makers think it is and are considering protectionist policies that *will* hurt the country, which would be easier, fixing the trade deficit or educating the policy makers? Explain your reasoning.

SPECIAL TOPIC *1*

Government Spending and Taxation

TRUE OR FALSE

T F

☐ ☐ 1. Government spending can be classified into the two broad categories of (1) government purchases of goods and services and (2) transfer payments.

☐ ☐ 2. The federal government accounts for approximately three-fifths of all government spending in the United States.

☐ ☐ 3. Federal spending on national parks, highways, education, and law enforcement together account for over 50 percent of the federal budget.

☐ ☐ 4. The largest single category of federal spending is national defense and the largest single category of revenue is the personal income tax.

☐ ☐ 5. The largest single category of state and local spending is education and the largest single category of revenue is user charges.

☐ ☐ 6. Federal government spending in real per capita terms has grown rapidly throughout the entire history of the United States.

☐ ☐ 7. Corrected for inflation, the average person today pays more federal taxes in one week than the average person in 1900 paid in an entire year.

☐ ☐ 8. Over the past 40 years, national defense expenditures as a share of the federal budget have risen while transfer payments as a share of the federal budget have fallen.

☐ ☐ 9. The administration, enforcement, and compliance costs of taxes in the United States amount to 12 to 15 cents for each dollar of revenue raised.

☐ ☐ 10. In 1999, the income tax payments of the richest 10 percent of Americans accounted for approximately 67 percent of all federal income tax revenue.

☐ ☐ 11. As a result of the Earned Income Tax Credit, a provision in the tax code providing for a credit or rebate to persons with low earnings, more than one-third of all taxpayers either had zero tax liability or actually received money from the IRS in 1999.

PROBLEMS AND PROJECTS

1. Exhibit 1 provides data on the federal government budget in fiscal years 1960 and 2000. Use the data provided to answer the following questions.
   a. Fill in the missing numbers for fiscal year 1960.
   b. Fill in the missing numbers for fiscal year 2000.

EXHIBIT 1

Federal Government Finances for Fiscal Years 1960 and 2000

	FISCAL YEAR 1960		FISCAL YEAR 2000	
	AMOUNT (IN BILLIONS)	PERCENT OF TOTAL	AMOUNT (IN BILLIONS)	PERCENT OF TOTAL
Total Receipts (Revenues)	$549.5	100.0%	$1,883.0	100.0%
Individual income taxes	241.8	44.0	899.7	47.8
Corporate income taxes	127.7	_____	189.4	10.1
Social Security revenue	87.3	15.9	636.5	_____
Other revenue	92.7	16.9	157.4	8.4
Total Outlays (Expenditures)	$547.7	100.0%	$1,765.7	100.0%
National defense	285.8	_____	274.1	_____
Health and Medicare	4.8	0.9	368.9	20.9
Income security (welfare)	44.0	8.0	258.0	_____
Social Security	68.9	_____	408.6	23.1
Net interest on the debt	41.0	7.5	215.2	_____
Other expenditures	103.2	18.8	240.9	13.6

c. What has happened to national defense expenditures as a percent of federal spending between 1960 and 2000?

d. What has happened to Social Security expenditures as a percent of federal spending between 1960 and 2000?

e. What has happened to payments for interest on the debt as a percent of federal spending between 1960 and 2000?

f. What has happened to health and Medicare spending as a percent of federal spending between 1960 and 2000?

g. What has happened to welfare spending as a percent of federal spending between 1960 and 2000?

h. What was the single largest expenditure category in 1960? in 2000?

i. What has happened to corporate income taxes as a percent of revenue between 1960 and 2000? Does this mean businesses are paying less of the tax burden in 2000 than in 1960?

j. What was the single largest revenue source in 1960? in 2000?

k. Given the nature of the data presented, why is it better to make comparisons using the percentages of the budget rather than using the dollar amounts?

2. Exhibit 2 provides data from the Internal Revenue Service on the amount of federal income tax paid by different income groups in 1999. Use the data provided to answer the following questions.
   a. Fill in the missing blanks for the percent of income tax paid by group.
   b. In 1980, the top 1 percent paid 19.10 percent of the federal income tax. What has happened to the share of income tax paid by this group since 1980?

EXHIBIT 2

Federal Income Tax Paid by Income Group in 1999

INCOME GROUP	TOTAL FEDERAL INCOME TAX PAID BY GROUP (IN MILLIONS)	PERCENT OF TOTAL FEDERAL INCOME TAX PAID BY GROUP
Top 1%	$317,419	_____
Top 5%	486,464	55.45
Top 10%	583,002	_____
Top 25%	732,890	_____
Top 50%	842,168	_____
Bottom 50%	35,124	4.00
Total all groups	877,292	100.00

   c. In 1980, the bottom 50 percent paid 7.00 percent of the federal income tax. What has happened to the share of income tax paid by this group since 1980?
   d. Based on this data, would you say the rich pay their fair share of taxes in the United States?

MULTIPLE CHOICE

1. Which of the following comprises the largest single category of federal expenditures?
   a. national defense
   b. Social Security
   c. health care
   d. highways

2. Which of the following comprises the largest single category of state and local expenditures?
   a. education
   b. highways
   c. public welfare
   d. police and fire protection

3. Which of the following comprises the largest single category of federal revenue?
   a. corporate income tax
   b. personal income tax
   c. customs duties
   d. Social Security payroll tax

4. Which of the following is the largest single category of state and local revenue?
   a. property tax
   b. user charges
   c. general sales taxes
   d. personal income taxes

5. For the first time in almost a century,
   a. the rapid growth of federal spending stopped during the 1990s.
   b. the slow growth of federal spending began to increase during the 1990s.
   c. state and local governments spent more than the federal government during the 1990s.
   d. national defense became the largest category of federal spending in the 1990s.

6. Which of the following is true regarding U.S. federal government expenditures?
   a. National defense has fallen from 52 percent of the federal budget in 1960 to 16 percent in 2000.
   b. Federal expenditures on income transfers and health care have risen from 22 percent of the budget in 1960 to 57 percent in 2000.
   c. Corrected for inflation, the average person today pays more federal taxes in one week than the average person in 1900 paid in an entire year.
   d. All of the above are true.

7. One dollar of tax revenue ends up costing citizens in the economy
   a. less than one dollar.
   b. exactly one dollar.
   c. more than one dollar.
   d. nothing.

8. In 1999, the income tax payments of the richest 1 percent of Americans accounted for what percent of all federal income tax revenue?
   a. 1 percent
   b. 16 percent
   c. 36 percent
   d. 56 percent

9. In 1999, the income tax payments of the poorest 50 percent of Americans accounted for what percent of all federal income tax revenue?
   a. 4 percent
   b. 25 percent
   c. 50 percent
   d. 76 percent

10. Estimates from the U.S. Treasury Department suggest that the typical family in the highest income quintile pays approximately what percent of their total income in federal taxes?
    a. 6 percent
    b. 25 percent
    c. 50 percent
    d. 76 percent

11. Estimates from the U.S. Treasury Department suggest that the typical family in the lowest income quintile pays approximately what percent of their total income in federal taxes?
    a. 6 percent
    b. 25 percent
    c. 50 percent
    d. 76 percent

12. Based on estimates from the U.S. Treasury Department, the federal tax structure is
    a. highly regressive.
    b. roughly proportional.
    c. highly progressive.
    d. regressive at lower incomes and progressive at higher incomes.

13. Because of which provision in the tax code did more than one-third of all tax-payers either have a zero tax liability or actually receive money from the IRS in 1999?
    a. Earned Income Tax Credit
    b. Standard Deduction
    c. Marginal Tax Rate
    d. Families with Low Income Credit

14. Government expenditures as a percent of GDP in the United States
    a. are very high in comparison to the rest of the world.
    b. are smaller than for most other high-income industrial countries.
    c. are much smaller today than they were a century ago.
    d. have risen rapidly during the 1990s.

15. A transfer payment is
    a. a purchase of a good or service by the government.
    b. money paid to a government employee.
    c. money used to finance the construction of roads.
    d. the taxing of income away from one individual to give it directly to another individual without requiring anything in return from the recipient.

16. Which of the following is an example of a government transfer payment?
    a. payments to Social Security recipients
    b. expenditures on benefits for unemployed workers
    c. agricultural subsidies
    d. all of the above

17. Which of the following most clearly distinguishes government from a private business?
    a. the power to tax
    b. the hiring of educated employees
    c. the production of goods and services
    d. the need to make managerial decisions

DISCUSSION QUESTIONS

1. Discuss the trends in the size of the U.S. federal government over its history. Was the growth rate of real per capita federal expenditures similar in the 1800s and the 1900s?

2. What are the major expenditure areas and revenue sources of the U.S. federal government and how has this changed over the past several decades?

3. How progressive is the U.S. federal tax system? How heavy is the burden of the federal income tax on the rich?

4. How do the types of expenditure programs and sources of revenue differ between the federal government and state and local governments in the United States?

SPECIAL TOPIC 2

The Internet: How Is It Changing the Economy?

TRUE OR FALSE

T F

☐ ☐ 1. On-line sales of goods and services to consumers totaled $45 billion in 2000.

☐ ☐ 2. In 2001 there were over 30 million Web sites.

☐ ☐ 3. Approximately 25 percent of the U.S. population uses the Internet.

☐ ☐ 4. People in Africa and the Middle East account for approximately half of all Internet users.

☐ ☐ 5. The Internet is beneficial because it lowers transaction costs in the economy, makes markets more competitive, and increases networking opportunities.

☐ ☐ 6. On-line sales account for a larger percentage of computer hardware and software sales than for automobile sales.

☐ ☐ 7. The Internet generally makes it more difficult for consumers to obtain access to some goods, particularly specialty products and customized goods with unique characteristics.

☐ ☐ 8. The Internet has generally benefited consumers but has been of little use in fostering transactions between business firms.

☐ ☐ 9. The Internet has rapidly become an important part of the job search process and helps to match job seekers with potential employers.

☐ ☐ 10. By helping to lower search time and improve the quality of the matching between potential employees and potential jobs, the Internet has created economic benefits in the labor market.

PROBLEMS AND PROJECTS

1. A lot can be learned by looking at the most popular search terms on the Internet and how they change from week to week. One such list for the Web site Yahoo! can be found at http://buzz.yahoo.com. Look at this Web page as you do this problem and answer the following questions.
   a. What are the top five search terms this week?
   b. Which search terms gained the most and which fell by the most from last week? Can you explain why?
   c. Which search terms have been in the top 20 list for the longest number of weeks?
   d. Of the search terms currently in the top 20, which do you expect will stay on the list for the longest number of weeks into the future?

2. Go to the Amazon.com Web site [http://www.amazon.com] and search in "Popular Music" for your favorite CD (or the one you listen to the most). Answer the following questions while you look at the Web page for your favorite CD.

   a. How much does this CD cost from Amazon.com? How does this compare to the price you paid for it? How would shipping and handling costs affect this comparison?

   b. Further down the Web page you will see a section titled "Customers who bought this title also bought:." These are the CDs most frequently purchased by other shoppers who also purchased your favorite CD. Do you like and/or own these CDs as well? If there is one you don't know about, or haven't heard, go to the page for it and listen to some of the song samples to see if you like it.

   c. Read the reviews at the bottom of the Web page for your favorite CD. Do you agree or disagree with them? Readers can rank the "helpfulness" of each review, and the average "helpfulness" is indicated by the number of stars colored orange out of the total of five stars. Do the reviews you agree with the most tend to have the highest number of stars?

3. Many students complain about the low prices they get when they go to sell their used textbooks. Because the Internet lowers transaction costs, it should be making it easier for students to buy and sell textbooks from one another without the use of a bookstore as a middleman.

   a. Visit the Student Book Exchange Web site [http://www.stubex.com]. How much are the textbooks you are using this semester selling for used on this Web site? Do you think you will sell your textbooks on-line or will you sell them back to your local college bookstore? How much more would you have to get for your textbook on-line to be willing to sell it there instead of back to your local student bookstore? What does this say about the value your student bookstore provides?

   b. At the University of Texas there is a Web site devoted to helping students trade used textbooks [http://www.cs.utexas.edu/users/emery/TEXbooks]. How do the resale prices at this Web site compare to the prices at the Student Book Exchange for your textbooks?

MULTIPLE CHOICE

1. In 2000, on-line sales of goods and services to consumers totaled
   a. $5 billion.
   b. $20 billion.
   c. $45 billion.
   d. $100 billion.

2. The Internet produces economic gains because it
   a. lowers transaction costs.
   b. makes markets more competitive.
   c. increases the ability of people to network.
   d. does all of the above.

3. In 1998, on-line trading accounted for approximately what percent of all non-institutional trading in stocks and options?
   a. 7 percent
   b. 37 percent
   c. 67 percent
   d. 97 percent

4. For which of the following products or services does on-line sales account for the largest percentage of total sales?
   a. computer hardware and software
   b. travel
   c. music and videos
   d. automobiles

5. For which of the following products or services does on-line sales account for the smallest percentage of total sales?
   a. computer hardware and software
   b. travel
   c. music and videos
   d. automobiles

6. On-line retail firms may have lower costs than traditional retail firms because
   a. it will often not be necessary for on-line firms to unpack or display products.
   b. there are fewer losses due to shoplifting for on-line retailers.
   c. on-line retailers can use low-cost warehouses rather than expensive stores to house their products.
   d. all of the above.

7. A major drawback with purchasing goods on-line is that
   a. consumers can't touch, taste, smell, or try the goods on before purchasing them.
   b. it is generally more difficult to find specialty products or customized goods.
   c. they generally cost more than goods available at local retail stores because on-line retail firms have to pay higher inventory costs.
   d. most major retailers do not have Internet sites.

8. Which of the following is true regarding job-posting Web sites?
   a. Job-posting Web sites contain more job openings and are easier to search than traditional newspaper help-wanted ads.
   b. Job openings posted on Web sites tend to be more current and updated than ones in traditional print sources, and they are also less costly for the advertiser.
   c. It is generally possible for job seekers to advertise their skills to employers on job-posting Web sites as well as the reverse.
   d. All of the above are true.

9. Which of the following economic benefits result from the use of the Internet in the job search process?
   a. Job seekers will obtain employment more quickly and thus the unemployment rate will be lower.
   b. On-line screening of candidates may contribute to a faster and higher quality of match between workers and employers, which should increase productivity in the economy.
   c. Job turnover will be lower because employed workers generally do not browse employment ads on the Internet.
   d. both a and b, but not c

10. In 1997, approximately what percent of workers provided part or all of their work at home or other locations through the use of the Internet?
    a. 5 percent
    b. 10 percent
    c. 20 percent
    d. 50 percent

11. The use of the Internet to work from home or another location is called
    a. Internetting.
    b. telecommuting.
    c. spiderwebbing.
    d. surfing.

DISCUSSION QUESTIONS

1. Some people claim that Internet sites such as eBay do not create meaningful economic value because people are simply trading their old "junk" for higher prices than it is worth. Evaluate this position from an economic standpoint; do you agree or disagree?

2. What cost advantages do on-line retailers have over traditional retail stores? What are some disadvantages to buying things on-line compared to buying from a traditional retail store?

3. How has the Internet changed the job search process? What potential economic gains are there from the use of the Internet in the labor market?

4. Does the Internet make markets more or less competitive? In what ways has the Internet changed the nature of retail competition?

The Economics of Social Security

TRUE OR FALSE

T F

☐ ☐ 1. The Social Security program in the United States takes the taxes collected from present workers and saves this money for their retirement.

☐ ☐ 2. When a current worker pays Social Security taxes, the majority of that money is directly paid out to current retirees rather than being saved.

☐ ☐ 3. The downward trend in the number of workers per retiree requires that higher Social Security tax rates be used just to maintain a constant level of benefits for retirees.

☐ ☐ 4. In terms of benefits received relative to taxes paid, today's workers will fare much better than workers have in the past.

☐ ☐ 5. For a worker aged 40 or younger, the rate of return they will receive on their Social Security contributions exceeds what could have been earned if they had invested the money personally.

☐ ☐ 6. The share of the population aged 70 or over will continue to rise as the baby boom generation ages.

☐ ☐ 7. Essentially, the surplus of the Social Security system exists only on paper. The federal government used this money to finance current government spending by issuing U.S. Treasury bonds.

☐ ☐ 8. For Social Security to spend its trust fund will require the federal government to either raise taxes or cut other spending to repay the trust fund money it has borrowed.

☐ ☐ 9. Because lower income persons tend to belong to demographic groups with a lower life expectancy, they will on average receive less benefits from Social Security than higher income persons who generally live longer.

☐ ☐ 10. Because of the shorter life expectancy for whites, the Social Security system adversely affects their economic welfare when compared to blacks.

☐ ☐ 11. Most married women who work will receive virtually no additional benefits relative to if they had not worked (and not paid Social Security taxes) at all.

PROBLEMS AND PROJECTS

1. Social Security is a "pay-as-you-go" system, so the money paid out in benefits to current retirees comes from tax collections on current workers. One of the main problems facing Social Security is the declining number of workers per retiree in the United States. Suppose that Social Security wishes to pay benefits of $15,000 per year to each retiree. If there were ten workers per retiree, this would mean each current worker would have to pay, on average, $1,500 in taxes per year to support this level of benefits for each retired person.
   a. In the 1950s, there were approximately 15 workers per retiree. How much would each worker in the 1950s have to pay in taxes each year to support a level of benefits equal to $15,000 per year per retiree?
   b. By 2000, this ratio had fallen such that there were approximately three workers per retiree. How much would each worker in 2000 have to pay in taxes each year to support a level of benefits equal to $15,000 per year per retiree?
   c. By 2030, this ratio will fall to approximately two workers per retiree. How much will each worker in 2030 have to pay in taxes each year to support a level of benefits equal to $15,000 per year per retiree?
   d. As this ratio falls in the future, the alternative to increasing taxes is to cut benefits. If the amount of *taxes* per worker is held constant between 2000 and 2030, by how much will benefits to each retiree have to be reduced?

2. Suppose you have been saving for a new boat by putting cash in an old shoe box in your house. So far you have saved $5,000. Your spouse, however, has been running a "deficit" and has borrowed all of the money and left IOUs (notes promising to repay the money) in the box.
   a. Technically do you have $5,000 saved for your boat?
   b. If you went to buy the boat and needed the money, what would it require your spouse do?
   c. How does this example differ from the Social Security trust fund, which has been "invested" in U.S. Treasury bonds?

3. Workers born between 1945 and 1964 will earn a real rate of return of about 1.8 percent from their Social Security contributions. This same money, if invested in the stock market, would have given approximately a 7 percent rate of return. A frequently used tool in finance is the "rule of 72," which states that the number of years it will take for an investment to double (with compound interest) is equal to 72 divided by the rate of return. With a rate of return of 1.8 percent, this implies that a given amount of money invested would double every 40 years. On the other hand, at a rate of return of 7 percent, the money would double almost every ten years.
   a. Using these values, if you placed $20,000 in a retirement account invested in the stock market at age 25, it would grow to $40,000 by the time you were 35, to $80,000 by the time you were 45, to $160,000 by the time you were 55, and to $320,000 by the time you retired at age 65. How does this compare to the amount you would have at age 65 had you earned the 1.8 percent offered by the Social Security program?
   b. If a worker selected a private retirement plan that was safer than the stock market and so only earned a 3.6 percent rate of return, how much additional money would they have at age sixty-five than at the 1.8 percent rate?
   c. Because Social Security pays current tax revenue out to current recipients ("pay-as-you-go" system), there is no real savings involved in the program. Many economists believe that the structure of the system has lowered the savings rate in our economy, which in turn lowers investment and

economic growth. The system is approximately 72 years old. Suppose that it has lowered our rate of economic growth by 1 percentage point per year. If these numbers were accurate, how much larger would our economy be today if Social Security had not been adopted?

    d. You may have heard that it is much better to save a little bit when you are younger than to save a lot when you are older. Use a 7.2 percent rate of return (so the money doubles every ten years) to figure out the following amounts. If you placed $10,000 in an account when you were 25, how much would you have in the account when you turned 65? How much would you have at age 65 if you had put $15,000 in when you were 25? Suppose you waited until age 35 to put money in an account. How much would you have to deposit at age 35 to have the same amount at age 65 as if you placed $10,000 in when you were 25? if you waited until age 45?

MULTIPLE CHOICE

1. Social Security
   a. collects taxes from current workers and invests this money to repay the workers when they retire.
   b. is based on the same principles as private insurance programs.
   c. is an intergenerational transfer program that takes money from current workers and transfers it to current retirees.
   d. is designed so that administrative decisions can be made independent of political concerns.

2. Which of the following best explains why the Social Security system is expected to face financial difficulties in the near future?
   a. Too much Social Security revenue was invested in the private sector rather than in government bonds.
   b. The federal government does not pay interest on the money it borrows from the Social Security system.
   c. The funds in the Social Security trust fund were invested in high-risk ventures that failed to pay off.
   d. The number of workers paying into the system is expected to decline relative to the number of retirees collecting benefits.

3. When the Social Security system enters its deficit years and the bonds held in the trust funds are drawn down,
   a. overall taxes will be reduced as the trust funds are used to pay benefits to retirees.
   b. the payroll taxes used to finance Social Security benefits can be reduced because the trust funds will be sufficient to pay the retirement benefits of the baby boom generation.
   c. income and other federal taxes will have to be raised (or additional funds will have to be borrowed) in order to redeem the bonds held by the trust fund.
   d. income taxes will have to be reduced in order to keep the revenues and expenditures of the Social Security system in balance.

4. In approximately what year will Social Security outlays begin to exceed revenues?
   a. 2006
   b. 2016
   c. 2050
   d. 3030

5. Which of the following is an issue when considering a shift to a retirement system based, at least partially, on personal savings accounts?
   a. Ensuring that individual investors do not take on too much risk in their investments.
   b. Deciding on what fraction of their payroll tax workers should be permitted to allocate to personal accounts.
   c. Finding a way to continue to pay out Social Security benefits to those who have already paid into the system when workers begin to channel their contributions into personal accounts.
   d. All of the above are issues regarding reforms involving personal savings accounts.

6. (I) Current Social Security retirees typically receive real benefits that are equal to three or four times the amount of their contributions into the system. (II) Current young workers can expect to receive real benefits less than their contributions into the system.
   a. I is true; II is false.
   b. I is false; II is true.
   c. Both I and II are false.
   d. Both I and II are true.

7. The surplus in the Social Security retirement system is currently held in the form of
   a. U.S. Treasury bonds.
   b. gold.
   c. U.S. corporate stock.
   d. cash reserves in major U.S. banks.

8. The Social Security system is currently generating tax revenues that exceed the benefits paid to recipients. This surplus is
   a. being invested in foreign bonds, which will provide Americans with a source of income when the baby boom generation retires.
   b. being invested in government bonds, which will require an increase in general tax revenues when the bonds come due.
   c. separated from other government revenue so politicians will not spend the money during the current period.
   d. being channeled into earmarked private savings accounts.

9. As the baby boom generation retires in the future, Social Security will have to
   a. reduce benefits to retirees.
   b. increase taxes on workers.
   c. borrow money.
   d. Some combination of a, b, and c will be utilized.

10. In 2002, the Social Security payroll tax did not apply to annual income above
    a. $15,900.
    b. $32,900.
    c. $84,900.
    d. $100,900.

11. Based on average life expectancy, which of the following groups would you expect to collect Social Security benefits for the greatest number of years?
    a. college graduates
    b. blacks
    c. persons with AIDS
    d. single males

12. Most married women who choose to work can expect to receive
    a. substantially higher Social Security benefits than if they had not worked and thus not paid into the system.
    b. substantially lower Social Security benefits than if they had not worked and thus not paid into the system.
    c. approximately the same Social Security benefits than if they had not worked and thus not paid into the system.
    d. benefits based on their husbands salary plus 50 percent of their own salary.

13. (I) Because married women are permitted to receive benefits based on either their own earnings or 50 percent of the benefits earned by their spouse, whichever is greater, the payroll tax takes a big chunk of the earnings of many working women without providing any significant additional benefits to them. (II) Because blacks have a shorter life expectancy, they are economically disadvantaged by Social Security relative to whites and Hispanics.
    a. (I) is true; (II) is false.
    b. (I) is false; (II) is true.
    c. Both (I) and (II) are false.
    d. Both (I) and (II) are true.

14. Which of the following countries has not taken steps to privatize its Social Security system?
    a. United States
    b. Mexico
    c. United Kingdom
    d. Chile

DISCUSSION QUESTIONS

1. If given a choice between remaining in the government Social Security program or switching to a private investment fund, which would you choose? What factors would be the most important in your decision?

2. The most popular reform option for Social Security involves using personal savings accounts. What do you see as the major advantages and disadvantages of switching to a system of personal savings accounts?

3. What is the difference between a "fully-funded" system and a "pay-as-you-go" Social Security system? How would the problems facing the Social Security system have been different if the system had been fully funded from the beginning?

4. Discuss how the differing life expectancies by race, gender, and education impact the Social Security benefits received by different groups. In addition, how does the calculation of benefits for married women affect their return from Social Security contributions?

SPECIAL TOPIC 4

The Stock Market: What Does It Do and How Has It Performed?

TRUE OR FALSE

T F

☐ ☐ 1. During the 1980s and 1990s, the real returns from stock market investment have been far worse than the long-term average of 7 percent.

☐ ☐ 2. An investor may lower the risk of his or her portfolio by holding shares of many different firms in unconnected industries.

☐ ☐ 3. While the stock market may vary substantially from day to day, if stocks are held over long periods of time the variation in return is relatively small.

☐ ☐ 4. About one-half of all households in the United States now own stock either directly or through investment in a mutual fund.

☐ ☐ 5. Periods of low inflation and low interest rates will generally be accompanied by a poorly performing stock market.

☐ ☐ 6. The random walk theory of the stock market suggests that current stock prices already reflect the best-known information about the future values of stocks.

☐ ☐ 7. The highest return and lowest risk can generally be earned by an investor who is willing to frequently buy and sell large quantities of individual stocks for quick profit.

☐ ☐ 8. A corporation can tie the compensation of top corporate officers to stock performance through the use of stock options.

☐ ☐ 9. Mutual funds allow small investors with limited investment budgets to obtain lower risk and more diversity in their portfolios than if the investors had to purchase individual stocks.

☐ ☐ 10. When a corporation originally issues stock, this is done in the primary market. The more familiar secondary markets are where investors trade the ownership rights embodied in stocks that were previously issued.

☐ ☐ 11. When a person purchases a stock, they are effectively lending a corporation money, which will be repaid to the stockholder at a future date.

195

PROBLEMS AND PROJECTS

1. Underlying the current price of a firm's stock is the present value of the firm's expected future net earnings or profit. For each of the following, indicate whether the change would result in an increase or decrease in the present value of a firm's future net earnings.

    _____ a. The interest rate increases.

    _____ b. There is an increase in the annual dividend the corporation is expected to pay.

    _____ c. The corporation withholds this year's dividend and uses the money to make an investment that is expected to be extremely profitable in the future.

2. Use the present value formula in the text to compute the current value of each of the following streams of future income.

    a. a payment of $100 one year from now and a payment of $100 two years from now, when the interest rate is 10 percent

    b. a payment of $100 one year from now and a payment of $100 two years from now, when the interest rate is 5 percent

    c. a payment of $150 one year from now and a payment of $50 two years from now, when the interest rate is 10 percent

    d. a payment of $100 one year from now and a payment of $150 two years from now, when the interest rate is 10 percent

    e. a payment of $150 one year from now and a payment of $150 two years from now, when the interest rate is 10 percent

MULTIPLE CHOICE

1. Investors can make their investments in corporate stocks less risky by
    a. purchasing shares of a mutual fund, which holds the stocks of many diverse corporations.
    b. buying stocks and holding them each for only for short periods of time.
    c. investing in firms that are in the same, rather than different, industries.
    d. none of the above.

2. Which of the following would reduce the risk of an investment in the stock market?
    a. investing in a portfolio of diverse firms
    b. holding the investment for a long period of time
    c. both a and b
    d. neither a nor b

3. Historically, when a diverse set of stocks are held over a lengthy time period, stocks have yielded a _____ rate of return and the variation in the rate of return has been _____. (Fill in the blanks.)
    a. low; low
    b. low; high
    c. high; low
    d. high; high

4. (I) The market for new issues of stock is called the primary market. (II) The New York Stock Exchange is an example of a secondary market in which previously issued shares are traded between investors.
   a. I is true; II is false.
   b. I is false; II is true.
   c. Both I and II are true.
   d. Both I and II are false.

5. An increase in interest rates coupled with higher inflation would tend to
   a. result in higher stock prices.
   b. result in lower stock prices.
   c. have a mixed result on stock prices as higher interest rates lower prices, while higher inflation raises prices.
   d. increase stock prices if corporate earnings were falling but decrease stock prices if corporate earnings were rising.

6. Because it is based on the present value of future earnings and dividends, the current price of stock would
   a. decline if interest rates fell.
   b. increase if expected future profits were to increase.
   c. increase if the time until a future dividend payment was suddenly delayed farther into the future.
   d. decrease if next year's expected dividend was larger.

7. A lower and more stable inflation rate results in
   a. a higher tax burden on capital gains.
   b. less uncertainty on investment and other long-term contracts.
   c. lower stock prices.
   d. all of the above.

8. According to the random walk theory, which of the following is true?
   a. Stock prices reflect all available information about factors that affect stock prices.
   b. Future movements of stock prices are unpredictable.
   c. Changes in stock prices are driven by surprise occurrences.
   d. all of the above

9. Which of the following is true?
   a. Lower corporate earnings would tend to cause an increase in stock prices.
   b. If baby boomers begin to withdraw their money from the stock market to pay for their retirement, the stock market should surge upward.
   c. Because the profitability of U.S. corporations underlies the stock market, changes in the wealth and prosperity of foreign nations generally do not affect U.S. stock prices.
   d. If inflation in the U.S. was to rise and become more unstable, stock prices would fall.

10. The real returns from stock market investment over the past 20 years have been
   a. roughly equal to the long-term average of 7 percent.
   b. higher than the long-term average.
   c. lower than the long-term average.
   d. negative in each year except 1991.

11. The current market value of a stock option contract to purchase 1,000 shares of IBM stock at a price of $100 that can be exercised five years from now would
   a. increase if the expected future price of IBM stock rose.

    b.   increase if the expected future price of IBM stock fell.
    c.   decrease if the expected future price of IBM stock rose.
    d.   remain unchanged regardless of the expected future price of IBM stock.

DISCUSSION QUESTIONS

1.   A friend of yours just inherited $100,000 and asks your opinion on the best way to invest the money for her retirement. She wants to earn the highest return possible but also wants to have a relatively low-risk investment. What advice would you give her? Would your advice depend on her current age?

2.   What factors have contributed to the relatively high performance of the stock market over the past 20 years? Based upon what might happen to these same factors in the future, how do you expect the stock market to perform in the near future?

3.   The random walk theory holds that all available information is already reflected in stock prices. Therefore, stock prices change due to new, surprise information. The result is that stock prices move in a random, unpredictable, fashion. What does this theory imply about
    a.   how well a person who picks stocks by throwing darts at the newspaper will do relative to someone who spends hours picking their stocks based upon detailed research?
    b.   how well someone will do who holds on to one portfolio of stocks for many years relative to someone who buys and sells stocks frequently?
    c.   the current price of the stock of XYZ corporation relative to the price of ABC corporation stock if XYZ is expected to earn more profits in the future than ABC?

The Federal Budget and the National Debt

TRUE OR FALSE

T   F

☐ ☐ 1. When the government runs a budget deficit, it increases the national debt.

☐ ☐ 2. Approximately 40 percent of the national debt is held by agencies of the federal government.

☐ ☐ 3. Financing current government expenditures by borrowing pushes the opportunity cost of the resources used onto future generations.

☐ ☐ 4. The larger the stock of physical capital available to future generations, the lower wages they will earn.

☐ ☐ 5. The traditional (or crowding-out) view holds that government borrowing increases interest rates, lowering investment and the future capital stock.

☐ ☐ 6. Privately held government debt is the term used to refer to the debt held by the citizens of foreign nations.

☐ ☐ 7. To understand how government debt influences future generations, its impact on capital formation must be determined.

☐ ☐ 8. According to the new classical view of government deficits, deficit and tax financing of government expenditures have equivalent macroeconomic effects.

☐ ☐ 9. The harm done to future generations by government borrowing is larger under the new classical view than under the traditional (or crowding-out) view.

☐ ☐ 10. As a share of GDP, the United States has a larger debt than any other country in the world.

☐ ☐ 11. The current inclusion of Social Security receipts and expenditures in the budget calculation makes the deficit appear smaller (or the surplus larger) than would otherwise be the case.

PROBLEMS AND PROJECTS

1. Exhibit 1 shows the first six years of annual budget data for the government of Grak, a country that recently gained its independence. Fill in the missing information.

EXHIBIT 1

	TOTAL REVENUE	TOTAL EXPENDITURE	SURPLUS (+) OR DEFICIT (−)	TOTAL DEBT (END OF YEAR)
Year 1	$150	_____	$ 0	$ 0
Year 2	_____	200	−50	50
Year 3	200	180	_____	30
Year 4	240	250	_____	_____
Year 5	250	280	−30	_____
Year 6	260	_____	_____	0

2. Exhibit 2 presents data for the U.S. federal government's receipts (revenue) and outlays (expenditures) for 1997 and 1998. In the exhibit is also shown the reported surplus or deficit for each year.

EXHIBIT 2

	FISCAL YEAR	
	1997	1998
Receipts		
Income Taxes	$919.7	$1,017.3
Social Security Revenue	539.4	571.8
Other Revenue	120.2	132.7
Total Receipts	$1,579.3	$1,721.8
Outlays		
National Defense	$270.5	$268.5
Social Security	365.3	379.2
Other Spending	965.4	1,004.9
Total Outlays	$1,601.2	$1,652.6
Surplus (+) or Deficit (−)	−$21.9	+$69.2
Excluding Social Security		
Total Receipts	_____	_____
Total Outlays	_____	_____
Surplus (+) or Deficit (−)	_____	_____

a. To examine the effect of the Social Security system on the reported figures, calculate total receipts and outlays each *excluding* Social Security and fill in this data in the space provided.

b. With these revised figures for receipts and outlays, calculate the budget surplus or deficit excluding Social Security.

c. How do your results compare to the reported surplus or deficit figures?

MULTIPLE CHOICE

1. Which of the following is a true statement about the federal deficit and the national debt?
    a. Both are "flow" concepts.
    b. The deficit is a "flow" concept and the debt is a "stock" concept.
    c. The deficit is a "stock" concept and the debt is a "flow" concept.
    d. Both are "stock" concepts.

2. The external debt is the portion of the national debt
    a. owned by foreigners.
    b. owned by the public instead of the Fed.
    c. owned by any party other than the Treasury Department.
    d. attributable to off-budget federal programs.

3. Privately held government debt is
    a. the portion of the national debt held by government agencies.
    b. the portion of the national debt that imposes a net interest burden on the federal government.
    c. the portion of the national debt held by foreign citizens.
    d. equal to the federal government debt minus any state and local government surpluses.

4. Domestically financed deficit spending shifts the cost of government spending to future generations by
    a. causing a higher future tax liability with no offsetting gains.
    b. shifting the opportunity cost of the resources used by government onto future generations.
    c. reducing the capital stock, lowering productivity and wages.
    d. all of the above.

5. According to the traditional view of deficit financing, an increase in debt-financed government expenditure
    a. causes interest rates to rise, private investment to fall, net exports to fall, and an inflow of foreign capital.
    b. causes interest rates to rise, private investment to fall, net exports to fall, and an outflow of domestic capital.
    c. causes interest rates to fall, private investment to rise, net exports to increase, and an inflow of foreign capital.
    d. causes interest rates to rise, private investment to fall, net exports to fall, and an outflow of domestic capital.

6. Since 1970, the federal debt has expanded rapidly because
    a. revenues have gone down, while expenditures have gone up.
    b. expenditures have risen faster than revenues.
    c. expenditures have increased slightly, while revenues have remained about the same.
    d. revenues have fallen faster than expenditures.

7. The difference between the federal budget deficit and the national debt is that the
   a. national debt is the cumulative effect of all prior surpluses and deficits.
   b. budget deficit is the cumulative effect of all prior debts and surpluses.
   c. debt includes all outstanding bonds, while the deficit excludes bonds held by government agencies.
   d. There is no difference.

8. Widespread acceptance of the Keynesian theory of fiscal policy
   a. caused most economists to reject the public choice view of budget deficits.
   b. relaxed the political pressure to balance the budget and hence paved the way for the continual budget deficits of recent decades.
   c. was based on the view that continual budget deficits would help stabilize the economy.
   d. increased the pressure for a constitutional amendment mandating that the federal government balance its budget.

The table below shows the revenues and expenditures for a new country during its first three years of existence. Use this data to answer questions 9 through 11.

YEAR	GOVERNMENT REVENUES	GOVERNMENT EXPENDITURES
First	$100	$110
Second	$150	$120
Third	$200	$250

9. In the first year, this country
   a. ran a deficit of $210.
   b. had a surplus of $10.
   c. ran a deficit of $10.
   d. had a surplus of $210.

10. In the second year, this country
    a. ran a surplus of $20.
    b. ran a surplus of $30.
    c. had a deficit of $20.
    d. had a deficit of $30.

11. Which of the following is correct regarding this government?
    a. In the third year, it had a $50 national debt and ran a $30 deficit.
    b. In the third year, it ran a $50 deficit and its national debt after the third year was $60.
    c. In the third year, it ran a $50 surplus and its national debt after the third year was $30.
    d. In the third year, it ran a $50 deficit and its national debt after the third year was $30.

12. Why are the bonds held by the Fed and government agencies excluded from the privately held debt figures?
    a. The U.S. Treasury does not have to pay off these bonds.
    b. These bonds were not issued by the Treasury.
    c. These bonds do not represent a net-interest obligation of the government.
    d. These bonds are not interest-bearing bonds.

13. In 2001 the **privately held** federal debt was approximately what percent of GDP?
    a.   17 percent
    b.   27 percent
    c.   47 percent
    d.   100 percent

14. The idea that a large public debt is "mortgaging the future of our children and grandchildren" is misleading because
    a.   it is the Federal Reserve that will be responsible for making interest payments on the debt.
    b.   future generations will have to bear the opportunity costs of the resources that are used today.
    c.   future generations will not owe any interest obligations on the debt.
    d.   future generations will inherit interest payments along with interest obligations.

15. Deficit spending and a large national debt can have important effects on future generations because they
    a.   allow generations to pass the opportunity costs of government spending onto future generations.
    b.   can significantly impact spending on capital formation.
    c.   pass costs onto future generations with no corresponding benefits.
    d.   will cause the government to go bankrupt

16. Currently, the Social Security trust fund is running a
    a.   deficit, which reduces the apparent size of the budget deficit.
    b.   surplus, which reduces the apparent size of the budget deficit.
    c.   surplus, which increases the apparent size of the budget deficit.
    d.   deficit, which increases the apparent size of the budget deficit.

17. If the revenues and expenditures of the Social Security trust fund were **not** included when calculating the budget deficit, the recalculated deficit would
    a.   be larger.
    b.   be smaller.
    c.   be unchanged.
    d.   actually be a surplus.

DISCUSSION QUESTIONS

1. Do you favor or oppose each of the following proposals for reducing the budget deficit? Why?
    a.   a balanced-budget amendment
    b.   a presidential line-item veto
    c.   an aggregate spending constraint adopted prior to the start of each fiscal year
    d.   inversely linking Congressional salaries to the size of the deficit

2. a.   How is a budget deficit financed by selling bonds to the Fed different from selling the bonds to another government agency?
    b.   How is a budget deficit financed by selling bonds to the Fed or another government agency different from selling the bonds to the public?
    c.   How is a budget deficit financed by selling bonds to a domestic resident different from selling bonds to a resident of a foreign country?

3. Do you think the budget deficit "problem" is overstated? Why or why not?

4. Do you prefer the traditional view of budget deficits or the new classical view? Which is most logically appealing to you? What evidence is there in support of each view?

5. "Debt financing is a way to make future generations pay for today's government spending. We are mortgaging our children's future." What is wrong with the economic thinking reflected in the quotation? What are some of the true costs of the national debt?

Labor Market Policies and the Natural Rate of Unemployment: A Cross-Country Analysis

TRUE OR FALSE

T F

☐ ☐ 1. Unemployment rates in Europe, Canada, and Australia are substantially higher than in the United States and Japan.

☐ ☐ 2. The high rates of unemployment in Europe are due to recessionary economic conditions and high rates of inflation.

☐ ☐ 3. Key differences in unionization, government regulation, and the level of unemployment benefits exist between Europe, Australia, and Canada versus the United States and Japan.

☐ ☐ 4. Countries with the higher rates of unemployment tend to also have a high proportion of employees whose wages are set by collective bargaining agreements.

☐ ☐ 5. The presence of high rates of unionization and collective bargaining allow market-determined wages to better allocate an economy's labor resources.

☐ ☐ 6. Severance pay is a payment that must be made to a worker when he or she is terminated from their employment.

☐ ☐ 7. Regulations requiring companies to pay workers dismissal (or severance) pay generally increase the cost of hiring and firing workers, making capital a more attractive resource for firms.

☐ ☐ 8. The "replacement rate" is the share of previous earnings replaced by unemployment benefits when a worker is unemployed.

☐ ☐ 9. Higher rates of unemployment benefits tend to encourage shorter spells of unemployment and shorter periods of job search among unemployed workers.

☐ ☐ 10. Countries with higher unemployment benefits tend to have higher rates of unemployment.

☐ ☐ 11. Solid labor market reforms, such as those in New Zealand and the United Kingdom, have resulted in lower rates of unemployment.

PROBLEMS AND PROJECTS

1. For each of the following factors, decide whether it would tend to increase (+) or decrease (−) the unemployment rate in the United States.

   _____ a. The U.S. federal government passes a new law forcing employers to pay each employee severance pay equal to two months regular wages when the employee is terminated.

   _____ b. The dollar value of unemployment benefits are reduced from their current levels.

   _____ c. The share of employees whose wages are determined by collective bargaining agreements falls because of declining unionization.

2. Exhibit 1 shows data on the unemployment rates and key indicators of the labor markets in the countries discussed in this application. Use the data to answer the following questions.

EXHIBIT 1

	AUSTRALIA	CANADA	JAPAN	UNITED STATES	FRANCE	GERMANY	ITALY	SPAIN	UNITED KINGDOM
Unemployment Rate (1991–1998)	9.6	10.0	3.0	5.9	11.6	8.0	10.6	20.9	8.7
Percent of employees whose wages are determined by collective bargaining (1995)	80.0	36.0	21.0	18.0	95.0	92.0	82.0	78.0	47.0
Restrictiveness of government dismissal regulations (1995)	1.5	0.6	0.5	0.0	2.1	1.4	11.6	5.2	3.6
Replacement rate of unemployment benefits (1995)	27.0	27.0	10.0	12.0	38.0	26.0	20.0	32.0	18.0

   a. Which two countries have the lowest unemployment rates?
   b. Which two countries have the lowest percent of employees whose wages are determined by collective bargaining agreements?
   c. Which two countries have the lowest government restrictions on dismissal?
   d. Which two countries have the lowest rate of unemployment benefits?
   e. How do your answers to b, c, and d compare with your answer to a?
   f. Which two countries have the highest unemployment rates?
   g. Which two countries have the highest percent of employees whose wages are determined by collective bargaining agreements?
   h. Which two countries have the highest government restrictions on dismissal?
   i. Which two countries have the highest rate of unemployment benefits?
   j. How do your answers to g, h, and i compare with your answer to f? Which factors do you think are most highly related to causing high unemployment rates?

MULTIPLE CHOICE

1. Which of the following countries had the lowest unemployment rate over the 1996 through 2000 period?
   a. Spain
   b. Germany
   c. United States
   d. Italy

2. Which of the following helps explain the higher unemployment rates in Europe than in the United States over the past two decades?
   a. Europe was in recession throughout this period, while the United States was not.
   b. Europe had high and variable inflation, while the United States did not.
   c. Europe was consistently above its natural unemployment rate, so this difference is simply a temporary phenomenon.
   d. None of the above.

3. Which of the following countries had a higher unemployment rate than the United States over the 1996 through 2000 period?
   a. Australia
   b. Germany
   c. France
   d. all of the above

4. In Germany and France, collective bargaining agreements set the wages of approximately _____ percent of employees. (Fill in the blank.)
   a. 10
   b. 20
   c. 30
   d. 90

5. Which of the following countries has the lowest share of employees whose wages are set by collective bargaining?
   a. Australia
   b. Canada
   c. Japan
   d. United States

6. Which of the following countries has the most generous unemployment benefits?
   a. France
   b. United Kingdom
   c. Japan
   d. United States

7. (I) Centralized wage setting will have smaller adverse effects in small countries with labor forces that are quite similar in skill levels. (II) Countries with more centralized wage setting tend to have a lower overall unemployment rate.
   a. Both I and II are true.
   b. Both I and II are false.
   c. I is true; II is false.
   d. I is false; II is true.

8. For which age group of workers do restrictive employee dismissal policies increase the unemployment rate the most?
    a. young workers
    b. middle-aged workers
    c. older workers
    d. The policies impact all workers the same.

9. Countries with higher unemployment rates tend to have _____ centralized wage setting, _____ restrictive employee dismissal policies, and _____ generous unemployment benefits. (Fill in the blanks.)
    a. less; more; more
    b. more; less; less
    c. less; less; less
    d. more; more; more

10. If an unemployed worker previously earned $1,000 per week at his job and is now receiving unemployment benefits of $600, the replacement rate of the unemployment benefits is
    a. 6 percent.
    b. 40 percent.
    c. 60 percent.
    d. 100 percent.

11. Compared to the United States and Japan, the labor markets in Europe, Canada, and Australia have
    a. higher unionization and collective bargaining.
    b. more generous unemployment benefits.
    c. more regulations about hiring and firing workers.
    d. all of the above.

12. Since 1980, the United Kingdom has _____ the generosity of its unemployment benefit program and the unemployment rate has _____. (Fill in the blanks.)
    a. decreased; decreased
    b. increased; increased
    c. increased; decreased
    d. decreased; increased

DISCUSSION QUESTIONS

1. Are the higher rates of unemployment in Europe, Canada, and Australia the result of short-run, temporary factors (such as a recession) or the result of bigger underlying problems that are raising the long-run natural rate of unemployment?

2. How does the generosity of unemployment benefits affect the rate of unemployment? Carefully discuss the linkage between job search time and the rate of unemployment in a country.

3. Why does centralized collective bargaining tend to raise the rate of unemployment? Does it make labor markets better or less able to adjust to changing economic conditions.

4. What is severance pay? How does it affect the cost of hiring new workers? the cost of terminating workers? the unemployment rate among which age groups are most affected by such policies?

5. Summarize the main reasons why Europe, Australia, and Canada have higher rates of unemployment than the United States and Japan. What reforms could these countries adopt to lower their unemployment rates?

The Phillips Curve: Is There a Trade-Off between Inflation and Unemployment?

TRUE OR FALSE

T   F

☐ ☐ 1. As it was originally developed by economist A. W. Phillips, the Phillips curve analysis indicates that higher inflation causes the rate of unemployment to rise.

☐ ☐ 2. The economic record of the 1970s strengthened the faith of economists in the Phillips curve analysis.

☐ ☐ 3. Unemployment will fall below the natural rate when inflation is less than expected.

☐ ☐ 4. The natural rate of unemployment can be defined as the unemployment rate present when inflation is neither rising nor falling.

☐ ☐ 5. The expansionary policies of the 1970s led to higher rates of both inflation and unemployment.

☐ ☐ 6. There is a permanent trade-off between inflation and unemployment. If we can live with higher inflation, we will have lower unemployment.

☐ ☐ 7. When inflation is greater than anticipated, unemployment falls below the natural rate.

☐ ☐ 8. Regarding the impact of expansionary policy on the economy, what matters is not the inflation produced, but how much that inflation differs from what people expected.

☐ ☐ 9. When people overestimate inflation, it means that actual inflation is higher than what was expected.

☐ ☐ 10. Expansionary policies will generally lead to inflation without permanently reducing unemployment below the natural rate.

PROBLEMS AND PROJECTS

1. Exhibit 1 illustrates the macroeconomy of Agar. Agar is currently experiencing stable 2 percent inflation, which people have come to expect. The economy is at full employment at point A. Phillips curve PC_2 represents the Phillips curve when 2 percent inflation is expected, PC_4 when 4 percent inflation is expected, and PC_6 when 6 percent inflation is expected.

   a. Suppose Agar's central bank wished to expand the economy and lower unemployment by increasing the growth rate of the money supply. The increase in the money supply results in inflation rising to 4 percent. If the people of Agar did not anticipate this and kept expecting 2 percent inflation, what would happen to unemployment in Agar? Which point in the diagram represents this outcome?

   b. Now, instead, suppose that the people of Agar correctly anticipated the new 4 percent inflation rate that would result from the expansion of the money

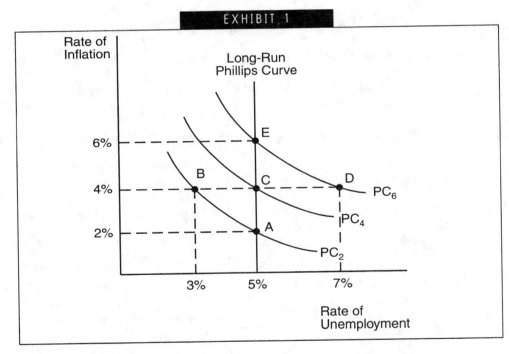

EXHIBIT 1

supply. What would happen to unemployment in Agar? Which point in the diagram represents this outcome?

   c. Finally, suppose instead that the people of Agar overestimated the effect of the monetary expansion and were expecting 6 percent inflation to result from the policy. What would happen to unemployment in Agar? Which point in the diagram represents this outcome?

   d. Using your answers above, decide whether unemployment is either below the natural rate, equal to the natural rate, or above the natural rate in each of the following cases: (1) Inflation is higher than was anticipated; (2) inflation is equal to what is anticipated; and (3) inflation is lower than was anticipated.

2. Exhibit 2 illustrates the macroeconomy of Vega. Vega is currently experiencing a high but stable 6 percent rate of inflation, which people have come to expect. The economy is at full employment at point E. Like in the previous problem, Phillips curve PC_2 represents the Phillips curve when 2 percent inflation is expected, PC_4 when 4 percent inflation is expected, and PC_6 when 6 percent inflation is expected.

   a. Suppose, to combat inflation, Vega's central bank reduces the growth rate of the money supply bringing the rate of inflation down to 4 percent. If the policy was unannounced and the people of Vega did not anticipate the lower rate of inflation (they kept expecting 6 percent inflation), what would hap-

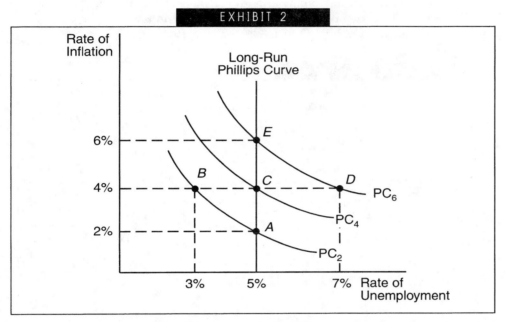

EXHIBIT 2

pen to unemployment in Vega? Which point in the diagram represents this outcome?

   b. Now, instead, suppose that the central bank had clearly announced their policy in advance so that the people of Vega correctly anticipated the new 4 percent inflation rate that would result from the reduced money supply growth. What would happen to unemployment in Vega? Which point in the diagram represents this outcome?

   c. Finally, suppose instead that based upon the announcement, the people of Vega believed that the effect of the policy would be a reduction in inflation down to 2 percent, when in actuality it only falls to 4 percent. What would happen to unemployment in Vega? Which point in the diagram represents this outcome?

   d. Using your answers above, decide whether unemployment is either below the natural rate, equal to the natural rate, or above the natural rate in each of the following cases: (1) Inflation is higher than was anticipated; (2) inflation is equal to what is anticipated; and (3) inflation is lower than was anticipated. How do your answers differ from those to problem 1, part d?

   e. If you were in charge of the central bank in a country with high inflation and wanted to reduce inflation with the least harm to the economy, do you think it is better to clearly announce your policy in advance or to do it secretly and catch people by surprise?

3. Exhibit 3 illustrates the macroeconomy of Lebos. The figure to the left represents the aggregate demand/aggregate supply model, while the figure to the right represents the Phillips curve model of the Lebos economy.

   a. Initially, Lebos is in macroequilibrium at a price level of P_{100} and a level of real GDP equal to the full-employment level at Y_1. In the recent past, Lebos has been experiencing stable prices and people have come to expect zero inflation in the future. Find the points in both diagrams that represent the current state of the economy and label these both point A.

   b. Suppose that the monetary authorities expand the money supply, increasing aggregate demand to AD_2 and real GDP to Y_2, which lowers unemployment to 3 percent. Find the points in both diagrams representing this new situation and label them point B. [Hint: The rate of inflation as the price level rises from an index of 100 to 104 is the percent change or 4 percent.]

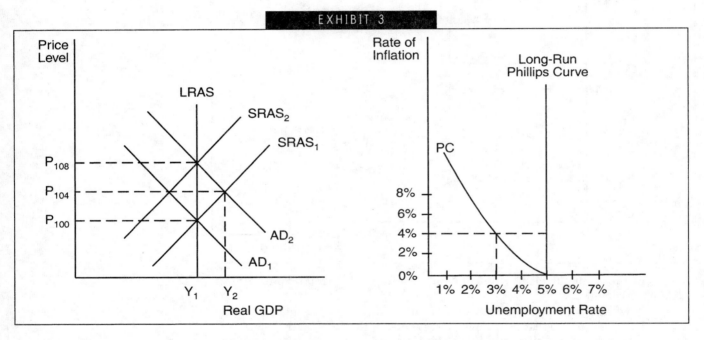

EXHIBIT 3

c. In the long run, the SRAS will react to the demand stimulus by shifting to $SRAS_2$ as the economy adjusts and people begin to expect the now higher rate of inflation. The price level will rise to P_{108} (another four percent increase), and real GDP will fall back to equal to the full-employment level at Y_1. Label the resulting long-run situation in the aggregate demand/aggregate supply diagram at the left by point C.

d. In the other diagram, illustrate how the Phillips curve will shift as the expected rate of inflation rises from zero to four percent. Find the resulting point in the Phillips curve diagram and label it C.

e. Based upon your answers, what has been the long-run effect of this expansionary monetary policy? Has it permanently lowered unemployment?

4. Consider the hypothetical information in Exhibit 4. (For now, ignore the incompleted part of the table and the diagram.)

   a. In the left-hand panel of Exhibit 4, plot the data for 1993–1995 and draw a Phillips curve through the plotted points. Do the same for the 2000–2002 data.

   b. Fill in the missing information in the table in Exhibit 4, and diagram the information in the right-hand panel in the exhibit.

c. Is there a stable trade-off between inflation and unemployment? Between unanticipated inflation and unemployment?
d. What is the economy's natural rate of unemployment?

EXHIBIT 4

YEAR	ACTUAL INFLATION RATE	ACTUAL UNEMPLOYMENT RATE	EXPECTED INFLATION RATE	ACTUAL MINUS EXPECTED INFLATION RATE
1993	3%	5%	3%	_____%
1994	2	8	3	_____
1995	4	4	2	_____
2000	8	5	8	_____
2001	7	8	8	_____
2002	9	4	7	_____

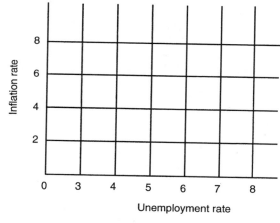
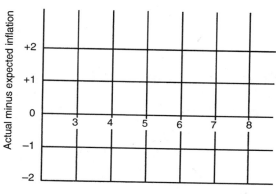

MULTIPLE CHOICE

1. The modern view of the Phillips curve indicates that expansionary macroeconomic policy
   a. will reduce the unemployment rate if policy makers are willing to accept the required rate of inflation.
   b. will reduce the unemployment rate only when people underestimate the inflationary effects of the expansionary policy.
   c. will reduce the unemployment rate only when people overestimate the inflationary effects of the expansionary policy.
   d. will reduce the unemployment rate if people accurately anticipate the inflationary effects of the expansionary policy.

2. Suppose Congress cuts taxes and that the monetary authorities accelerate the annual growth rate of the money supply from 5 to 10 percent. If decision makers overestimate the impact of these policy changes on the price level,
    a. the unemployment rate will rise.
    b. the unemployment rate will fall.
    c. there will be no effect on the unemployment rate.
    d. the unemployment rate will fall if the change in monetary policy dominates but will increase if the change in fiscal policy dominates.

3. Anticipation of an increase in the rate of inflation will
    a. cause the short-run Phillips curve to shift upward (to the right).
    b. cause the short-run Phillips curve to shift downward (to the left).
    c. reduce the long-run normal rate of unemployment.
    d. cause the rate of inflation to slow, other things constant.

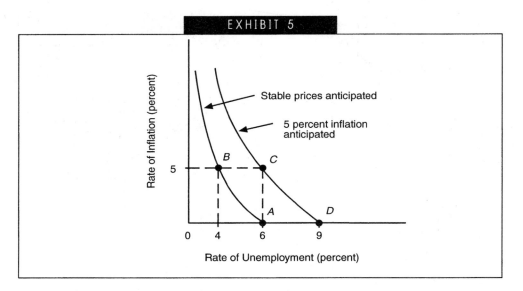

EXHIBIT 5

Use the Phillips curve diagram in Exhibit 4 to answer questions 4 through 6. Assume 6 percent is the natural rate of unemployment.

4. Suppose the economy is initially experiencing stable prices and 6 percent unemployment (point A). If people continue to expect prices to remain stable (zero inflation), but the monetary authorities expand the money supply causing 5 percent inflation, the economy will move to point
    a. A.
    b. B.
    c. C.
    d. D.

5. Continuing with the previous question, in the long run, people will begin to expect the now higher rate of inflation and will adjust their behavior accordingly. This will result in a movement in the long run to point
    a. A.
    b. B.
    c. C.
    d. D.

6. Now return to the original starting point at A, and instead, suppose the original expansion in the money supply had been fully and correctly anticipated by people. The short-run effect of the policy if it were fully anticipated would have been a movement to point
   a. A.
   b. B.
   c. C.
   d. D.

7. The Phillips curve depicts the relationship between
   a. the federal debt and unemployment.
   b. wage rates and aggregate demand.
   c. the equilibrium level of income and the employment rate.
   d. inflation and unemployment.

8. If people anticipate that expansionary macroeconomic policy will lead to a higher (larger increase) price level than actually occurs, the expansionary policy will
   a. temporarily decrease unemployment.
   b. leave unemployment unchanged.
   c. temporarily increase unemployment.
   d. reduce the natural rate of unemployment.

9. During the 1960s, most economists believed macropolicy
   a. that caused inflation would permanently reduce unemployment.
   b. that caused inflation would permanently increase unemployment.
   c. could not be utilized to reduce unemployment.
   d. did not affect inflation.

10. What does a vertical Phillips curve in the long run imply?
    a. In the long run, the rate of unemployment will converge toward zero.
    b. Higher inflation does not permanently reduce the rate of unemployment.
    c. Higher inflation increases the rate of unemployment.
    d. Higher inflation lowers the rate of unemployment.

11. When persons overestimate inflation (when actual inflation is lower than was expected), actual unemployment will
    a. exceed the natural rate of unemployment.
    b. equal the natural rate of unemployment.
    c. fall below the natural rate of unemployment.
    d. decrease if the government is running a budget deficit and increase if a budget surplus is present.

12. Which of the following is true?
    a. When the inflation rate is steady—when it is neither rising nor falling—the actual rate of unemployment will equal the economy's natural rate of unemployment.
    b. When the inflation rate is higher than was anticipated, unemployment will exceed the natural rate.
    c. Demand stimulus policies will lead to inflation without permanently reducing the unemployment rate.
    d. Both *a* and *c* are true; *b* is false.

13. If a shift to a more expansionary monetary policy leads to an unanticipated acceleration in inflation,
    a. actual unemployment will decline in the short run.
    b. the natural rate of unemployment will decline.
    c. the real interest rate will rise in the short run.
    d. the nominal interest rate will fall in the long run.

EXHIBIT 6

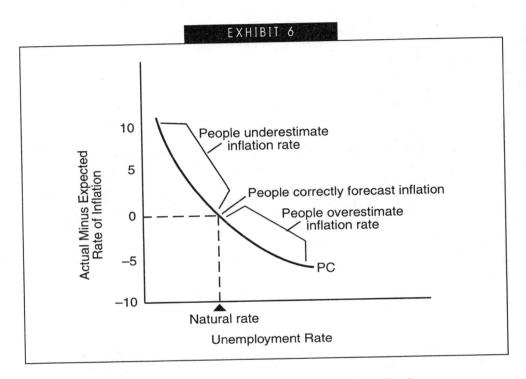

Use the Modern Expectational Phillips curve diagram in Exhibit 6 to answer questions 14 and 15.

14. According to the modern expectational Phillips curve, unemployment will temporarily be above the natural rate of unemployment when
    a. any inflation is present.
    b. people expected inflation to be higher than what actually occurred.
    c. people expected inflation to be lower than what actually occurred.
    d. people correctly anticipated the inflation rate.

15. According to the modern expectational Phillips curve, actual unemployment will generally fall below the natural rate of unemployment if
    a. inflation falls to zero.
    b. inflation exceeds what was anticipated by decision makers.
    c. inflation is les than anticipated by decision makers.
    d. people fully anticipate the inflationary side effects of expansionary macroeconomic policies.

DISCUSSION QUESTIONS

1. Prior to the experience of the 1970s, most economists and policy makers believed that a lower rate of unemployment could be attained if we were willing to live with a higher rate of inflation.

a. Discuss this trade-off within the context of the original Phillips curve.

b. How did the experience of the 1970s change this view?

c. What does modern economic analysis suggest about this relationship? Be sure to address the role of expectations in your answer.

2. For each of the following, (1) discuss how the unemployment rate will change, particularly with respect to the natural rate; (2) show using a Phillips curve diagram; and (3) discuss whether the outcome is sustainable in the long run.

a. Inflation is lower than was expected.

b. Inflation is higher than was expected.

c. Inflation is equal to what was expected.

CHAPTER ONE

TRUE OR FALSE

The following are true: 1, 3, 5, 7, 9, 11, 13, 15

The following are false:

2. The opportunity cost is the value of the next best alternative that you forgo to attend class that day (such as the value of sleeping later, or watching television).

4. The value of a good is subjective; it differs across individuals. Some people like liver, while others hate it.

6. The resources devoted to education have alternative uses, thus public education is not free to society. It is a scarce or economic good.

8. Economizing behavior suggests you will purchase whichever is the *least* expensive.

10. *Ceteris paribus* means everything else is held constant.

12. This is a normative statement because it is an opinion.

14. Association is *not* causation.

PROBLEMS AND PROJECTS

1. a. (6) The lost manufacturing jobs were a secondary effect of the tax.
   b. (3) Incentives matter; as the benefits rise, the incentive to take the time to pick it up does as well. However, one could also relate this to guidepost (4) in a similar manner.
   c. (2) Economizing behavior suggests you will attempt to get the most out of your limited budget.
   d. (5) The deaths are the cost of waiting to acquire more information about the drug.
   e. (7) Value is subjective; the tomato and onion are worth different amounts to the husband and wife. This is what creates the opportunity for trade.
   f. (1) Bill Gates has a very high opportunity cost of his time spent making the wine, thus the wine is very costly to produce.
   g. (8) The test of a theory (and its eventual acceptance) is dependent upon its ability to predict real-world events.
   h. (4) The marginal cost of the trip to the beach is lower from the grandmother's house. However, one could also relate this to guidepost (3) in a similar manner.

2. a. (5) Only information worth the cost of acquiring should be collected.
   b. (6) This would cause secondary effects that would harm the poor. For example, those making less than $10,000 per year would have trouble finding someone who would rent housing to them.
   c. (1) While it becomes free to the student, it is still costly to society in terms of other forgone activities (other things that could have been produced with those resources).
   d. (2) You would prefer the one that is the least expensive.
   e. (3) Incentives matter—they predictably influence behavior, even for criminals. (2) Individuals choose purposefully would also apply.
   f. (4) The tuition and books are expenses that are not relevant for the current decision to attend class—they are not *marginal* costs.
   g. (7) Value is subjective.
   h. (8) If it predicts well, the theory should be considered accurate.

3. a. (3) What is true for one individual is not necessarily true for the group. In fact, probably no one would play if the top prize was winning your $1 back!
   b. (1) The advent and popularity of computers is an event which is affecting the relationship; we have not held all else constant.

c.   (2) Better students tend to ask more questions. This does not imply that asking more questions will *cause* you to be a better student.

4. b.   There is a direct (or positive) relationship.
    c.   1/15 is the slope; the car gets 15 miles per gallon; the slope is 1 divided by miles per gallon.

5. b.   Inversely (or negatively) related.
    d.   Increase by 200 thousand tons (from 600 to 800).
    e.   Decrease by 100 thousand tons (from 800 to 700).

MULTIPLE CHOICE

1. b.   Scarcity and poverty are not the same thing.

2. a.   Economics is about the choices people make because of scarcity.

3. c.   This is the definition of scarcity.

4. d.   Again, this is a definition. Economizing behavior extends to a broad range of human activity.

5. a.   The statement concerns what the government *ought* to do.

6. c.   Choices a and b are violations of guideposts; choice d misunderstands what economists mean by the term scarce.

7. a.   Scarcity prompts competitive behavior regardless of what allocation system is adopted.

8. b.   Someone must incur the cost of producing a scarce good, regardless of who actually consumes it.

9. d.   Goods will always be scarce regardless of whether there is poverty. Scarcity and poverty are not the same.

10. b.   There is as much air freely available from nature as we would like to consume.

11. d.   This is an example of thinking at the margin.

12. c.   All other answers are characteristics of both micro and macro.

13. a.   This is the definition of opportunity cost.

14. d.   In all three, individuals are acting in accord with the incentives.

15. b.   The total cost of 9 gallons plus the car wash is $14.50 (9 × $1.50 = $13.50 for the gas plus $1 for the car wash), while the total for 10 gallons plus the car wash is $15.00 (10 × $1.50 = $15.00 for the gas, and the car wash is free). Thus, buying the extra gallon only adds $0.50 ($15.00 − $14.50) to her total cost.

16. b.   Both positive and normative economics deal with costs, benefits, and theory.

17. c.   This is a subjective opinion.

18 a.   The other answers are counter to the economic way of thinking.

19. c.   This is the only statement that could be tested with data.

20. c.   This is the definition of *ceteris paribus*.

21. b.   This is the definition of utility.

CHAPTER TWO

TRUE OR FALSE

The following are true: 2, 3, 5, 7, 9, 10, 11, 13

The following are false:

1. Opportunity cost is the value of the highest valued alternative forgone as the result of washing your car (say an afternoon at the movies with friends), *not* the undesirable non-money aspects of the choice.

4. As long as trade is voluntary, both parties gain from trade.

6. The value of property is determined by how much it is valued by others not by the owner. Thus, private property rights create an incentive for owners to use their property in ways that are most highly valued by others.

8. Middlemen play an important role in coordinating the economic activities of others. By bringing buyers and sellers together, they help create economic value by providing a service.

12. Capitalism is the use of unregulated market prices and the decentralized decisions of private property owners to allocate resources. Socialism uses the political process and government planning to allocate resources.

14. Increased technology increases a country's productive capacity, and thus shifts the production possibilities curve outward.

PROBLEMS AND PROJECTS

1. a. Because Susan will have to quit her job, she will forgo earning $20,000 per year, or a total of $80,000 over the four years. This is her opportunity cost of attending college and should be added to the table.
   b. Because room and board and transportation are costs that she will have regardless of whether she keeps working or goes to college, they are not relevant in the decision. They are not marginal costs of college because they do not change with her decision. If the drive to the university was longer than to her current job, her transportation expenses might increase and this is relevant, however, we do not have the information to know this here.
   c. For the per-year amounts, adding $20,000 and subtracting transportation ($557) and room and

board ($4,434) yields a new per-year total of $22,743. For four years, this is a total of $90,972 ($22,743 × 4)
   d. Her forgone earnings account for 87.9 percent of her cost of going to college ($20,000 ÷ $22,743).
   e. Because earnings rise with age, the cost of college (the opportunity cost component of forgone earnings) rises with age. College is thus more expensive for older students.

2. a. (1) They are attempting to make the home more attractive to others to increase its market value.
   b. (4) You are held accountable for the damages you cause.
   c. (2) Commonly owned property is not taken care of as well as private property.
   d. (3) Commonly owned property is not conserved as well as private property. It is generally used up much more quickly.
   e. (2) or (3) Cows, pigs, and chicken are privately owned, while whales and elephants are not. Thus, they are better managed and better conserved through breeding to maintain future stocks.
   f. (2) Rented property is given less care because the occupant does not own the property and will not bear the full cost of the reductions in the value of the property from misuse and damage.
   g. (1) The selling value of the automobile is determined by how much others value the car. When Sam does things to his property that are not valued by others, he bears the cost.

3. a. The plane cost $450, the bus $200, so the plane is $250 more than the bus ($450 − $200).
   b. The plane takes 6 hours, the bus 56 hours, so the plane saves 50 hours of Bob's time.
   c. For 50 hours to be worth $250 requires that each hour be valued at $5 per hour ($5 = $250 ÷ 50).
   d. Fly. In fact, if Bob values his time at any rate more than $5 per hour he should fly.

4. b. 4; 3; 1
   c. 10; 8; 2
   d. Larry
   e. Larry's is 1, Sam's is 1/2 (Hint: For Sam, you must divide both sides by two to get this answer from the exhibit which shows that 2 chairs = 1 table.); Sam
   f. If Larry specializes in tables, he produces 4 tables and no chairs. Sam specializes and produces 10 chairs and no tables. Together they have produced 10 chairs and 4 tables, which is one more table *and* one more chair than if they do not specialize.

5. a. 3

b. 2

c. Brazil

d. United States

e. The United States should specialize in producing coffee, Brazil in tobacco, and the two countries should trade. As a result, both countries will be better off.

6. a. yes; yes; no

b. 900 million bushels; 200 million bushels

c. 100 million bushels; 1 bushel of wheat (Hint: 100 corn = 100 wheat, so dividing both sides by 100 gives 1 corn = 1 wheat.)

d. No, point E is unattainable because the country does not have enough resources to simultaneously produce this much of both goods.

7. a. (3)

b. (1)

c. (5)

d. (4)

e. (2)

8. a. (1) C = 3, I = 5; (2) C = 5, I = 3

b. Any of the points on the curve between C = 3, I = 5 to C = 5, I = 3 (the portion that includes C = 4, I = 4).

MULTIPLE CHOICE

1. c. Opportunity cost is the value (or utility) of the highest valued forgone alternative (such as, building more interstate highways).

2. c. The opportunity cost of time spent not working is the wage forgone.

3. a. For saving 20 hours of time to be worth $200 requires that each hour be valued at at least $10 ($10 = $200/20).

4. a. Specialization by comparative advantage raises available output.

5. d. The rational choice is the alternative that is most highly valued.

6. d. Answers *a* through *c* are the three basic questions listed in the text.

7. b. Private property rights allow an owner to gain when they use their property in ways that others value.

8. a. Ken gains $2,000 ($7,000 − $5,000) and Monica gains $1,000 ($8,000 − $7,000).

9. b. When the political process replaces market forces in allocating resources, political influence will be the primary determinant of allocations.

10. a. Specialization and trade result in gains at all levels from individuals to nations.

11. c. Points inside the curve represent output possibilities when resources are not being fully utilized.

12. c. Transaction costs are the costs of searching out and conducting a transaction.

13. a. Middlemen specialize in providing information and arranging trades, so you will not have to.

14. d. These are simply the three characteristics of private property rights given in the text.

15. b. Only if all resources are currently being used does it require taking resources away from the production of another good to expand production in another area.

16. d. All of these items shift the production the possibilities curve outward.

17. b. The alternative to the date is to have $10 worth of other goods and play tennis.

18. d. Point A is efficient because it is on the curve, meaning all resources are employed; point B is inefficient because it is inside the curve, meaning the country is not using all of its resources; while point C is unattainable because the country does not have enough resources to produce this much of both goods.

19. d. The extra cost of driving is = $200 (4 hours × $50 per hour)

20. b. Specialization according to comparative advantage maximizes total output.

21. a. One party of an exchange benefiting does not imply that others lose.

22. c. These are the two important aspects of voluntary exchange given in the text.

23. d. In Lebos, 2F = 2C or equivalently 1F = 1C, while in Slavia 1F = 2C. These numbers are fond by taking the differences in the numbers between rows.

24. c. Because the opportunity cost of producing food is lower in Lebos. Slavia has the comparative advantage in clothing.

CHAPTER THREE

TRUE OR FALSE

The following are true: 1, 2, 3, 5, 7, 8, 9, 13.

The following are false:

4. Relatively inelastic refers to when consumer purchases are not very responsive. The correct answer is relatively *elastic*.

6. A decrease in supply results in a higher price.

10. Lower prices for wine will cause a mvoement along the supply curve (a decrease in quantity supplied), not a shift in the supply curve (a decrease in supply).

11. A change in the cost of production results in a shift in the supply curve, not just a movement along the curve. Thus, it results in a change in supply, not just a change in quantity supplied.

12. The higher lumber prices would cause a decrease in the supply of new housing. This would result in higher prices, but only a reduction in *quantity* demanded, not demand (in other words, the demand curve does not shift).

14. The market is able to coordinate complex economic activity through the use of price signals. This is the "invisible hand."

PROBLEMS AND PROJECTS

1. c. $12
    e. $15
    f. There has been a change (an increase) in demand (a shift to the right of the demand curve), showing that consumers are willing to buy more shoes at all prices.
    g. There has been a change (an increase) in quantity supplied (a movement along the original supply curve) as producers expand output at the higher price.

2. a. 40 cents; 10
    b. 70 cents; 12
    c. Yes, lower bun prices would also cause the demand for hot dogs to increase.

3. a. increase
    b. increase
    c. decrease
    d. increase
    e. increase: increase
    f. increase
    g. increase

4. b. 0; −; +; −
    c. −; 0; −; −
    d. +; 0; +; +
    e. 0; +; −; +

5. a. Quantity will fall by 5 (from 25 to 20) along demand curve D_1.
    b. Quantity will fall by 15 (from 25 to 10) along demand curve D_2.
    c. Demand curve D_2 shows a demand more responsive to price.
    d. Demand curve D_2 is relatively elastic; demand curve D_1 is relatively inelastic.

MULTIPLE CHOICE

1. d. A below-equilibrium price results in an excess of quantity demanded relative to quantity supplied.

2. d. Higher income would increase the demand for automobiles, causing an increase in price.

3. a. Consumer surplus arises when a consumer purchases an item for a price lower than the maximum price they would be willing to pay.

4. a. When cigar prices rise, smokers will substitute cigarettes for cigars.

5. d. If consumers expected the price to fall in the near future, they would hold off their purchases until later, causing the *current* demand to decline.

6. a. Because Budweiser is a substitute for Miller, higher Budweiser prices will cause people to substitute to Miller beer.

7. d. These are true statements of what the height of both the demand and supply curves represent.

8. a. Travelers will substitute bus, train, and air travel for auto travel.

9. b. Lower coffee prices will cause consumers to buy more coffee and, thus, more cream. The demand for cream will increase (shift to the right).

10. b. As price falls toward equilibrium, quantity demanded rises and quantity supplied falls.

11. d. This is the law of supply, which relates to the actions of sellers not buyers.

12. c.   He is the seller, so it is producer surplus of the difference between the actual selling price and the minimum price he would accept. Thus, $2,600 − $2,000 = $600.

13. d.   This is the definition of economic efficiency along with the second part that no activity generating more cost than benefit be undertaken.

14. c.   A shift to the right of the demand curve results in a higher price and a higher quantity.

15. a.   The area below the demand curve and above the price is consumer surplus, while the area above the supply curve and below the price is producer surplus.

16. b.   Lower consumer income has caused a decrease in the demand for new cars. As a result, the price of new cars has fallen, which has caused a reduction in quantity supplied by producers.

17. c.   The tax raises price causing *quantity demanded* (not demand) to fall.

18. c.   Response *a* would lower price; *b* lowers quantity; *d* raises quantity but results in little change in the price.

19. c.   A decrease in supply results in a higher price (which reduces quantity demanded, not demand).

20. a.   Lower cattle feed prices reduce the cost of producing beef, causing an increase in supply and a lower price.

21. a.   The demand for a good is generally more elastic in the long run than in the short run. Purchases will fall by more in the long run as consumers find additional substitutes.

22. b.   The invisible hand shows that markets direct self-interested individuals to pursue activities that are beneficial to society.

23. d.   The existing supply of plywood is now not sufficient to meet the increased demand to rebuild homes, so the price rises due to the higher demand.

24. c.   An increase in demand results in a higher price and a movement upward along the given supply curve. This is an increase in quantity supplied, not an increase in supply.

CHAPTER FOUR

TRUE OR FALSE

The following are true: 1, 4, 5, 9, 10, 12, 13, 15

The following are false:

2. Higher demand for housing would increase (not decrease) the demand for lumber.

3. Interest rates would fall as the market would need to induce more individuals to borrow the excess money now available for loans.

6. A depreciation of the dollar would make U.S. products less expensive to foreigners, causing U.S. exports to increase. However, note that it would make foreign products more expensive to U.S. citizens, causing U.S. imports to fall.

7. A price ceiling that sets the price below equilibrium causes a shortage, not a surplus.

8. Shortages are caused by prices being set below equilibrium.

11. Because market prices will change, the burden of a tax can be shifted to other parties. The actual burden of a tax, in fact, will not depend on whether the tax is legally imposed on the buyer or seller.

14. A proportional tax is one in which everyone pays the same percent of their income in taxes. A tax that took the same dollar amount from everyone would instead be regressive because it would take a smaller percentage of a rich person's income.

PROBLEMS AND PROJECTS

1. a(i). An increase in the supply of accountants (shift to the right of the supply curve) would lower the equilibrium wage and raise equilibrium employment.
   a(ii). This would decrease the demand for accountants, lowering the equilibrium wage and equilibrium employment.
   b(i). This would decrease the demand for loanable funds, lowering the equilibrium interest rate and quantity of loanable funds.
   b(ii). This would increase the supply of loanable funds, causing the interest rate to fall, and the equilibrium quantity to rise.
   c(i). This would increase the demand for the Mexican peso, causing the peso to appreciate (increase in value), and increasing the quantity traded.

c(ii). This would increase the supply of pesos onto the foreign exchange market, causing the peso to depreciate (decrease in value), and increasing the quantity traded.

2. a. $250; 500
   b. fall to 200, rise to 800, a shortage of 600 units of rental housing
   c. it would fall
   d. it would fall
   e. other non-price factors (such as discrimination) would become more important

3. a. $4; 5,000
   b. rise to 7,000; fall to 3,000
   c. a surplus of labor, a situation also known as unemployment
   d. better off as they retain their jobs at a higher wage rate
   e. worse off as they are no longer able to find jobs, not only lowering their current income but also reducing job training opportunities, which will reduce their future employment prospects

4. a. $1.50
   b. $2.25, risen by $.75
   c. $1.25 ($2.25 − $1.00), fallen by $.25 from the pretax level of $1.50
   d. Buyers are now paying $.75 more, while sellers receive $.25 less, so buyers bear the larger burden of the tax.
   e. Tax revenue is $200 ($1 × 200) which is the rectangle from $1.25 to $2.25 in price and 0 to 200 in quantity.
   f. Consumption falls by 50 units (250 − 200), and the deadweight loss is the triangular area to the right of the tax revenue box.
   g. Had the tax been imposed on buyers, the price would have fallen to $1.25. Sellers would receive $1.25 from each sale, but buyers would pay $1.25 plus the tax of $1, or $2.25.
   h. The burden is identical to when the tax is imposed on sellers.

5. a. 20 percent ($10,000 ÷ $50,000)
   b. 15 percent ($15,000 ÷ $100,000)
      10 percent [($15,000 − $10,000) ÷ ($100,000 − $50,000) = ($5,000 ÷ $50,000)]
      90 percent [100 percent − MTR = 100 percent − 10 percent]
      regressive because the ATR falls with income (15 percent now versus 20 percent before)
   c. A regressive tax means the average tax rate (the percent of income paid in taxes) falls with income, not that the dollar amount of tax paid falls.
   d. 20 percent ($20,000 ÷ $100,000)

20 percent [($20,000 − $10,000) ÷ ($100,000 − $50,000) = ($10,000 ÷ $50,000)]

80 percent [100 percent − MTR = 100 percent −20 percent]

proportional because the ATR stays the same (still 20 percent)

e. 35 percent ($35,000 ÷ $100,000)

50 percent [($35,000 − $10,000) ÷ ($100,000 − $50,000) = ($25,000 ÷ $50,000)]

50 percent [100 percent − MTR = 100 percent − 50 percent]

progressive because the ATR rises with income (35 percent now versus 20 percent before)

f. 60 percent ($60,000 ÷ $100,000)

100 percent [($60,000 − $10,000) ÷ ($100,000 − $50,000) = ($50,000 ÷ $50,000)]

0 percent [100 percent − MTR = 100 percent − 100 percent]

progressive because the ATR rises with income (60 percent now versus 20 percent before)

No, she will earn no additional take home pay because taxes take all of her raise.

6. a. $0, 500, 800, 900, 800, 500, 0

c. $3

d. lowering the tax to $3 would increase revenue from $500 to $900.

MULTIPLE CHOICE

1. a. The demand for resources will increase when the demand for the product rises.

2. a. A higher demand for loans will increase the interest rate.

3. a. When the peso appreciates, foreign goods become less expensive to Mexicans (thus Mexican imports will rise), but Mexican goods become more expensive to foreigners (so Mexican exports will fall).

4. a. Markets eliminate shortages by price rising to ration the available gasoline among the consumers desiring it.

5. d. Price floors create a surplus, also known as unemployment in this context.

6. c. This is kind of a trick question. A price ceiling sets a maximum legal price, so when it is set above equilibrium it has no effect on the market. The market will remain in equilibrium as long as the equilibrium price remains less than the legal maximum. A price ceiling set below the equilibrium price creates a shortage, while a price floor (a minimum legal price) set above equilibrium creates a surplus.

7. d. There will be a reduction in the future supply of rental housing.

8. d. All of the other answers are false statements and show the harmful secondary effects of making a market illegal.

9. c. The price is now $.40 higher to consumers than in the absence of the tax, while sellers are receiving $.05 less from each gallon sold (they now receive $1.20 minus the $.45 tax, or $.75).

10. b. The deadweight loss (or excess burden) is the lost gains from trade when market quantity falls.

11. a. A relatively inelastic demand means that most of the tax will be borne by consumers as the sellers pass the tax along to buyers in the form of higher prices.

12. d. A regressive tax requires that the percentage of income paid in taxes falls with income, not the dollar amount of taxes paid.

13. b. The average tax rate is 10 percent at all income levels shown. Since it remains the same as income rises, the tax is proportional.

14. a. The Laffer curve shows that revenue can rise when high tax rates are reduced.

15. a. When tax rates are high, lowering them will increase revenue, but when tax rates are already low, lowering them further will reduce revenue.

16. d. The marginal tax rate is the change in tax liability ($12,000 − $5,000 = $7,000) divided by the change in income ($30,000 − $20,000 = $10,000), so $7,000 ÷ $10,000 = 70 percent.

17. b. The minimum wage is a minimum legal price, thus a price floor. A price ceiling is a maximum legal price (for example, a cap on the maximum professional sports players' salaries).

18. d. Under both, the quantity traded falls as the quantity traded is determined by the lower of quantity demanded or quantity supplied.

19. a. The tax would increase price and lower the amount purchased.

20. b. The tax is borne less heavily by the elastic side of the market and more heavily by the inelastic side of the market.

CHAPTER FIVE

TRUE OR FALSE

The following are true: 1, 2, 3, 5, 6, 8, 9, 11, 12

The following are false:

4. Public goods are goods that have two characteristics: joint-in-consumption and nonexcludable. The government provides both public goods and private goods as do private markets. Mail delivery, for example, is a private good provided by government.

7. Poor information is present in many real-world markets.

10. This is an example of a private market providing a solution to the information problem.

13. The free rider problem happens when nonpaying customers *cannot* be excluded.

14. This is true for private markets, but the public sector breaks this link. Some people get more benefits from government than they pay for in terms of taxes, while others pay more than they receive.

15. There is always an opportunity cost associated with the government use of resources. Scarcity remains as someone must bear the cost of the government-provided goods.

PROBLEMS AND PROJECTS

1. a. yes, yes, public
   b. yes, no, private
   c. no, no, private
   d. no, no, private
   e. yes, yes, public
   f. yes, no, private
   g. no, no, private
   h. yes, no, private

2. a. P = $120; Q = 4,000 tons/year
   b. P = $130; Q = 3,000 tons/year (*Hint:* Add $20 to each price and graph the new supply curve. It will appear parallel to the original supply curve but shifted upward by $20. Find the efficient point at the intersection of the new supply curve and the original demand curve.)
   c. When producers and consumers do not bear the full cost of their actions, they will tend to overproduce (and overconsume) the good relative to what would be efficient.

   d. A tax of $20 per ton would shift the original supply curve upward (see Chapter 4), and it would match the supply curve reflecting the true social cost of production. The resulting private market equilibrium would match economic efficiency.

3. a. P = 50; Q = 26
   b. 32
   c. a subsidy of $24 million to a team locating in the city
   d. No, it will result in a number of teams exceeding the efficient amount.

4. a. efficient, rule 1
   b. inefficient, rule 2
   c. efficient, rule 1
   d. inefficient, rule 2
   e. inefficient, rule 2
   f. efficient, rule 1
   g. inefficient, rule 2
   h. inefficient, rule 2
   i. efficient, rule 1

MULTIPLE CHOICE

1. d. Government mandated price ceilings reduce efficiency.

2. b. The inability of private firms to exclude nonpaying customers creates a free rider problem. The firm will not be able to generate enough revenue to produce the good efficiently.

3. a. Competition over scarce resources is present in both sectors.

4. d. Scarcity implies that opportunity costs are always present when a good is produced either in the private or public sectors.

5. d. Your purchasing a hamburger is not likely to affect other third parties.

6. a. Externalities are costs that you impose on others such as pollution and congestion for which you do not have to pay compensation.

7. a. These are the two rules for efficiency listed in the book.

8. b. National defense is the only one meeting both criterion for a public good.

9. a. When private markets do not fully reflect the social costs, the good or service will be overprovided.

10. c.   All externalities are the result of poorly defined or poorly enforced private property rights.

11. d.   These are the two characteristics of a good that make it a public good.

12. d.   Brand names are one way private markets attempt to overcome information problems.

13. c.   The ability to legally use coercive force is a unique feature of government.

14. c.   The external benefit is the benefit that goes to others in the form of a reduced likelihood of catching the flu.

15. a.   National defense is under the protective function.

16. d.   Markets underprovide goods that generate external benefits and overprovide goods that generate external costs.

17. a.   All externalities are the result of poorly defined or poorly enforced private property rights.

18. b.   Nonexcludability gives individuals an incentive to free ride, that is to consume without paying.

19. d.   These are the primary functions of government listed in the book.

CHAPTER SIX

TRUE OR FALSE

The following are true: 1, 2, 4, 6, 7, 10, 11, 12, 14, 15

The following are false:

3. These are methods legislators use to get the special interest issues for their district passed in the legislature by gaining the votes of other members of the legislature.

5. Information is costly to acquire. With little personal benefit from being informed, voters will generally gather little information and be rationally ignorant.

8. The costs to any one individual are small, so they will not devote resources to fighting it.

9. Only one-sixth of all transfer dollars go to programs that are "means-tested," the rest are directed toward people who qualify based on criteria other than poverty. Transfers are directed to those interest groups with the most political power.

13. It is called logrolling. Pork-barrel legislation is combining many separate special interest issues together on a single bill.

PROBLEMS AND PROJECTS

1. a. A is efficient (benefits of $200 exceed costs of $150); B is inefficient (costs of $120 exceed benefits of $100).
   b. Under the equal tax plan, Adam would vote for proposal A because his benefit is $140 while his tax is only $50. Bob and Cathy would vote against proposal A. So, proposal A would fail to gain a majority and would not pass. Proposal B would pass as both Bob and Cathy would vote in favor of it, while Adam votes against it.
   c. No. The efficient proposal A fails, while the inefficient proposal B passes.
   d. Proposal A would now pass unanimously (all three in favor), while proposal B would now fail unanimously (all three against).
   e. Yes. When taxes are divided in proportion to benefits received, all voters will benefit from an efficient project and will all be opposed to an inefficient project.

2. a. Only the new dam for district C is efficient (the total is positive). The totals for the other two are

negative (the costs outweigh the benefits), so they are inefficient.
   b. In all three cases, only one representative gains from each project. Thus, each would receive one yes vote and two no votes. All three would fail.
   c. You gain $10 from the road in district A and lose only $5 from paying for B's park. You would be better off ($10 − $5 = +$5). Similarly, the representative from B gains $9 from the park and loses only $6 from your road. B would agree to the trade because $9 − $6 = +$3. With both you and B voting for these projects, they would both pass by a majority (2 to 1).
   d. A bill containing all three would give each representative the total that can be found by summing each row. Representative A would value the total bill at +$3 (+ $10 − $5 − $2), B would value it at +$1 (−$6 + $9 − $2) and C at +$2 (−$6 − $5 + $13). All three would vote unanimously in favor of the pork-barrel bill, and it would pass.

3. a. (2); b. (3); c. (1); d. (3); e. (1)

4. a. Types 1 and 3 where the costs and benefits are either both widespread or are both concentrated. This is the most similar to benefits-received principle of taxation.
   b. Type 2
   c. Type 4
   d. Type 2
   e. Type 4
   f. Type 1
   g. Type 2
   h. Type 4
   i. Type 2
   j. Type 3

MULTIPLE CHOICE

1. d. This is the special interest effect described in this chapter.

2. c. Of these groups, the remainder are large and unorganized.

3. a. The effect says politicians count the current more than the future and are best off for reelection purposes giving easy-to-see current benefits financed by uncertain future costs.

4. c. The costs of gathering information are worthwhile only if there are direct personal benefits.

5. b. Only one-sixth of all transfer dollars go to programs that are "means-tested," the rest are directed toward people who qualify based on criteria

other than poverty. Transfers are directed to those interest groups with the most political power.

6. d. The ability of individuals to move from one local area to another effectively creates competition among localities that leads them to be more efficient.

7. a. Remember only voters from your district get to vote for your reelection.

8. d. Public choice theory applies basic economic principles to the individuals involved in the public sector decision-making process.

9. a. Incentives matter—it is the basic postulate of economics and is the key premise economists use in analyzing the behavior of individuals in the public sector.

10. d. A politician must win votes to get elected.

11. a. This is demonstrated in the problem and projects section in problem number 1.

12. c In this way it most closely resembles taxes reflecting benefits received.

13. a. The political process has a bias toward adopting projects with concentrated benefits and widespread costs even when they are unproductive.

14. d. This is the definition of pork-barrel legislation.

15. a. This is the definition of logrolling.

16. d. When the government begins giving away more money, more resources will be devoted by individuals to capture this additional money that is now "up for grabs."

17. d. This is the definition of the shortsightedness effect.

18. b. Just like markets, governments can be inefficient. When special interests gain the upper hand in the political process, government action will retard our welfare.

CHAPTER SEVEN

TRUE OR FALSE

The following are true: 1, 2, 4, 5, 9, 11, 12

The following are false:

3. The motorcycle only counted in the GDP of the year in which it was sold new.

6. Transfers of money are not counted toward GDP to avoid double counting. The money will eventually be counted when it is spent on goods and services by the person who receives it. GDP is a measure of current production, so the money only counts when it is associated with the production of new output.

7. Only the incomes of those living within the boarders of the domestic country are included in GDP. Note, however, this income would be counted in *GNP*.

8. This is a purely financial transaction and does not count toward GDP, which is a measure of production. Note, however, that any commission paid to a stockbroker for their current services would be counted toward GDP.

10. Nominal GDP reflects changes in both output and prices, whereas real GDP reflects changes in output only and is thus a better measure.

PROBLEMS AND PROJECTS

1. a. $9,873
   b. $9,873
   c. Total output can be measured either by adding up all money spent on purchasing output or by adding up all of the income generated by the money spent on the output. All money spent on output eventually flows to someone as income.
   d. $651
   e. Net exports is exports minus imports or $1,103 – $1,467 = –$364
   f. $9,861; 8,744; 7,981

2. a. The real values are found by dividing each nominal wage by the price index for the same year then multiplying by 100. So $0.75 $\times$ (100 $\div$ 29.9) = $2.51, $3.00 $\times$ (100 $\div$ 90.9) = 3.30, and $6.50 $\times$ (100 $\div$ 177.1) = 3.67.
   b. Bob had the highest real wage ($3.67) and thus had the most purchasing power with his hourly wage.

c. $0.75 $\times$ (177.1 $\div$ 29.9) = $4.44 is the real 2001 equivalent of what Bob's grandfather made in 1961.

3. a. $5,986 for nominal GDP; 91.8 for GDP deflator; 7,066 for real GDP.
   b. 5.6 percent for nominal GDP; 2.4 percent for GDP deflator; and –0.5 percent for real GDP.
   c. Inflation fell each year relative to the year before.
   d. Changes in nominal GDP include both the change in prices and the change in output, while real GDP measures only the change in output. So, during a period of inflation, the change in real GDP is smaller than the change in nominal GDP. In fact, a rough approximation for this relationship is percent change in nominal = percent change in prices + percent change in real, which can be seen in the data in the table as being fairly close to the true values.
   e. The negative growth in real GDP shows that the economy was in a recession during 1991. Growth was a positive 3.1 percent in 1992, so the economy was out of the recession and in an expansionary period.

4. a. 0   j. +
   b. +   k. 0
   c. 0   l. +
   d. 0   m. 0
   e. 0   n. +
   f. +   o. +
   g. 0   p. +
   h. 0   q. +
   i. 0

MULTIPLE CHOICE

1. c. Real GDP is what GDP is "really" worth, that is, adjusted for price changes.

2. b. $RealGDP_{00} = NominalGDP_{00} \times (GDPdeflator_{95} \div GDPdeflator_{00}) = \$2,500 \times 1/2 = \$1,250.$

3. d. The sale of the house does not count, but the Realtor's commission does count.

4. b. They measure the cost of purchasing a given bundle of goods in each year.

5. a. See answer 2. Remember, the price index from the same year as the nominal figure goes on the denominator of the fraction, while the year you are converting to goes in the numerator of the fraction.

6. c.   The others represent current production of a final good.

7. b.   Earnings of citizens are counted in GNP; earnings within a country's borders are counted in GDP.

8. b.   Net exports = exports – imports = 40 – 75 = –35.

9. c.   GDP = personal consumption expenditures + gross investment + government consumption and gross investment + net exports = 900 + 200 + 300 – 35 = 1,365.

10. a. GDP does count the value in the year it was produced. GDP is a fairly good measure of current production when that production occurs in legal market exchange.

11. a. Comparisons of dollar values through time are wrong and incorrect unless they have been adjusted for inflation first.

12. b. The percentage change in nominal is approximately equal to the sum of the percentage change in prices plus the percentage change in the real value. Thus, prices increased by approximately 3 – 1 = 2 percent.

13. a. Measured GDP would fall as individuals shifted their economic activity towards leisure, household production, and the underground economy to avoid taxation. All of these activities would still be part of "total economic activity," however.

14. c. GDP counts only production within the domestic borders.

15. b. The commission is payment for a service that is being provided during this year, so it is counted toward GDP.

16. b. The improvements to the car are part of this year's production of goods and services and are thus added toward GDP.

17. b. This is the definition of GDP. Remember, only final goods and only domestically produced goods are counted.

18. b. The value of a price index in its base year is always 100.

19. c. The percentage change in the price index is (107 – 100) ÷ 100 = 7 percent.

20. b. Convert the 1929 value into a 2001 value by 0.65 × (177.1 ÷ 17.1) = $6.73.

21. d. Convert the 1990 value into a 2000 value by 3 × (200 ÷ 100) = $6.

22. a. There are three ways to work this problem. First, you could convert the 2001 value to 2000 dollars with $15,600 × (100 ÷ 103) = $15,145.63, then find the percent by which this exceeds his 2000 salary with (15,145.63 – 15,000) ÷ 15,000 = 0.97 percent, which is roughly 1 percent. Alternatively, you could have converted his 2000 salary into 2001 dollars, then found the percentage change (15,600 – 15,450) ÷ 15,450 = 0.97 percent. Finally, the easiest method is to recall that the percentage change in the real value is equal to the percentage change in the nominal value (15,600 – 15,000) ÷ 15,000 = 4 percent minus the percentage change in the price index (103 – 100) ÷ 100 = 3 percent, so 4 percent – 3 percent = 1 percent.

23. d. Household production is considered nonmarket production because there is no money exchanged for the service. Because of the lack of a recorded transaction *measured,* GDP does not include it even though it is current production.

24. c. Its most useful purpose is to inform us about how current output and production compare to recent periods in the past (i.e., compared to last year).

25. d. All of the statements are true regarding GDP per capita.

CHAPTER EIGHT

TRUE OR FALSE

The following are true: 1, 2, 4, 5, 7, 8, 9, 11, 14.

The following are false:

3. Frictional and structural unemployment are present regardless of the state of the economy. They are due to natural phenomenon in labor markets.

6. The remaining twenty-five persons are either unemployed or are out of the labor force. The unemployment rate would be equal to the number unemployed divided by the labor force.

10. The natural rate is composed of frictional and structural unemployment. Cyclical unemployment is excluded.

12. The inflation rate is the percentage change in the price index, or $(132 - 120) \div 120 = 12 \div 120 = 0.1 = 10$ percent.

13. Inflation is an increase in all prices, including wage rates, so inflation causes consumer prices and worker incomes to rise simultaneously.

15. Actual GDP will exceed potential GDP during an economic boom.

PROBLEMS AND PROJECTS

1. a. *F*; b. *S*; c. *F*; d. *C*; e. *O*; f. *C*; g. *O*; h. *O*

2. a. 150, 80, 60 (The labor force is equal to employed plus unemployed.)
   b. 33.3 percent, 5 percent, 10 percent (The unemployment rate is unemployed divided by labor force.)
   c. Bela has the lowest unemployment rate, Abos the highest.
   d. 75 percent, 80 percent, 60 percent (The labor force participation rate is the labor force divided by population.)
   e. 50 percent, 76 percent, 54 percent (The employment to population ratio is employed divided by population.)
   f. The unemployment rate is measured as a percent of the labor force while the employment rate is measured as a percent of the population.

3. a. *R*; b. *R*; c. *F*; d. *B*

MULTIPLE CHOICE

1. d. Due to the lack of information, it takes time for both employees and employers to find a good match.

2. d. Unemployment is calculated as a percent of the labor force.

3. b. Inflation refers to a *process* of *general* rising prices.

4. a. This is the definition of the natural rate.

5. b. $(165 - 150) \div 150 = 15 \div 150 = 0.1 = 10$ percent

6. b. It is the labor force (which is employed plus unemployed) divided by the population.

7. c. Structural refers to a mismatch of skills with job openings.

8. b. During a recession, output (GDP) will be less than the full employment or potential level.

9. c. On the contrary, long-term contracts become more uncertain because individuals are uncertain what prices will be in the future. Most individuals avoid uncertainty.

10. b. They are a normal part of dynamic labor markets.

11. a. The economy is contracting between the boom and the recession.

12. a. During an expansion, the economy is growing, so output rises and unemployment falls.

13. d. A mismatch of skills is structural unemployment.

14. d. None of the ones listed are classified as unemployed.

15. c. The labor force is the number employed plus the number unemployed, so $120 + 30 = 150$.

16. b. The unemployment rate is the number unemployed divided by the labor force, so $30 \div 150 = 0.2 = 20$ percent.

17. c. The labor force participation rate is the labor force divided by the population, so $150 \div 200 = 0.75 = 75$ percent.

18. b.   The employment/population ratio is the number employed divided by population, so $120 \div 200 = 0.6 = 60$ percent.

19. b.   Both can affect the natural rate of unemployment.

20. b.   In a boom, output is greater than normal. Both *c* and *d* refer to recessions, and *a* is wrong because it is not the natural rate that changes.

21. c.   A key term here is sustainable. The economy's maximum sustainable output rate is the full employment, or potential level. When the economy is operating at that level, the actual unemployment rate will equal the natural rate.

CHAPTER NINE

TRUE OR FALSE

The following are true: 2, 5, 8, 9, 11, 12, 13, 14

The following are false:

1. Being vertical, it shows that real output is the same regardless of the price level in the long run.

3. It is when imports of goods and services are greater than exports.

4. Bond prices will decrease when interest rates rise. They move in opposite directions.

6. It shows the relationship between the aggregate quantity of goods and services demanded and the price level, not the interest rate.

7. The real interest rate equals the money (or nominal) interest rate *minus* inflation, or alternatively, the money interest rate equals the real interest rate plus inflation. It can be written either way by rearranging the terms in the equation.

10. When the dollar appreciates, U.S. goods become more expensive to foreigners (so our exports will fall). On the other hand, foreign goods become less expensive to U.S. citizens (so our imports increase). This is why net exports fall when the dollar appreciates.

15. The aggregate demand curve slopes downward because of the real balance effect, the interest rate effect, and the international substitution effect.

PROBLEMS AND PROJECTS

1. a. For 1991, AD and SRAS should cross to the left of LRAS, for 1997 they should cross at a point equal to LRAS, and for 2000 they should cross to the right of LRAS. The values for LRAS come from the potential GDP column, while the value where AD crosses SRAS comes from the actual GDP column.
   b. 4.9 percent (Remember, the natural rate is the rate present when the economy's real output equals the full-employment or potential level of GDP.)
   c. 1991, 1991, yes, recession
   d. 2000, 2000, yes, boom
   e. 1997, 1997, yes, "at full employment"

2. a. 1.4 percent; 8.8 percent; 6.8 percent; 4.1 percent; rising; falling

b. between 1979 and 1982 a decrease, between 1998 and 2001 an increase

3. a. real GDP = 310; P = 120
   b. The LRAS should be a vertical line at output of $330.
   c. A recession; output is below the full employment level.

4. a. 0; the money amount repaid is the same as the money amount loaned.
   b. 5; negative (while he can buy ten pizzas now with the $100, you will only be able to buy five pizzas one year from now with the $100 he returns to you, so you are losing purchasing power meaning a negative real interest rate)
   c. 0; $200 (the original $100 plus $100 of money interest)
   d. You (the lender) are worse off, you will be able to buy eight pizzas with $200 if the price is $25 versus ten pizzas if the price is $20. Your friend (the borrower) is better off because he is having to repay you less in real terms. The real interest rate has fallen and the nominal interest rate is unchanged (it was fixed in the contract).
   e. You might have agreed to a contract where he repays you $250 (enough to buy ten pizzas). Higher expected inflation would increase the nominal interest rate you agree to so that the real interest rate is unaffected.

5. a. $20; saving = income − taxes − consumption ($100 − $10 − $70)
   b. $15; business borrowing = savings − government borrowing ($20 − $5)
   c. $25; total revenue = taxes from households + business taxes + borrowing ($10 + $10 + $5)
   d. $110; GDP = C + I + G + NX ($70 + $15 + $25 + $0)
   e. $100; total inflow = $110 + $15 = $125 and of this, $10 goes for taxes and $15 is spent on business investment leaving $125 − $10 − $15 = $100
   f. Yes. Household income is primarily based on business income from the sale of goods and services to other households (consumption), other businesses (machines and other investment goods), the government, and foreign economies (net exports—not shown). Real income is primarily dependent on real output.

6. a. Either household net saving must increase or business investment must fall (or some of both happens).
   b. Business investment must fall by an offsetting amount. Savings is required for investment. To have higher investment and higher growth requires a higher level of savings. As a politician, to have higher growth you would want to use

government tax and expenditure policy to encourage households to save more.

MULTIPLE CHOICE

1. b. Note that *d* represents the price variable in the aggregate goods and services market.

2. a. The real interest rate represents the burden in terms of the purchasing power of money.

3. c. Current output takes place where AD = SRAS. Long-run equilibrium (consistent with being at the natural rate of unemployment) occurs when all three curves intersect.

4. a. Bond prices (their current value) falls as interest rates rise.

5. c. The inflationary premium reflects the expected rate of inflation. When it is zero, the two interest rates are the same using the equation.

6. d. This is the price of loanable funds in the loanable funds market.

7. d. In equilibrium, the net inflow of capital offsets the balance of trade (net exports).

8. a. These are the major markets in the circular flow diagram.

9. c. The purchasing power of any given amount of money falls when prices rise.

10. d. These are the three reasons why the AD curve slopes downward.

11. c. Inflation higher than expected will lower the real interest rate, lowering the burden on buyers and lowering the reward to lenders.

12. d. The money interest rate is the real interest rate plus inflation.

13. a. Your real return will be the nominal interest rate minus what part of it is eaten up by inflation (5 percent – 3 percent = 2 percent).

14. a. The expected rate of inflation equals the nominal interest rate minus the real interest rate.

15. b. When borrowing, you want the lowest *real* interest rate (nominal minus inflation).

16. c. It now takes more U.S. dollars to buy an English pound, so the dollar has fallen in value (it has depreciated). The English will find U.S. goods cheaper for them to buy.

17. b. A depreciation makes domestic goods less expensive for foreigners (increasing exports) and it makes foreign goods more expensive to domestic citizens (lowering imports).

18. c. A trade deficit is when imports exceed exports. It would create a positive net inflow of foreign capital to offset the trade deficit.

19. a. A vertical long-run supply curve shows that in the long run, aggregate supply does not depend on the price level. One reason why is stated in the answer.

20. a. A higher price level will increase output in the short run, but not the long run once resource prices have adjusted to the higher price level.

21. c. The short-run aggregate supply curve intersects the long-run aggregate supply curve when the price level is equal to the expected price level. At higher prices, the economy moves up along the short-run aggregate supply curve expanding output past its long-run capacity.

22. a. These are part of the definition of long-run equilibrium.

23. b. When exports are greater than imports, net exports are positive and there is a trade surplus. To offset this there must be an outflow of capital (a negative net capital flow).

24. a. These are the two basic policies the government can use to alter the macroeconomy.

CHAPTER TEN

TRUE OR FALSE

The following are true: 1, 3, 4, 6, 8, 10, 11, 14

The following are false:

2. This would decrease aggregate demand, not short-run aggregate supply.

5. A depreciation of the dollar would increase net exports causing aggregate demand to rise, not fall. The statement would be true if it said an appreciation of the dollar.

7. It would decrease the short-run aggregate supply, not the long-run aggregate supply.

9. Real output would rise, not fall.

12. An economic boom is not sustainable in the long run.

13. There is a large debate among economists as to how rapidly and effectively the self-correcting mechanism works.

PROBLEMS AND PROJECTS

1. a. −, 0, 0, −, −
   b. 0, +, +, −, +
   c. +, 0, 0, +, +
   d. +, −, 0, +, 0 (Expected rate of inflation shifts both AD and SRAS.)
   e. 0, −, 0, +, − (Remember, oil is a resource.)

2. a. Economy a is in a short-run equilibrium but not a long-run equilibrium; the current level of GDP is below the full-employment level; the current rate of unemployment is above the natural rate; the economy is in a recession. Economy b is in both short-run equilibrium and long-run equilibrium; the current level of GDP is equal to the full-employment level; the current rate of unemployment is equal to the natural rate; the economy is neither in a recession nor a boom. Economy c is in a short-run equilibrium but not a long-run equilibrium; the current level of GDP is above the full-employment level; the current rate of unemployment is below the natural rate; the economy is in a boom.
   b. Resource prices will fall, shifting SRAS to the right (an increase in SRAS), restoring full employment at a lower price level (at the point where the AD crosses LRAS in the figure).

   c. Nothing. The economy is currently in a *sustainable* long-run equilibrium that will remain unless the economy is disturbed by another event.
   d. Resource prices will rise, shifting SRAS to the left (a decrease in SRAS), restoring full employment at a higher price level (at the point where the AD crosses LRAS in the figure).

3. a. +, +, − (increase in consumption and investment increases AD)
   b. −, −, + (lower real wealth lowers consumption and decreases AD)
   c. +, +, − (increase in exports, reduction in imports, increase in AD)
   d. +, −, + (reduces SRAS)
   e. −, +, − (increases SRAS)
   f. −, +, 0 (increases LRAS and SRAS)
   g. +, 0, 0 (increases AD *and* decreases SRAS at the same time)
   h. −, −, + (decrease in consumption and investment decreases AD)
   i. −, −, + (lowers exports, thus lowering AD)

4. a. T
   b. T
   c. F (toward *B* because it would increase AD)
   d. T
   e. F (resource prices would rise, not fall)
   f. F (toward *F*, not *J*)
   g. T
   h. T
   i. F (toward *F*, not *J*)
   j. F (increase in SRAS, not a decrease)
   k. F (decrease in AD, not SRAS)
   l. T

MULTIPLE CHOICE

1. b. All of the others will increase AD.

2. b. An increase in the LRAS shifts the SRAS curve with it. Increases are shifts to the right.

3. a. It states that current consumption is based upon permanent or lifetime income.

4. b. During a recession, businesses lower their investment spending, which reduces the real interest rate.

5. c. The market will adjust (i.e., the self-correcting mechanism) to either stimulate or slow the economy to where unemployment equals the natural rate and real GDP equals the full-employment level.

6. c. If we are producing beyond capacity, there is strong demand for resources that places upward pressure on wages and resource prices.

7. c. It would shift SRAS to the right, lowering the price level and increasing real GDP. The actual unemployment rate would fall, and the natural rate does not change.

8. d. The aggregate demand curve shifts to the left, lowering real GDP and increasing unemployment.

9. a. The SRAS curve shifts to the right, real GDP rises, and the price level falls.

10. a. This is the self-correcting mechanism.

11. c. This is a favorable supply shock.

12. d. AD shifts to the right, SRAS to the left, so the price level rises while real GDP stays unchanged.

13. a. Optimism stimulates current investment and consumption.

14. c. This increases our long-run productive capacity, shifting LRAS to the right (an increase). Any shift in LRAS pulls the SRAS with it.

15. b. This would shift AD, not SRAS.

16. a. This would shift LRAS and SRAS, not AD.

17. d. A shift to the left of AD causes all three.

18. b. It would shift SRAS to the left, causing output to fall and prices to rise. Sometimes we interpret these within a more dynamic framework as a reduction in the growth of output and an increase in inflation.

19. a. If it is fully anticipated, decision makers on the AD side will expect the price level to rise as a result of this event. Thus, the higher expected rate of inflation will cause a simultaneous shift to the right of AD, resulting in a higher price level and no change in real GDP.

20. a. It would reduce net exports of the U.S., causing AD to decline.

21. b. An anticipated change is one that people expect.

22. a. It will increase U.S. net exports, increasing AD. This will result in higher real GDP (which means higher employment or lower unemployment). This will only last until the self-correcting mechanism begins acting to move the economy back to the original output level.

23. a. A shift to the right of AD increases the price level.

24. a. Both *b* and *c* shift SRAS, not LRAS, and *d* causes a decrease in LRAS, not an increase.

25. d. This has permanently increased our productive capacity, increasing LRAS. SRAS always shifts along with LRAS.

CHAPTER ELEVEN

TRUE OR FALSE

The following are true: 3, 4, 5, 6, 7, 9, 11, 12, 13

The following are false:

1. In the Keynesian model, an increase in savings is a reduction in consumption, which reduces aggregate expenditure and causes equilibrium income to fall.

2. Keynes believed that inflexible wages and prices prevented the economy from automatically restoring full employment.

8. MPC = the *change* in consumption divided by the change in disposable income.

10. It shows a negative relationship.

PROBLEMS AND PROJECTS

1. a. 2/3
   b. 1/1.5 = 2/3
   c. 0
   d. (4 − 1)/4 = 3/4

2. a. 3; 3; 1; 4
   b. The multipliers would fall because the imports would act as a leakage on the multiplier.

3. a. Round 2: 100; 50
   Round 3: 50; 25
   Round 4: 25; 12.5
   Round 5: 12.5; 6.25
   Subtotal: 387.5; 193.75
   Grand Total: 400; 200

4. a. 400
   b. If output is at 800, the corresponding aggregate expenditures are 600 (see diagram). Firms are producing 200 too much, causing inventories to rise past their planned levels. Firms will cut back production, and the economy will move toward equilibrium.
   c. The slope of the planned aggregate expenditure function is due to the marginal propensity to consume. When income (real GDP) rises by 400, aggregate expenditures rise by 200 due to the increase in consumption. Therefore, the MPC is 200/400 = 1/2.

5. a. Savit (additional income) 12.5; 6.25; 3.13; 1.56; 1.56; 50.0

   Savit (additional consumption) 6.25; 3.13; 1.56; 0.78; 0.78; 25.0
   Spendit (additional income) 22.5; 20.25; 18.23; 16.40; 147.6; 250.0
   Spendit (additional consumption) 20.25; 18.23; 16.40; 14.76; 132.9; 225.0
   b. Spendit. In each round more money is spent, creating a larger expansion of income.
   c. 1/2; 9/10

6. Increase by $20 trillion.

MULTIPLE CHOICE

1. c. The multiplier is used to derive the total end effect of a change in autonomous expenditure.

2. d. Prior to Keynes, economists thought aggregate demand played no important role in the macroeconomy.

3. c. This is the definition of Keynesian equilibrium.

4. b. Remember (from Chapter 8) that the resource costs of production are also incomes.

5. a. The multiplier = $1/(1 − MPC) = 1/(1 − 3/4) = 4$.

6. b. The notion "supply creates its own demand" is Say's Law, which Keynes attacked.

7. b. The others do affect consumption, but this is the *primary* determinant.

8. c. It raises expected profits; others (including *b*) might *lower* investment.

9. d. The higher the MPC, the more income there is to spend in the next round.

10. c. A consumption function relates consumption to income.

11. c. MPC = additional consumption/additional income = 200/300.

12. c. This was one of Keynes' major challenges to classical thinking.

13. b. It may lead to increased borrowing or less saving currently.

14. d. This is a major conclusion of Keynesian economics.

15. b.   The multiplier applies: $(1/(1 - 0.75)) \times (\$12$ million) = \$48 million.

16. c.   A greater MPC raises the multiplier, which equals $1/(1 - MPC)$.

17. a.   Multiplier is 5, so if autonomous spending rises by 80, real output will rise by 400.

18. c.   This is how the Keynesian theory is presented within the AD/AS model.

19. c.   Simultaneously high inflation and unemployment, known as stagflation, occurred during the 1970s and was unable to be explained by the model.

20. d.   Inventories will rise, and production will be reduced because total spending is *less* than total output.

21. d.   Supply (the production of goods and services) produces income for households that is sufficient to purchase all output. Thus, supply creates its own demand, this is Say's Law.

22. b.   Autonomous expenditures are expenditures that do not depend on the level of income.

23. c.   180 consumption + 75 investment + 40 government + (20 − 40) net exports = \$275

24. a.   Spending is not sufficient to purchase all output, so inventories accumulate.

25. d.   When planned expenditures equal output produced.

26. d.   The multiplier is $1/(1 - 3/4) = 4$, so \$25 creates a total of $4 \times \$25 = \$100$.

27. d.   The economy is operating along the vertical portion of the aggregate supply curve, so output cannot increase. Only inflation will occur. The multiplier is only relevant when there exists unemployed resources.

CHAPTER TWELVE

TRUE OR FALSE

The following are true: 2, 4, 5, 6, 8, 9, 10, 11, 13

The following are false:

1. Crowding out is when high interest rates caused by government borrowing reduce private consumption and investment expenditures.

3. The full-employment level of output is fixed by resources and technology. General countercyclical fiscal policy cannot alter this. However, one could argue that this statement is true in that changes in marginal tax rates in the supply-side view are an example of fiscal policy that could increase the economy's long-run level of output.

7. Higher interest rates would tend to decrease private consumption and investment.

12. Fiscal policy is subject to severe timing problems, even more so than monetary policy because of the long decision-making time of Congress.

14. Modern views (new classical and crowding-out) suggest that fiscal policy is much less potent than was thought in Keynesian theory.

PROBLEMS AND PROJECTS

1. a. K
    b. CO
    c. NC
    d. NC
    e. CO
    f. SS
    g. SS
    h. K

2. a. recession
    b. B (SRAS would shift to the right until it crossed AD along LRAS.)
    c. Lower taxes and/or increase government spending; budget deficit
    d. C (AD would shift to the right until it crossed SRAS along LRAS.)
    e. same output, but at a different price level
    f. No, fiscal policy would not be able to shift AD, it would stay where it is.
    g. Nothing, allow the self-correcting mechanism to work.

3. a. boom
    b. Raise taxes and/or decrease government spending; budget surplus
    c. First, SRAS would shift to the left until it crossed AD along LRAS. Then AD would shift to the left, sending the economy into a recession.
    d. This ends up destabilizing the economy rather than helping it.

4. a. +
    b. 0
    c. −
    d. +
    e. +
    f. −
    g. +
    h. + (but by less than in the Keynesian view)
    i. 0

MULTIPLE CHOICE

1. d. Government expenditure and tax policy constitute fiscal policy.

2. d. All of the choices are theoretically possible, although there is controversy about which is most likely.

3. d. A balanced budget means spending equals tax revenue.

4. a. The higher demand for loanable funds increases the real interest rate; private borrowing for consumption and investment fall. With lower investment, there will be a lower capital stock in the future.

5. c. Lower C and I partially offset the higher G in the aggregate demand equation.

6. a. The public will have to pay higher taxes later to repay the debt, so they save accordingly now.

7. d. This is not a government program that changes spending and taxes over the business cycle in accordance with countercyclical fiscal policy.

8. a. If the self-correcting mechanism works rapidly, the economy will have already adjusted by the time fiscal policy hits.

9. a. A surplus is when spending is less than revenue.

10. b. They increase spending automatically (and/or cut taxes) during a recession, sending the budget toward a deficit situation.

11. c. This would reduce AD bringing the economy back toward full employment.

12. a. This would increase AD to move the economy toward full employment.

13. b. Lower interest rates make it less attractive for foreigners to invest in the U.S., so the demand for the U.S. dollar on the foreign exchange market will fall. In fancy terms, there will be a capital outflow and the dollar will depreciate. In turn this will make U.S. goods cheaper to foreigners, increasing our exports, and it will make foreign goods more expensive to U.S. citizens, decreasing our imports. Thus, there will also be an increase in net exports.

14. d. Under the new classical view, fiscal policy has no real effect on AD, the real interest rate, or the economy.

15. d. Again, the new classical view is that fiscal policy has no real effects.

16. c. They carry out countercyclical fiscal policy automatically.

17. d. These are the reasons why supply-siders stress lowering marginal tax rates.

18. c. The long-run growth effects take a while to appear.

19. c. According to the Keynesian view, running a deficit would have expanded the economy.

20. d. Both b and c are part of the modern synthesis view listed in the book, but a is not, it is incorrect.

21. c. Deficits cause higher real interest rates. An appreciation of the dollar will make our goods more expensive relative to foreign goods, causing a reduction in net exports.

22. a. Keynesians think we should use budget deficits and surpluses to stabilize aggregate demand in the economy.

23. c. The crowding-out view says that it will be at least partially offset by reductions in private investment caused by higher interest rates. The new classical view holds that it will have no effect as it is completely offset by reductions in current consumption (because of higher savings in response to the deficit).

24. d. Automatic stabilizers increase spending during recessions and cut it during booms.

CHAPTER THIRTEEN

TRUE OR FALSE

The following are true: 2, 3, 7, 8, 10, 11

The following are false:

1. M2 includes even more (such as time deposits) and thus is a broader definition than M1.

4. Fiat money is money that has neither intrinsic value nor is backed by a commodity; our paper money is an example of fiat money.

5. A bank must keep only a percent of the money deposited on reserve. This percent is given by the required reserve ratio.

6. The bank would have to keep 5 percent, or $5 on reserve. It could use the other $95 to make a loan.

9. The value of money is not fixed but is rather determined by supply and demand. Higher prices, for example, lower the value of money because they lower its purchasing power.

12. This would reduce the money supply, not increase it, because it would discourage loans.

13. This would reduce the money supply because when the Fed sells bonds, it would receive money from the sale, which is then taken out of circulation.

14. Unlike the Fed, the U.S. Treasury does not change the supply of money by buying (retiring) or selling (issuing) bonds. The treasury will use the money collected from selling bonds to finance current government spending, which keeps it in circulation. The Fed would withdraw this money from circulation.

PROBLEMS AND PROJECTS

1. a. M1
   b. M2
   c. neither
   d. M1
   e. neither
   f. M1
   g. neither
   h. M1
   i. M2
   j. neither

2. a. $1 \div 0.20 = 5$

b. It should buy (sometimes we say purchase) bonds.

c. $10 billion (with a multiplier of 5, $10 billion would create $50 billion)

d. 10; buy; $5 billion; the multiplier rises and the amount to buy falls

3. a. $-$; 0
   b. 0; +
   c. +; + (note that the Fed is *buying* these bonds)
   d. 0; 0
   e. $-$; 0
   f. +; 0
   g. 0; $-$

4. a. increase the money supply
   b. Round 1: 10,000; 2,000; 8,000
      Round 2: 8,000; 1,600; 6,400
      Round 3: 6,400; 1,280; 5,120
      Round 4: 5,120; 1,024; 4,096
      Total: 50,000; 10,000; 40,000

MULTIPLE CHOICE

1. c. Open market operations refer to the Fed buying and selling U.S. government securities, such as treasury bonds, treasury bills (T-bills), treasury notes, etc. To increase the money supply, it must buy government securities. If you are having trouble with this, just remember that when the Fed sells you a bond, they *take* your money so there is less money supply, and when they buy your bond, they *give* you new, freshly printed money.

2. a. The multiplier is $1 \div 0.05 = 20$; so $20 \times \$10$ million = $200 million. If the Fed buys bonds, it will increase the money supply, not decrease it.

3. a. The Fed has this responsibility.

4. d. See the text discussion on ambiguities in measuring the money supply.

5. c. $100 is 20 percent of $500 (figured as $100 ÷ $500).

6. c. Fiat money is money with no backing or intrinsic value.

7. b. It is the most flexible, hence, the most often used.

8. a. Do not confuse this with the discount rate. The federal funds rate is a market-determined interest rate that banks charge each other for loans. The

discount rate is set by the Fed and is the rate the Fed charges banks for loans.

9. b. These are the three functions of money listed in the book.

10. a. Choices c and d reduce the money supply; b is not under the control of the Fed who sets only monetary policy, not fiscal policy.

11. b. Potential deposit multiplier = 1 ÷ required reserve ratio.

12. d. Excess reserves and cash held out of the system lower the amount of loans made and thus lower the expansion generated.

13. d. To decrease the money supply, the discount rate should be increased, the reserve ratio increased, and the Fed should sell bonds.

14. c. Answer *a* is the medium of exchange function of money, while *d* is the store of value function of money.

15. d. The value of money is what it can buy. If prices rise, the same amount of money will buy fewer goods.

16. d. Credit cards do not represent an asset. They are not part of the money supply.

17. d. All of the ones listed are in M2.

18. a. Excess reserves are money the bank has on reserve over and above the amount it needs to meet its reserve requirement. This money can be loaned out if the bank wishes to do so.

19. b. The multiplier is 1 ÷ 0.20 = 5.

20. d. The Fed selling bonds lowers the money supply but does not affect the national debt.

21. c. When the U.S. Treasury issues and sells new bonds, it increases the national debt but does not affect the money supply.

22. c. Savings deposits are in M2 but not in M1.

23. b. Having a central bank that is insulated from political pressures is what is meant by independent. Evidence shows that countries with independent central banks have better economic performance, particularly with respect to inflation.

CHAPTER FOURTEEN

TRUE OR FALSE

The following are true: 1, 2, 3, 4, 8, 12, 13

The following are false:

5. The quantity theory of money states that it will cause a proportional change in prices (P) and leave output (Y) unchanged.

6. A vertical supply curve indicates that the quantity of money supplied does *not* depend on the interest rate but is set by the Fed.

7. Both anticipated and unanticipated policy have the same effect in the long run, but they have different effects on the economy in the short run.

9. While the decision lag is shorter for the Fed, there are still "long and variable" lags in the time it takes for changes in the money supply to have an impact on the economy.

10. It would be 2 percent. The growth rate version of the equation of exchange states that $\%\Delta M + \%\Delta V = \%\Delta P + \%\Delta Y$, where $\%\Delta$ stands for "percent change." So, the inflation rate [$\%\Delta P$] may be found as $\%\Delta P = \%\Delta M + \%\Delta V - \%\Delta Y$, here this is 2 percent = 5 percent + 0 percent – 3 percent.

11. An expansion in the money supply is "expansionary monetary policy," while a reduction in the money supply is "restrictive (or contractionary) monetary policy."

14. The short run impacts will differ (unanticipated changes real output, but anticipated only changes prices). The long-run impacts will be the same (only change prices).

PROBLEMS AND PROJECTS

1. All three of the remaining blocks have the same answers. The real interest rate will remain unchanged, real GDP will remain unchanged, unemployment will remain unchanged, and the price level (inflation) will increase in all three cases. The only time monetary policy impacts "real" variables in the economy is when it is unanticipated, and then only in the short run.

2. a. II; 2 (V = nominal GDP ÷ M, so 9,963 ÷ 4,945 = 2.01)
   b. I; 30 (Y = M × V ÷ P, so 600 × 5 ÷ 100 = 30)

c. III; 4 percent [$\%\Delta P = \%\Delta M + \%\Delta V - \%\Delta Y$, so 7 percent + 0 percent – 3 percent = 4 percent, note that when velocity is constant, III may be simplified to $\%\Delta P = \%\Delta M - \%\Delta Y$]

d. III; –2 percent (This is "deflation," a falling price level, of 2 percent, see derivation in part *c*.)

e. III; 3 percent (From the derivation in part *c* above, to get $\%\Delta P = 0$ with constant velocity requires $\%\Delta M = \%\Delta Y$. This is known as the constant growth rate rule favored by the monetarists.)

f. I; 16 (This is the strict quantity theory of money. With constant output and velocity, doubling the money supply doubles the price level.)

g. I; price level rises to 6 in the short run and to 10 in the long run.

3. a. S_1 shifts left (decreases) in both, causing the interest rates to rise.
   b. Higher interest rates reduce consumption and investment, so AD shifts to the left (a decrease in AD). Real GDP falls and the price level falls.

4. a. higher real GDP and a higher price level
   b. No, eventually SRAS will shift to the left restoring output to the full-employment level (Y_f) and moving the economy to an even higher price level.
   c. The economy would have moved directly to the long-run outcome shown by part b, with a higher price level and output remaining at the full-employment level (Y_f). This would happen because both SRAS and AD would immediately shift in the short run.

5. a. An anticipated decrease causes a simultaneous decrease in AD and increase in SRAS. Real GDP is unchanged and the price level falls
   b. In the short run, AD would decrease (shift to the left). Real GDP would fall and the price level would fall as well. In the long run, SRAS will shift to the right moving the economy back to an output level of Y_f with a higher price level.
   c. Both achieve a lower price level in the long run, but the unanticipated case causes a short-run recession to get there, while the anticipated case does not. The Fed should announce this policy to avoid the recession.

MULTIPLE CHOICE

1. b. The nominal (money) interest rate represents the price (in terms of opportunity cost) of holding money. A lower price would increase the quantity demanded.

2. c. Using the growth rate version of the equation of exchange, if velocity is constant, inflation will be zero when the growth rate of the money supply equals the growth rate of output.

3. b. Under the strict quantity theory of money, whatever happens to the money supply happens to prices as well (in other words, a "proportional change in prices").

4. b. You could use the formula, or just remember that under the quantity theory, if money supply doubles (from $200 to $400 million), prices will double as well (from 120 to 240).

5. b. MV = nominal GDP, so V = nominal GDP ÷ money supply. Do not mix up real GDP, which is Y, with nominal GDP, which is PY.

6. b. % ΔP = % ΔM − % ΔY when velocity is constant, so 9 percent − 3 percent = 6 percent.

7. a. Answers *b* and *c* are stated in reverse (that is, they would be true if the question read "unexpectedly *decreases* the money supply").

8. b. It would lower the supply of loanable funds, increasing the real interest rate and thus lowering consumption, investment, and aggregate demand and output as well.

9. a. In the short run ("initially"), if it is unanticipated, it will have its impact on real output. The major impact on prices will come in the long run.

10. c. If it is anticipated, it has no effect on anything "real" (such as real GDP, real interest rates, or employment/unemployment); it only impacts prices.

11. c. Both are true statements of the impact of monetary policy.

12. d. Interest rates will fall as the supply of loanable funds rises, and the lower interest rate will stimulate consumption and investment spending.

13. a. Once the economy returns to long-run equilibrium, prices are higher and output returns to full employment.

14. a. This is a definition. In the equation, M stands for money supply, V for the velocity of money, P for the price level, and Y for real GDP. Together, PY stands for nominal GDP.

15. c. Demand curves show the relationship between the price and quantity demanded.

16. c. from the equation: 3 percent − 5 percent = −2 percent

17. c. This is the quantity theory of money.

18. c. This is the primary belief of monetarists.

19. d. Announcing the policy will make it anticipated so that it affects only prices and not real output. Otherwise, the money supply cut would reduce real GDP in the short run.

20. c. AD will increase moving to this point.

21. d. In the long run, SRAS will decrease moving toward this point.

22. d. If anticipated, AD increases and SRAS decreases simultaneously.

23. d. Everything happens in the short run when it is anticipated; there are no further movements.

24. d. Comparing the answers above, as well as your prior understanding of this issue, leads to the conclusion that all are true.

CHAPTER FIFTEEN

TRUE OR FALSE

The following are true: 1, 2, 3, 6, 7, 8, 10, 11, 12, 13, 14

The following are false:

4. This is a nonactivist policy because it relies on a rule rather than discretion.

5. Forecasting models are wrong on many occasions. A famous quote is that the index of leading indicators has accurately forecast thirteen of the last eight recessions (in other words, it forecast seven recessions that did not occur).

9. This is a nonactivist policy because it relies on a rule rather than discretion.

PROBLEMS AND PROJECTS

1. a. 10 percent, the same as last year
    b. 3 percent (13 percent nominal minus 10 percent inflation)
    c. 9 percent (13 percent nominal minus 4 percent inflation)
    d. Unhappy; she is paying a real interest rate three times higher than she expected.

2. a. SRAS would shift to $SRAS_2$ and the economy would move to point B.
    b. expansionary fiscal policy (tax cuts and/or spending increases) and expansionary monetary policy (increasing the money supply)
    c. AD would shift to AD_2 and the economy would move to point C.
    d. SRAS would have already shifted to $SRAS_2$, moving the economy to point B, so the economy would then experience AD moving to AD_2, resulting in point D.

3. a. No. After moving to point B, SRAS would shift to the left bringing the economy back to Y_f at a higher price level.
    b. Yes, but the only way the economy could be moved to point B on a sustainable basis would be if the LRAS curve shifted right. Increased productivity or economic organization (among other things) could permanently increase our productive capacity, shifting the LRAS to the right.

4. a. B
    b. C
    c. C

d. C

e. This statement is true. In the long run, both result in point C. The only difference is whether we move directly there in the short run (rational expectations) or whether we move to point B in the short run first (adaptive expectations).

5. a. B
    b. NA
    c. A
    d. NA
    e. B
    f. NA
    g. B
    h. NA

MULTIPLE CHOICE

1. c. Activists want to actively use monetary and fiscal policy to offset the effects of the business cycle.

2. d. All three are discretionary expansionary policy actions.

3. d. Nonactivists emphasize that discretionary actions do more harm than good.

4. b. It is a composite index used to forecast the future direction of the economy.

5. d. It might not have been a very "Great Depression" had it not been for the perverse monetary and fiscal policies followed during that time.

6. b. This is the rational expectations view and is reflected in the policy ineffectiveness theorem.

7. c. Problems with lags, and issues of potency seriously bring into question the effectiveness of fiscal policy.

8. d. See question 5.

9. a. Activists want to use fiscal and monetary policy to stabilize the economy, nonactivists do not.

10. b. This is how even good intentioned policy can end up making the economy worse.

11. d. This is the time used up in the decision-making process. It is much shorter for monetary than fiscal policy.

12. c. A vote-seeking politician would want the positive short-run effects to be present on the day of the election.

13. a. Adaptive expectations is that the inflation rate will be whatever it has been in the recent past (period 2).

14. c. This is a definition.

15. a. If people can correctly anticipate policy, it becomes ineffective even in the short run.

16. a. In the short run, AD will fall, lowering output. In the long run, SRAS will adjust and output will return to its old level, but inflation (the price level) will be lower.

17. b. Both SRAS and AD shift downward, so output remains unchanged and the price level (inflation) falls.

18. b. This is the policy ineffectiveness theorem.

19. a. These are some of their major positions.

20. c. A monetary rule does not allow any discretionary actions that have the *potential* (and there is the main debate) to help the economy.

21. c. Under adaptive expectations, people base it on whatever it was in the recent past.

22. c. Under rational expectations, people use all available information when forming their expectations.

23. d. All are true and this summarizes the graphical representation of both viewpoints.

CHAPTER SIXTEEN

TRUE OR FALSE

The following are true: 1, 3, 4, 7, 8, 10, 11, 12, 13, 14

The following are false:

2. It will rise. The growth in per capita GDP is roughly equal to the growth rate of GDP minus the growth rate of population.

5. Over time, small differences in growth rates lead to large differences in size.

6. Some have growth rates far exceeding developed nations, while others lag far behind.

9. These policies will reduce the rate of economic growth.

PROBLEMS AND PROJECTS

1. a.   B
    b.   C
    c.   F
    d.   H
    e.   J

2. a. $104,700 ($50,000 × 2.094); $219,200 ($50,000 × 4.384)
    b. $28,600 more ($133,300 instead of $104,700); $136,150 more ($355,350 instead of $219,200)
    c. $22,650 less ($82,050 instead of $104,700); $84,600 less ($134,600 instead of $219,200)
    d. $14,340 more ($15,151.50 versus $811.50). So after one hundred years, Country 1's economy is now almost nineteen times larger than Country 2's.
    e.   twenty-five years (At which time the LDC would have obtained an income level of $33,860 relative to the developed country's $32,820.)

MULTIPLE CHOICE

1. c.   High tax rates discourage productivity, investment, and work effort, reducing growth.

2. a.   The growth in per capita GDP is roughly equal to the growth rate of GDP minus the growth rate of population.

3. d.   The others would retard economic growth.

4. a.   The others would retard economic growth.

5. d.   These are several of the important reasons why open capital markets increase growth.

6. d.   These essential functions of government enhance growth.

7. b.   When government gets too large, it begins to lower growth.

8. d.   Economic freedom as measured in the book is associated with higher levels of income and also higher rates of growth.

9. d.   As a result of all of these factors, Ireland's rate of economic growth has increased substantially.

10. a.   A large government that goes beyond certain core functions generally reduces economic growth.

11. b.   Free trade promotes growth because it allows for specialization by comparative advantage.

12. d.   These policies are consistent with the listed keys to economic growth. The others would lower growth.

13. c.   This would lower economic growth (it is against having open and free capital markets).

14. b.   This is found by the growth rate rule given in the textbook. You can approximate this with the following: years = 70 ÷ growth rate.

15. d.   There is no clear pattern for all LDCs.

16. a.   Small government and low tax rates increase growth.

17. d.   Stable prices mean low inflation, and an important part of this is keeping the variation of inflation from year-to-year small and predictable.

CHAPTER SEVENTEEN

TRUE OR FALSE

The following are true: 3, 4, 5, 6, 8, 11, 12, 13

The following are false:

1. Both countries benefit from free trade.

2. Specific domestic producers of goods that are imported may "lose," and domestic consumers of goods that are exported may "lose," but in both cases the gains of the "winners" outweigh the losses to the "losers."

7. Even countries with an absolute advantage in all goods can gain by trading for goods in which they have a comparative disadvantage.

9. Jobs would be lost in the industries that were protected by the tariffs, but they would be more than offset by gains in other industries.

10. NAFTA has resulted in trade expansions that have benefited all three countries involved.

PROBLEMS AND PROJECTS

1. a. For Lebos, a line from 160 food and zero clothing (point E) in the upper left to zero food and 160 clothing (point A) in the lower right. For Egap, a line from 40 food and zero clothing (point E) in the upper left to zero food and 120 clothing (point A) in the lower right.
    b. D; 40 food; 40 clothing; 40F = 40C
    c. 10 food; 30 clothing; 10F = 30C
    d. Lebos: 1F = 1C; Egap: 1F = 3C; Lebos gives up the least clothing to produce one food and thus has a comparative advantage in food. In terms of one clothing, Lebos: 1C = 1F, Egap: 1C = 1/3F, so Egap has the lowest opportunity cost of producing clothing.
    e. 40 clothing (point D) for Lebos; zero clothing (point E) for Egap
    f. 160; 40; 80
    g. Compared with part e, Lebos has the same amount of food (120) but has more clothing (80 versus 40). Lebos is better off.
    h. From part g, Egap has sent Lebos 80 clothing in exchange for 40 food. So, Egap now has 40 clothing left (it produced 120 and traded away 80) and 40 food. Compared with e, Egap has the same amount of food (40) but more clothing (40 versus zero). Egap is better off.

2. a. $1,500 and 8,000 (where Arcadia's quantity demanded equals Arcadia's quantity supplied)
    b. Total quantity demanded: 6,000; 8,000; 10,000; 12,000; 14,000; 16,000. New equilibrium $2,000 and 10,000 (where total quantity demanded equals Arcadia's quantity supplied).
    c. Price has risen from $1,500 to $2,000; quantity produced has risen from 8,000 to 10,000; quantity of other goods must have fallen (moved along production possibilities curve).
    d. At the new price of $2,000, Arcadians demand only 7,000 compared with 8,000 prior to trade and the higher price. With trade, Arcadia exports 3,000 computers (it produces 10,000 and domestic consumers buy 7,000 of them leaving 3,000 for exports).
    e. hurts domestic citizens (higher price and lower consumption) and helps domestic producers (higher price and higher sales)

3. a. $700; 70; 70
    b. $500 is the new price; 90 is the quantity demanded (consumed); 90 is the total quantity supplied; 50 is supplied by domestic suppliers (found along the domestic supply curve); 40 is imported (the difference between total supply of 90 and domestic supply of 50).
    c. Price rises to $600; quantity demanded (and consumed) falls to 80; domestic production expands to 60; amount imported falls to 20.
    d. Everything would be identical with a 20-unit quota as it is with the tariff.

4. a. U.S.; U.S.; South Korea; U.S.
    b. South Korea
    c. U.S. production: −8; +80
       U.S. trade: +10; −50
       U.S. consumption: +2; +30
       S. Korea production: +16; −32
       S. Korea trade: −10; +50
       S. Korea consumption: +6; +18

MULTIPLE CHOICE

1. d. Restrictions on imports create benefits only to domestic producers in the import competing industries. Consumers and producers in export industries are made worse off. The losses outweigh the gains and the country is worse off.

2. c. Buy goods abroad when they are cheaper than alternative domestic products.

3. b. It will fall by 4 units from a total of 8 to a total of 4.

4. c. From above 2 food equals 4 clothing. Dividing both sides by 2 gives 1 food equals 2 clothing.

5. b. Slavia has the comparative advantage in food, Italia in clothing. Remember that low opportunity cost producer and comparative advantage mean the same thing.

6. d. Slavia specializes in food, Italia in clothing, and they trade.

7. b. With free trade, all nations that are involved benefit.

8. a. This is a restatement of the law of comparative advantage.

9. d. They are both levied on imports. A tariff is a tax, while a quota is a limit on the quantity.

10. a. With less foreign competition, the price to domestic consumers will rise, which allows the relatively inefficient U.S. firms to stay in business with their higher costs.

11. a. There is a link between a nation's imports and its exports. Imports give foreign countries the money to buy domestic exports. Lower imports mean lower exports.

12. b. They are harmful by wasting our resources in areas where we are relatively unproductive, thus lowering our standard of living. Consumers pay higher prices for goods (and thus cannot afford as many goods to consume), and only domestic producers in the specific industries gain (producers in export industries suffer).

13. c. Many tariffs originally put in place to protect infant industries remain in place forever. It is always politically costly to remove the tariff because of the special interest groups involved.

14. b. The evidence shows that these bad economic policies lead to lower levels of income and economic growth in the long run.

15. b. Consumers will benefit from lower prices; our resources will be redirected to more efficient uses.

16. a. Increased competition lowers price; increased imports generate higher exports.

17. d. Domestic producers would want to stop this action even though domestic consumers would gain substantially. Dumping is selling goods at prices below cost.

18. c. Foreign competition lowers price, which lowers domestic quantity supplied.

19. b. Higher demand raises price, lowering domestic consumption but increasing domestic production (the difference is exported).

20. c. This is the *basic* lesson of comparative advantage.

21. c. The other three are listed in the textbook as "partially valid" reasons for adopting trade restrictions. Their validity is hotly debated.

22. a. Use a horizontal line at P_W to find the answers. Domestic supply is where this line crosses the domestic supply curve, while domestic consumption is where the horizontal line crosses domestic demand. The difference between these values ($100 - 30 = 70$) is the value of imports.

23. d. All are correct. Use a horizontal line at $P_W + t$ to find these values as is described in the answer for question 22.

24. d. All are correct. A + B + C + D represents the loss in consumer surplus, C the revenue to the government, and A the gain in producer surplus (domestic).

25. a. A quota equal to the new level of imports with the tariff (30 units) would produce the same price and level of imports.

CHAPTER EIGHTEEN

TRUE OR FALSE

The following are true: 1, 2, 8, 10, 11, 12

The following are false:

3. A balance-of-payments equilibrium is automatic under purely *flexible* exchange rates. With fixed exchange rates, central banks must buy and sell foreign currency to maintain balance.

4. The exchange rate will move to ensure a balance-of-payments equilibrium.

5. The foreign exchange market is ruled by supply and demand as is any other market.

6. Black markets in foreign currency arise when the official exchange rate differs substantially from the exchange rate that would be set by the market.

7. When a country's balance of trade is in deficit, its current account is nearly always in deficit as well. However, the balance of payments must always balance to zero so this implies a capital account surplus.

9. When the U.S. imports more than it exports, Americans are able to consume more than they otherwise would. The long-term desirability of a trade deficit depends on the underlying causes of the trade deficit.

13. There is no more reason to expect bilateral trade to balance between nations than between individuals.

PROBLEMS AND PROJECTS

1. a. About 270,750 Mexican pesos [$30,000 × 9.025 or $30,000 ÷ 0.1108]
    b. About 70 U.S. dollars [80 × 0.8764 or 80 ÷ 1.141]
    c. About 29,936 Canadian dollars [2,500,000 ÷ 132.700 × 1.589]
    d. 83.5 [132.700 ÷ 1.589] per Canadian dollar or 0.0120 Canadian dollars per yen, which is exactly what the true exchange rate was between these two currencies on this date.
    e. The euro and the Japanese yen have depreciated relative to the U.S. dollar, while the Mexican peso has appreciated.

2. b. 0, −, depreciate
    c. −, +, appreciate

    d. +, − , depreciate
    e. −, +, appreciate
    f. +, +, indeterminate (could either appreciate or depreciate)
    g. 0, 0, no change

3. a. (1) −25.3; (2) 36.1; (3) 3.7; (4) 4.5
    b. There has been a rising current account deficit and a rising capital account surplus to offset it.

MULTIPLE CHOICE

1. d. One dollar now buys more yen, and one yen now buys fewer dollars.

2. b. Capital would leave the U.S. and flow toward England, thus an increase in the supply of dollars and an increase in the demand for the pound. The others would cause an appreciation of the dollar.

3. b. Every dollar traded results in obtaining 100 yen, so 20,000 U.S. dollars would exchange for 2,000,000 yen.

4. d. All would either reduce the supply of dollars or increase the demand for dollars, leading to an appreciation of the dollar.

5. b. If the dollar depreciates, it exchanges for fewer units of foreign currency. Foreign goods become more expensive to U.S. citizens, and U.S. goods become less expensive to foreigners.

6. b. The expansion in the supply of dollars will cause a depreciation, making exports less expensive and imports more expensive.

7. d. Flexible exchange rates make the balance-of-payments accounts automatically balance.

8. c. A trade deficit is when imports exceed exports.

9. a. The others would supply the foreign currency and create a demand for dollars.

10. a. This is a listing of the two main factors responsible for the trade deficits of the United States. The other answers are the two trade balance fallacies discussed in the chapter. They are both incorrect.

11. b. The trade deficit is not an obligation or a government account. It is simply an aggregate number, such as the number of people who migrated out of (or into) your state this year. The balance of

payments must balance, so a current account deficit means a capital account surplus.

12. c. Otherwise, the free market value will differ substantially from the official value causing major balance of payments and official reserve problems.

13. b. Cheaper foreign currency means cheaper foreign goods and services.

14. d. Demand for foreign currency will rise and the supply of foreign currency will fall as investors in all countries shift investment to foreign countries. The domestic currency depreciates as a result.

15. a. An increase in supply (of anything) tends to decrease price (cause depreciation).

16. b. Depreciation makes foreign goods more expensive and domestic goods cheaper.

17. b. Increased exports of U.S. wine and fewer imports of French wine would reduce the trade deficit and thus also reduce the current account deficit.

18. a. Higher real interest rates lead to an increased demand for U.S. assets and an increased demand for U.S. dollars in order to buy those assets.

19. b. Higher prices raise demand for foreign exchange (imports) and lower supply (exports).

20. c. Higher prices and output cause depreciation, while higher interest rates cause appreciation, but all induce a deficit in the current account.

SPECIAL TOPIC ONE

TRUE OR FALSE

The following are true: 1, 2, 5, 7, 9, 10, 11.

The following are false:

3. These items account for less than 10 percent of the budget. Spending on income transfers, health care, national defense, and interest on the national debt together account for just over 85 percent of federal spending.

4. National defense accounts for only 16 percent of the federal budget. Social Security is the largest program comprising 23 percent of the federal budget. The personal income tax is the largest source of federal revenue, accounting for almost half of all federal revenue.

6. Federal spending remained roughly constant with not much growth throughout the 1800s, and only beginning in the 1900s did spending begin to grow rapidly.

8. It is just the opposite—transfers have grown rapidly and defense has fallen substantially.

PROBLEMS AND PROJECTS

1. a. 23.2 (127.7 ÷ 549.5), 52.2 (285.8 ÷ 547.7), 12.6 (68.9 ÷ 547.7)
    b. 33.8 (636.5 ÷ 1,883.0), 15.5 (274.1 ÷ 1,765.7), 14.6 (258.0 ÷ 1,765.7), 12.2 (215.2 ÷ 1,765.7)
    c. fallen from 52.2 percent of the budget to 15.5 percent of the budget
    d. risen from 12.6 percent of the budget to 23.1 percent of the budget
    e. risen from 7.5 percent of the budget to 12.2 percent of the budget
    f. risen from 0.9 percent of the budget to 20.9 percent of the budget
    g. risen from 8.0 percent of the budget to 14.6 percent of the budget
    h. national defense in 1960, Social Security in 2000
    i. fallen from 23.2 percent of revenue to 10.1 percent of revenue; no, because business cannot pay taxes, only people can—business taxes are borne by consumers, workers, and/or shareholders
    j. individual income taxes are the largest revenue source in both years
    k. because the data are in nominal terms and they are not corrected for inflation

2. a. 36.18 (317,419 ÷ 877,292), 66.45 (583,002 ÷ 877,292), 83.54 (732,890 ÷ 877,292), 96.00 (842,168 ÷ 877,292)
    b. risen
    c. fallen

d. There is, of course, no right answer to this question, but most people examining this data are surprised to see that the rich pay such a large share of the tax burden.

MULTIPLE CHOICE

1. b. Social Security accounts for approximately 23 percent of the federal budget, while national defense is about 16 percent.

2. a. Education is the largest category, accounting for almost 30 percent of state and local expenditures.

3. b. The personal income tax is the largest source of federal revenue, accounting for almost half of all federal revenue.

4. b. User charges account for approximately 28 percent of state and local revenue.

5. a. In fact, real per capita federal spending was actually slightly lower in 2000 than in 1990.

6. d. All of these statements are true regarding the federal budget.

7. c. Taxes impose compliance and administration costs as well as creating an excess burden through the elimination of productive exchanges.

8. c. This is the IRS data given in the textbook; it is also given in problem 2 in the problems and projects section.

9. a. This is the IRS data given in the textbook; it is also given in problem 2 in the problems and projects section.

10. b. This is the U.S. Treasury Department data given in the textbook.

11. a. This is the U.S. Treasury Department data given in the textbook.

12. c. The percent of income taken by federal taxes rises sharply with income.

13. a. The Earned Income Tax Credit is a provision in the tax code that provides a credit or rebate to persons with low earnings and is phased out as earned income rises.

14. b. Relative to other major industrial countries, the United States has a low level of government spending as a share of GDP.

15. d. Transfer payments involve the redistribution of income.

16. d. All of these are examples of transfer payments that tax income away from some individuals and transfer it to others.

17. a. No private business can legally use coercive force to require a person to pay for something like the government can.

SPECIAL TOPIC TWO

TRUE OR FALSE

The following are true: 1, 2, 5, 6, 9, 10.

The following are false:

3. Approximately 60 percent of the population, or 170 million people, in the United States use the Internet.

4. Only 1 percent of Internet users are from Africa and another 1 percent are from the Middle East. The United States accounts for 32 percent of Internet users.

7. The Internet generally makes it easier for consumers to do this.

8. The Internet has also made it easier for businesses to purchase from each other.

PROBLEMS AND PROJECTS

1. The answers to this problem will depend on the list as you do this problem.

2. The answers to this problem will depend on your favorite CD. Generally I own most of the other CDs listed in the section of what others bought, and frequently I find a new one I didn't know about that I really like.

3. Without the college bookstore acting as a middleman, you should be able to get a higher used price for selling your textbooks on-line; however, the transaction cost of having to ship your book or find the seller may be high enough that this is not worth it to you. The bookstore provides value because it acts as a middleman helping to lower the transaction costs for buyers and sellers trading used books.

MULTIPLE CHOICE

1. c. This is the data given in the book, and this figure is projected to rise to $269 billion by 2005.

2. d. These are the three major sources of economic gains from the Internet listed in the textbook.

3. b. This is a number given in the text.

4. a. Computer hardware and software has the highest percent of on-line sales.

5. d. Automobiles have the smallest on-line sales of those listed, but food and garden/hardware are even lower.

6. d. All of these are reasons why on-line retail stores can potentially have lower costs.

7. a. This is one of the drawbacks to purchasing on-line. A potential solution, employed by Gateway Computers, is to have only a few items on display in hybrid stores that act as showrooms.

8. d. All of these are advantages of job-posting Web sites over traditional newspaper ads.

9. d. Job turnover may increase because many employed workers routinely search for new jobs on the Internet.

10. b. This was the 1997 figure, but it is rising rapidly.

11. b. Telecommuting is the use of the Internet to work from home or another location.

SPECIAL TOPIC THREE

TRUE OR FALSE

The following are true: 2, 3, 6, 7, 8, 9, 11

The following are false:

1. The system takes the current tax revenue and pays it out to current retirees. Only recently has Social Security began to save a fraction of current revenue in anticipation of the retirement of the baby boom generation.

4. Current workers will fare much worse than those before them.

5. A worker aged thirty-five can expect a rate of return of about 2 percent, about one-fourth that of an average stock market return.

10. On average, blacks have a shorter life expectancy than whites so Social Security adversely affects the economic welfare of blacks relative to whites.

PROBLEMS AND PROJECTS

1. a. Taxes of $1,000 per worker would support a benefit level of $15,000 per retiree in the 1950s.
   b. Taxes of $5,000 per worker would support a benefit level of $15,000 per retiree in 2000.
   c. Taxes of $7,500 per worker would support a benefit level of $15,000 per retiree in 2030.
   d. Benefits would have to be cut from $15,000 to $10,000 per retiree.

2. a. Yes, technically you have savings of $5,000, and your spouse has a debt of $5,000.
   b. Your spouse would have to run a "surplus" (spend less than he or she earns) to repay the money.
   c. It is the same. The Social Security trust fund holds U.S. Treasury bonds, which will have to be repaid by the federal government (either through higher taxes or spending cuts in other areas) when Social Security needs to use the money in the trust fund. In essence, it is no different that if the surplus had never been saved.

3. a. At 1.8 percent, the money would have doubled once by age sixty-five, so you would have only $40,000 instead of $320,000. While this is an oversimplified problem, the amount is similar to the real difference, which amounts to about $200,000 for the average baby boomer.
   b. At 3.6 percent, the money would double every twenty years. So $20,000 invested at age twenty-five would grow to $40,000 at age forty-five and to $80,000 at age sixty-five. This is double the amount that would be present at a 1.8 percent return ($80,000 versus $40,000).
   c. The economy would be double its current size.
   d. $160,000; $240,000; $20,000; $40,000

MULTIPLE CHOICE

1. c. This is what is meant by a pay-as-you-go system.

2. d. The ratio was sixteen workers per retiree in the 1950s, three workers per retiree in 1998, and will fall to two workers per retiree by 2025.

3. c. By using the trust fund to purchase bonds, the money was available for the government to spend on other current programs. When these bonds come due, the federal government will have to repay this money it has borrowed from the Social Security trust fund.

4. b. This is when Social Security will begin to draw down the trust fund.

5. d. All of them are discussed in the book as issues regarding a switch to personal savings accounts.

6. d. A young worker today is expected to earn a negative real rate of return on their contributions, meaning that the real value of the benefits received will be less than the real value of the taxes paid.

7. a. These are essentially IOUs from the federal government that will have to be repaid in the future.

8. b. To repay the bonds, the government will have to either raise taxes or cut spending.

9. d. These are the only options available besides substantial reform.

10. c.   Above this level of income, total annual Social Security taxes remain constant.

11. a.   Blacks have a lower life expectancy than whites or Hispanics, life expectancy rises with education, and females have a longer life expectancy then males.

12. c.   A spouse can collect benefits based upon either their own average annual salary, or 50 percent of their spouse's average annual salary. A married woman who does not work will receive the same benefits as if she had worked and earned an average annual salary equal to 50 percent of her husband's.

13. d.   Both of the statements are true.

14. a.   All of the other countries have taken steps toward privatization.

SPECIAL TOPIC FOUR

TRUE OR FALSE

The following are true: 2, 3, 4, 6, 8, 9, 10

The following are false:

1. Real returns have averaged far greater than the 7 percent long-term average.

5. These will generally lead to good performance of the stock market.

7. The highest returns with the least risk are made by holding a diversified portfolio of stocks over a long period of time.

11. They are buying ownership rights in the assets of a corporation.

PROBLEMS AND PROJECTS

1. a. decrease
   b. increase
   c. increase

2. a. $173.55 = (\$100 \div (1.10)^1) + (\$100 \div (1.10)^2)$
   b. $185.94 = (\$100 \div (1.05)^1) + (\$100 \div (1.05)^2)$
   c. $177.69 = (\$150 \div (1.10)^1) + (\$50 \div (1.10)^2)$
   d. $260.33 = (\$100 \div (1.10)^1) + (\$150 \div (1.10)^2)$
   e. $214.88 = (\$150 \div (1.10)^1) + (\$150 \div (1.10)^2)$

MULTIPLE CHOICE

1. a. Answers b and c would increase risk.

2. c. Both will lower risk.

3. c. This is even true compared to investing in U.S. Treasury bonds.

4. c. Both are true.

5. b. The recent good performance of the stock market has been partially due to the opposite case.

6. b. The others are the opposite of what is true.

7. b. Answers a and c are opposite of what is true.

8. d. The random walk theory is consistent with all of the statements.

9. d. The others are the opposite of what is true.

10. b. Real returns have averaged far greater than the 7 percent long-term average.

11. a. The value of the option to purchase the stock would increase.

SPECIAL TOPIC FIVE

TRUE OR FALSE

The following are true: 1, 2, 5, 7, 8, 11.

The following are false:

3. When current resources (labor, machines, buildings, etc.) are used to produce government goods, the forgone production in other areas must be forgone today. This opportunity cost cannot be pushed into the future.

4. A larger capital stock means higher labor productivity and thus *higher* wages.

6. Privately held debt is the portion owned by all private investors, domestic and foreign (in essence, all debt not owned by U.S. government agencies). External debt refers to the portion owned by foreign investors.

9. Under the traditional view, investment is crowded out and the future capital stock is lower. This is not true under the new classical view.

10. We are about average.

PROBLEMS AND PROJECTS

1. Year 1: Total expenditure is $150 (equal to revenue because no surplus or deficit).
   Year 2: Total revenue is $150 ($50 less than total expenditure with a $50 deficit).
   Year 3: +$20 surplus (amount by which revenue exceeded expenditures)
   Year 4: −$10 deficit (revenue minus expenditure) and $40 debt ($30 old debt plus $10 more from this year's deficit)
   Year 5: $70 debt ($40 old debt plus $30 more from this year's deficit)
   Year 6: $190 total expenditure and $70 surplus (necessary to pay debt down to zero)

2. a. Total receipts: $1,039.9; $1,150.0
      Total outlays: $1,235.9; $1,273.4
   b. −196.0; −123.4
   c. In 1997 the actual deficit was larger than reported, and in 1998 there was actually a deficit despite a reported surplus.

MULTIPLE CHOICE

1. b. The debt is the total amount owed at any one point in time. The deficit (or surplus) is the annual amount by which the debt changes.

2. a. External debt is debt owned by foreigners.

3. b. It is the portion not owned by government agencies but by private investors. It represents a true net interest burden from the government to persons.

4. c. Answers a and b are untrue myths about the burden of the debt addressed in this application chapter.

5. a. Higher government borrowing pushes up interest rates, reducing private borrowing and investment. The inflow of foreign capital looking to earn the higher interest rate offered in the U.S. will appreciate the dollar, reducing net exports.

6. b. Expenditures have risen very rapidly, much more so than revenue.

7. a. The national debt is the sum of all prior deficits and surpluses.

8. b. Prior to the acceptance of Keynesian theory, the general practice was to follow a balanced budget except in war time or other emergencies. Keynesian theory called for deficits to be run to actively manage the state of the economy.

9. c. In year 1, expenditures of $100 exceed revenue of $100 by $10, thus a deficit.

10. b. In year 2, revenue of $150 exceeds expenditure of $120 by $30, thus a surplus.

11. d. In year 3, there is a $50 deficit ($250 expenditure versus $200 revenue). The national debt is the sum all of the deficits and surpluses over all three years (−10 + 30 − 50 = −30).

12. c. The interest on these bonds will be paid from one agency of the government to another.

13. b. This is a statistic given in the text.

SPECIAL TOPIC SIX

TRUE OR FALSE

The following are true: 1, 3, 4, 6, 7, 8, 10, 11

The following are false:

2. Their economies have not been in recessions, and their rates of inflation have been low and steady. These are not causing the difference in unemployment rates.

5. They make labor markets less flexible and cause higher rates of unemployment.

9. Higher benefits encourage longer spells of unemployment and thus raise the unemployment rate.

PROBLEMS AND PROJECTS

1. a. +
   b. −
   c. −

2. a. Japan, United States
   b. Japan, United States
   c. Japan, United States
   d. Japan, United States
   e. They are the same. The countries with the lowest unemployment rates (Japan and the United States) also have the lowest unemployment benefits, the lowest collective bargaining, and the least restrictive government policies on dismissal.
   f. Spain, France
   g. France, Germany
   h. Italy, Spain
   i. France, Spain
   j. The countries with the two highest unemployment rates (Spain and France) also tend to have high values for these other variables; high unemployment benefits seem to be the most highly correlated.

MULTIPLE CHOICE

1. c. The United States had the lowest unemployment rate of the countries listed.

2. d. The difference is not the result of these factors but is rather due to structural factors in the labor markets differing.

3. d. All of them had higher unemployment rates.

4. d. Almost the entire labor force has wages set by collective bargaining.

5. d. The United States just slightly beats out Japan as having the lowest percent.

6. a. France has the highest, with a replacement rate of 38 percent.

7. c. Smaller countries have less adverse effects, but in general, higher degrees of centralized wage setting raise unemployment rates.

8. a. It raises the cost of replacing long-time workers with new workers.

9. d. Higher levels of these factors tend to raise unemployment rates.

10. c. The replacement rate is the percent of previous income that is replaced by the unemployment benefits ($600 ÷ $1,000 = 60 percent).

11. d. Higher levels of these factors tend to raise unemployment rates. The United States and Japan have much lower unemployment rates.

12. a. The lowering of benefits has reduced the unemployment rate.

SPECIAL TOPIC SEVEN

TRUE OR FALSE

The following are true: 4, 5, 7, 8, 10.

The following are false:

1. The Phillips curve originally suggested that higher inflation would lower the rate of unemployment.

2. The stagflation of the 1970s (simultaneously high inflation and high unemployment) was contrary to what the Phillips curve predicted and thus resulted in a rejection of the Phillips curve analysis.

3. It will fall below the natural rate when inflation is higher than is anticipated (in other words, inflation is underestimated).

6. "Permanent" suggests "long run." In the long run, there is no trade-off even if one exists in the short run. In the long run, the rate of unemployment will hover around the natural rate regardless of the rate of inflation.

9. Overestimate means that the estimate (or anticipated rate) was higher than what actually occurred. Alternatively, it means that what actually occurred was lower than was anticipated.

PROBLEMS AND PROJECTS

1. a. Unemployment would fall to 3 percent, and the economy would be at point *B*.
   b. Unemployment would stay at 5 percent, and the economy would be at point *C*.
   c. Unemployment would rise to 7 percent, and the economy would be at point *D*.
   d. (1) When inflation is higher than was anticipated (in other words, people underestimate inflation), unemployment will fall below the natural rate. (2) When inflation is equal to what was anticipated (in other words, people correctly estimate inflation), unemployment will equal the natural rate. (3) When inflation is lower than was anticipated (in other words, people overestimate inflation), unemployment will rise above the natural rate.

2. a. Unemployment would rise to 7 percent, and the economy would be at point *D*.
   b. Unemployment would stay at 5 percent, and the economy would be at point *C*.
   c. Unemployment would fall to 3 percent, and the economy would be at point *B*.
   d. Same as answers to problem 1, part d above.

e. The rise in unemployment can be avoided by announcing the policy in such a manner as to help people in the economy to accurately anticipate the new inflation rate.

3. a. In the AD/AS diagram, point *A* is where AD_1 crosses $SRAS_1$. In the Phillips curve diagram, point *A* is where the two curves meet at the bottom along the horizontal axis at 0 percent inflation and 5 percent unemployment.
   b. In the AD/AS diagram, point *B* is where AD_2 crosses $SRAS_1$. In the Phillips curve diagram, point *B* is along PC at 4 percent inflation and 3 percent unemployment.
   c. In the AD/AS diagram, point *C* is where AD_2 crosses $SRAS_2$.
   d. The Phillips curve will shift to the right so that it now crosses the vertical long-run Phillips curve at an inflation rate of 4 percent. The resulting point *C* will be at this point where the new curve crosses the long-run curve.
   e. It has caused an increase in inflation but has not resulted in any long-run change in the unemployment rate.

4. a. There should be two distinct Phillips curve lines, one for 1993–1995 and another for 2000–2002.
   b. 0, −1, +2, 0 −1, +2
   c. No; yes
   d. 5%

MULTIPLE CHOICE

1. b. Only when inflation is higher than was anticipated (in other words, inflation was underestimated) will unemployment fall below the natural rate.

2. a. Because the effects were overestimated, unemployment rill rise, which is the exact opposite of what policy makers were trying to do. This is why expectations are so important in conducting macropolicy.

3. a. An increase in the expected rate of inflation shifts the short-run Phillips curve to the right.

4. b. Because expectations did not change, we move along the original curve. Note inflation was higher than expected, so unemployment fell below the natural rate.

5. c. People will eventually come to expect the higher rate of inflation, shifting the Phillips curve to the right and moving the economy to point C.

6. c.   When people correctly anticipate the higher rate of inflation, the curve shifts and unemployment remains at the natural rate.

7. d.   These are the two variables plotted in the diagram.

8. c.   Here people have overestimated inflation.

9. a.   This was the prediction of the original Phillips curve.

10. b.   The vertical curve shows that the rate of unemployment will hover around the natural rate in the long run regardless of the rate of inflation.

11. a.   When people overestimate inflation, unemployment rises above the natural rate.

12. d.   Answer b is the opposite of what is true.

13. a.   Inflation will be higher than was anticipated, so unemployment will temporarily fall below the natural rate.

14. b.   Unemployment will be above the natural rate when people overestimate the inflation rate—that is, the inflation rate turns out to be lower than was anticipated, or alternatively that people expected inflation to be higher than what actually occurred.

15. b.   Unemployment will fall below the natural rate when people underestimate the inflation rate—that is the inflation rate turns out to be higher than was anticipated, or alternatively that people expected inflation to be lower than what actually occurred.